BUSINESS ENGLISH

Second Edition

A Complete Guide To Developing An Effective Business Writing Style

by

Andrea B. Geffner

Former Dean,
Taylor Business Institute, N.Y.
Vice President,
ESCO, Inc., N.Y.

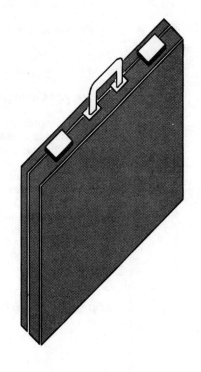

BARRON'S Barron's Educational Series, Inc.

For Marcus from the beginning

All inquiries should be addressed to:
Barron's Educational Series, Inc.
250 Wireless Boulevard
Hauppauge, New York 11788

Library of Congress Catalog Card No. 92-36563
International Standard Book No. 0-8120-1441-3

Library of Congress Cataloging-in-Publication Data

Geffner, Andrea B.
    Business English : a complete guide to developing an
effective business writing style / by Andrea B. Geffner. —
2nd ed.
            p.   cm.
    Includes index.
    ISBN 0-8120-1441-3
    1. English language—Business English.   2. English
langugage—Rhetoric.   3. Business writing.   I. Title.
PE 1479.B87G4   1993
808'.06665—dc20   92-36563
                                                  CIP
                                                  AC

PRINTED IN THE UNITED STATES OF AMERICA

456   100   98765432

CONTENTS

Part Two

CORRESPONDENCE

Part Three

WORDS AT WORK

TABLE OF
MODEL LETTERS

PREFACE

The last years of the twentieth century have been a time of breathtaking technological advancement. From fax machines to voice mail, from computer mail to cellular phones, much of the technological revolution has centered on our communications tools. The speed with which we can transmit information increases almost daily. The facility with which we can organize and utilize this information improves with every new generation of "hardware."

Yet, despite the proliferation of fast-paced telecommunications, the individual who can write clear, comprehensible prose is a vital part of any business team. The assumptions behind *Business English* are that solid control of the English language is a highly marketable skill in today's workplace, and that the ability to compose effective business communications is in greater demand today than ever before.

To meet this demand, a business writer must master the fundamentals of English in addition to the fine points of style. Thus, the first half of this book focuses on broad areas of grammar, sentence structure, and mechanics, with an eye toward minimizing error. To encourage self-checking and to provide immediate reinforcement of these skills, answers for this section are included at the back of the book. The second half of the book discusses the various categories of business correspondence, providing the reader with an overview of the styles and formats appropriate to each.

It is hoped that the reader will discover through this book not only a facility with language, but an awareness of the value of the written word.

Part One
GRAMMAR AND SENTENCE STRUCTURE

1.
IDENTIFYING VERBS AND SUBJECTS

When we speak, we use words to express ideas. But we can give extra structure to our ideas by means of pauses, facial expressions, and body movements. In writing, we have none of these tools; we must rely almost exclusively on the words we choose in order to get our meaning across.

Because language, whether spoken or written, is simply a method for transmitting thoughts and feelings from one person's mind into another person's mind, we must agree on certain ground rules so that we can understand each other most efficiently. Thus, the word *apple* (either printed on this page or said out loud) will signify the same thing to all English-speaking people. We agree on the meanings of words so that we can communicate.

Similarly, we agree on a standard form of grammar. The *order* in which we use words contributes as much meaning to a sentence as do the definitions of individual words. For example, the sentence "Sam sees the tree" conveys a different meaning from "The tree sees Sam." In fact, the first sentence makes sense to us; the second one doesn't.

The reason for this is the first principle of English sentence structure:

> EVERY SENTENCE MUST HAVE AT LEAST TWO PARTS, A
> SUBJECT AND A VERB.

In both the above sentences, *sees* is the verb; but in the first sentence *Sam* is the subject while in the second sentence *The tree* is the subject. So the sentences mean two different things.

Recognizing Verbs

The VERB is the part of the sentence that indicates what someone or something DOES or IS or HAS:

> My accountant *filled* out my income tax return.
> His method *is* more efficient than mine.
> He *has* a lot of information to save me money.

Often, the VERB is the word that shows *action*. In the following sentences, the verbs are underlined:

> A cashier sells.
> A bricklayer builds.
> A teacher instructs.
> A gymnast jumps.
> Mechanics repair.

Tailors <u>sew</u>.
Farmers <u>plant</u>.
Philosophers <u>think</u>.

The VERB in the last example is different from the others. It expresses action, but not the kind of action you can see or hear; "think" shows mental activity, something that happens in a person's mind.

> ACTION VERBS CAN BE DIVIDED INTO VERBS OF PHYSICAL ACTION AND VERBS OF MENTAL ACTION.

The VERBS in the following sentences express mental action:

Ruth *believes* in equal pay for equal work.
Her boss *agrees* with her.
She *chooses* to pay female employees as much as males.
Ruth *considers* this quite fair.
She *hopes* to stay there for many years.

★ EXERCISE 1

Each of the words on the right may be substituted for one word in the sentence to the left. Identify that word. Then write your new sentences by making the substitutions.

1. Hal opens the mail for his boss every day.

answers / screens / sorts

a. _____*Sort*_____

b. _____

c. _____

2. The retiring president of our company greeted her successor.

selected / resented / instructed

a. _____

b. _____

c. _____

3. The members of the board adjourned the meeting.

attended / scheduled / missed

a. _____

b. _____

c. _____

4. The woman at the reception desk looks tired.

feels / seems / was

a. _____

b. _____

c. _____

5. My landlord has twelve buildings in this city.

owns / possesses / rents

a. _____

b. _____

c. _____

6. Lea ordered a fax machine for the office.   purchased / bought / requisitioned

   a. _____

   b. _____

   c. _____

7. The doctor called his answering service before leaving the hospital.   checked / contacted / canceled

   a. _____

   b. _____

   c. _____

8. The bank reduced Alan's credit line.   increased / froze / reevaluated

   a. _____

   b. _____

   c. _____

9. Paul deserved a promotion.   wanted / expected / requested

   a. _____

   b. _____

   c. _____

10. Before the interview, I retyped my resume.   updated / expanded / reworded

    a. _____

    b. _____

    c. _____

★ EXERCISE 2
Fill in the blanks with one word.

1. Wendy _____is_____ an interior designer.

2. Her specialty _____is a_____ corporate design.

3. She _____lives_____ in a large metropolitan community.

4. She _____serve_____ several clients every day.

5. She _____takes_____ her work very seriously.

6. Wendy's friend Bruce _____is_____ an architect.

7. He _____lives_____ in the same community.

8. He _____refers_____ some of his clients to Wendy.

9. Sometimes he _____seeks_____ Wendy's advice.

10. Wendy and Bruce _____communicate_____ well together.

★ EXERCISE 3
Find the verbs in this letter
and underline them.

Dear Sir:

On April 12, I ordered a microwave oven from your store. The model number was 129-C. According to your Spring catalog, it cost $425.95. I received the oven on April 25.

However, on May 1, your bill arrived. It listed the oven at $460.95. This is $35 more than the original price.

I enclose a check for $425.95. Please credit my account for the $35 discrepancy. I appreciate your attention to this matter.

Sincerely yours,

Many verbs consist of more than one word. Consider these examples:

> John *is learning* data processing.
> I *am studying* DOS.
> Rose *has taken* computer courses in the past.
> She *will graduate* before us.

You will notice that in these sentences the verbs contained two words. But a verb may consist of three or four words, too:

> Alex *has been working* for five years.
> He *may be promoted* next month.
> Then he *will be running* the credit department.
> Roger *will have been transferred* by that time.
> He *should have been promoted* long ago.

★ EXERCISE 4
Identify the words in these sentences for which the words on the right may be substituted. Then write your new sentences, making the substitutions.

1. David has worked for his father for five years.

   had worked / will work / was working

   a. _____
   b. _____
   c. _____

2. The producer has been auditioning actors all week.

   will be auditioning / would have auditioned / was auditioning

   a. _____
   b. _____
   c. _____

3. A good secretary must be precise and fastidious.

   should be / has to be / ought to be

   a. _____
   b. _____
   c. _____

4. The unemployment rate <u>has</u> been rising over the past decade.

has risen / has climbed / has been fluctuating

a. _____

b. _____

c. _____

5. I will have finished my assignment by Friday.

should have finished / will have completed / will have submitted

a. _____

b. _____

c. _____

6. Since childhood, Sandy has wanted to become a nurse.

had wanted / has been planning / has hoped

a. _____

b. _____

c. _____

7. The sales representative took my order by telephone.

filled / verified / processed

a. _____

b. _____

c. _____

8. I am looking forward to my vacation.

was looking / have been looking / had been looking

a. _____

b. _____

c. _____

9. Two new salespersons have been hired.

were hired / will be hired / must be hired

a. _____

b. _____

c. _____

10. Our company has moved to a new location.

had to move / may have to move / will be moving

a. _____

b. _____

c. _____

★ EXERCISE 5
Underline the verbs in this letter.

Gentlemen:

I am writing in response to your ad in Sunday's newspaper. I would like to apply for the position of executive secretary.

I have been a secretary for the past six years. Most recently, I have been working as an assistant to the vice-president of ESCO, Inc. In addition to general secretarial duties, my responsibilities in this capacity have included the management of the office in the absence of my employer.

I have studied secretarial skills at Westside Business Institute, and I have completed 75 credits toward my B.A. degree.

I am enclosing my resume for your consideration. My complete job history is included. A list of references will be provided on request.

Yours truly,

Another difficulty with verbs is that a sentence may contain more than one:

Gerald *types* and *takes* dictation.
He *works* hard but *earns* little money.
He *wants* to quit his job and *look* for another.

★ EXERCISE 6
Underline all of the verbs in these sentences.

1. Aurora studied computer programming first and then looked for a job.
2. During his summer vacations, Jimmy has driven a cab, delivered milk, and sold shoes.
3. Mr. Alberts asked me for a copy of the annual report and told me where to look.
4. On her lunch hour, Lea went to Colony's and bought a new dress.
5. I typed and proofread the letter before the end of the day.
6. Georgette called in sick and took the day off.
7. After the interview, John was offered the job and accepted it.
8. Blossom saved her money, quit her job, and opened an antique shop.
9. Marc placed an ad in the newspaper and received dozens of responses the first week.
10. A banker for many years, Mr. Seymour retired and moved to Venice.

Recognizing Subjects

The SUBJECT of a sentence is the word doing the action of the verb.

The SUBJECT must always be a NOUN or a PRONOUN. A noun is the name of a person, place, thing, or idea. A PRONOUN is a substitute for a noun used to avoid repetition.

Remember: Not every noun in a sentence is a subject. The SUBJECT is only the noun performing the action of the VERB.

In the following sentences, all the subjects have been underlined:

A woman sat at a computer.
She keyed in her password.
The screen went blank.
A virus had attacked.

If you identify the VERB in a sentence first, you can then find the SUBJECT by asking WHO or WHAT is doing the action of the VERB.

April sings with a band.
VERB? Sings
Who sings with a band?
SUBJECT? April

★ EXERCISE 7
In these sentences, underline the verb and then circle the subject.

1. John is a computer programmer.
2. He likes his job.
3. He had planned to become a teacher.
4. But computer science is a fascinating field.
5. His plans had to be changed.
6. Marie is a bookkeeper.
7. She enjoys her job a great deal.
8. Mathematics always had been her strong subject.
9. So she went to school and developed her specialty.
10. The atmosphere and salary of her job are satisfying to her.

As you probably noticed, there are two subjects in the last sentence of the previous exercise. Just as a sentence may have more than one verb, so *a verb may have more than one subject.*

Here are some examples (the subjects have been underlined):

Wordprocessing and shorthand are two highly marketable skills.
Study, hard work, and patience are necessary to master
    them.
A pleasant job and a good salary can be the rewards for a
    diligent student.

★ EXERCISE 8
In these sentences, underline the verbs and circle the subjects.

1. Mr. and Mrs. Price are buying a house.
2. Their real estate agent and their banker are helping to arrange the mortgage.
3. The agent and the Prices' lawyer disagree over the terms of the sale.
4. The Prices and the banker are eager about the deal.
5. The agent, the banker, the lawyer, and the Prices all will be happy after the settlement of the purchase.
6. Regina and her boss were discussing her salary.
7. Accuracy, thoroughness, and conscientiousness were her reasons for a raise.
8. Poor sales and high expenses were his justification for low salaries.
9. Regina and her employer met frequently to discuss her salary.
10. Her raise will begin on the first of the month.

★ **EXERCISE 9**
In this letter, underline the verbs and circle the subjects.

Dear Madam:

We would like to introduce you to Dark Lady, a new fragrance by Leonard of London.

Dark Lady is named for William Shakespeare's mysterious love. Its bouquet is steeped in the poetry and romance of the Bard's greatest heroines. One drop mingles all the flowers of Ophelia's garland. Rosemary, violets, and pansies evoke remembrance, faithfulness, and thought. The greatest loves and lyrics of four hundred years blend in a crystal vial.

Dark Lady perfume and cologne are now available at all our fine stores. For a limited time, we are offering a special bonus. A half-ounce purse-atomizer and a floral silken pouch are yours with any Dark Lady purchase of $10 or more.

Of course, this and all your purchases can be charged and ordered by phone.

Yours truly,

Principal Parts of the Verb

Before we begin to study longer sentences, we must make one more point about verbs.

Every VERB has FIVE PRINCIPAL PARTS. These are the INFINITIVE, the PRESENT TENSE, the PAST TENSE, and the TWO PARTICIPLES.

A Model Verb

Infinitive:	to go
Present Tense:	go
Past Tense:	went
Present Participle:	going
Past Participle:	gone

Of these five parts, only the PRESENT TENSE and the PAST TENSE can be the VERB of a sentence. The other parts can only act as the verb in a sentence when they are accompanied by a helping verb (like *to be* or *to have*).

> The bill *was paid.*
> The paid bill *was entered* on the books.

In the first sentence, *was paid* is the verb. In the second sentence, *paid* is not the verb; *was entered* is the verb and *bill* is its subject. In the second sentence, *paid* is a PAST PARTICIPLE (with *no* helping verb) describing *bill*.

Remember: PARTICIPLES are words that look like verbs but aren't.

★ EXERCISE 10

In these sentences, find the word (or words) for which the verbs on the right may be substituted. Then write your new sentences, making the substitutions. Watch out for participles.

1. The person chosen for the job had known the boss before.

had hated / had avoided / had assisted

a. _____

b. _____

c. _____

2. The woman typing the letter is tired.

will be paid / was fired / is thinking

a. _____

b. _____

c. _____

3. Waiting for a bus, I saw my friend.

met / encountered / delayed

a. _____

b. _____

c. _____

4. Caught for her mistakes, Jane apologized.

was embarrassed / cried / quit

a. _____

b. _____

c. _____

5. The broken intercom was repaired this morning.

will be repaired / must be repaired / won't be repaired

a. _____

b. _____

c. _____

6. The calculator is on the desk.

was / can be found / must be used

a. _____

b. _____

c. _____

7. The waiting room is filled with people.

was filled / is crowded / will be filled

a. _____

b. _____

c. _____

8. The accountant working on my
   taxes is astute.

   seems / was /
   appeared to be

   a. _____

   b. _____

   c. _____

9. The skyscraper, built in 1924,
   will be torn down.

   was torn /
   has been torn / is being torn

   a. _____

   b. _____

   c. _____

10. Tied up with work, the executive
    missed her luncheon engagement.

    had to miss / canceled /
    postponed

    a. _____

    b. _____

    c. _____

Thus PRESENT PARTICIPLES and PAST PARTICIPLES can be used to describe, or modify, nouns. When a PRESENT PARTICIPLE is used without a helping verb (and so is *not* the main verb in a sentence), it can also be used as a SUBJECT. For example:

> *Walking* is good exercise.
> *Typing* 90 words per minute is remarkable.

The INFINITIVE of a verb is also used this way. Without a helping verb, the INFINITIVE can be a SUBJECT:

> *To get* a good job requires a good skill.
> *To pay* bills promptly is a good policy.

★ **EXERCISE 11**
In these sentences, underline all verbs and circle all
subjects.

1. Bicycling to my job keeps me healthy.
2. Writing checks makes me frugal.
3. Balancing my checkbook makes me proud.
4. To answer the treasurer's mail is the responsibility of his assistant.
5. To admit one's errors indicates maturity.
6. To lose one's job is a traumatic experience.
7. Waiting on lines infuriates me.
8. Smoking cigarettes is hazardous to your health.
9. To find a good job demands perseverance.
10. To operate this computer requires special training.

★ **EXERCISE 12**
Using each of the following present participles, write three sentences. In one, use the participle as the verb (with a helping verb); in another, use the participle as the subject; and in the last, use the participle to describe the subject.

Example:
Answering
a. Verb: *I have been answering the telephones all morning.*
b. Subject: *Answering telephones bores me.*
c. Describing word: *The answering machine was disconnected.*

1. Selling
   a. Verb: _____
   b. Subject: _____
   c. Describing word: _____

2. Speaking
   a. Verb: _____
   b. Subject: _____
   c. Describing word: _____

3. Paying
   a. Verb: _____
   b. Subject: _____
   c. Describing word: _____

4. Writing
   a. Verb: _____
   b. Subject: _____
   c. Describing word: _____

5. Looking
   a. Verb: _____
   b. Subject: _____
   c. Describing word: _____

★ **EXERCISE 13**
Using each of the past participles given, write two sentences. In one, use the participle as a verb (with a helping verb); in the other, use the participle to describe the subject.

Example:
Elected
a. Verb: *The attorney was elected to the town council.*
b. Describing word: *Elected officials have a responsibility to the public.*

1. Lost
   a. Verb: _____
   b. Describing word: _____

2. Tired
   a. Verb: _____
   b. Describing word: _____

3. Printed
   a. Verb: _____
   b. Describing word: _____

4. Opened
   a. Verb: _____

   b. Describing word: _____

5. Advertised
   a. Verb: _____

   b. Describing word: _____

★ **REVIEW EXERCISES**

A. In each sentence, underline the verb and circle the subject.

1. Mr. Munson was studying the stock market.
2. He was considering an investment.
3. For many years, his money had been in a savings bank.
4. In a bank, money is insured.
5. Nowadays, however, it earns little interest.
6. Mr. Munson would like to be earning more.
7. Even a time-deposit account would have paid higher interest.
8. So now he wants to invest in stocks.
9. But he knows the market is risky.
10. Before investing, he will be careful.

B. In each sentence, underline the verb and circle the subject.

1. Income-generating home offices are a growing phenomenon.
2. By the mid-1990s, more than 40 million U.S. households will contain a home office.
3. Some people perform all of their work in a home office.
4. They run home-based businesses ranging from baby-sitting agencies to financial consultants.
5. Other people do some of their work in a home office.
6. For example, they may manage a part-time business from home in order to earn extra income.
7. Corporate home workers are another example.
8. Employed by an outside company, these people do some or all of their work from home.
9. Current technology has made this kind of home office possible.
10. Employees at home can communicate electronically with the main office.
11. In fact, computers are used by more than half the home offices in the U.S.
12. In addition, home-based workers rely on telephones, modems, facsimilie machines, and scanners.
13. This information technology enables them to remain competitive.
14. Many home-based businesses are not computerized.
15. In the future, they may find it difficult to compete.

C. In this letter, underline all the verbs and circle all the subjects.

Dear Mr. Morris:

With the value of the dollar suffering abroad, many Americans are reconsidering that long-saved-for trip to Paris. Therefore, I am submitting a copy of my article, "Paris on a Budget," for your consideration. The readers of <u>Tourist</u> magazine may find it helpful.

Based on my own recent experiences, the article is a guide for the tourist on a tight budget. It suggests moderately priced but comfortable hotels and boarding houses. It recommends inexpensive but delightful restaurants. Free or nearly free places to go and things to do are listed also. All details and prices have been researched carefully.

Your consideration of my article is appreciated greatly. You are welcome to make any necessary editorial revisions.

Sincerely yours,

D. Underline all the verbs and circle all the subjects in this memorandum.

TO: Mr. Eric Bayer

FROM: Norma Charles

DATE: November 30, 19--

SUBJECT: Location for company Christmas party

At your request, I have investigated possible locations for our company Christmas party. Several places nearby are equipped to handle 175 people. The two most reasonable are the following:

1 Villa di Rome serves excellent, reasonably priced food, liquor not included. A live band is provided. The cost is $30 per person.

2 Blossom's offers a sumptuous buffet and an open bar. A dance floor is available, but not a live band. The cost is $35 per person.

I will be happy to discuss either of the places at your convenience.

NC

E. Underline all verbs and circle all subjects in this news release.

<u>For Immediate Release</u>   6/3/--

LORNA TELLMAN WINS PUBLIC SERVICE AWARD

Smallwood, June 3, 19--. Lorna Tellman was awarded the Annual Public Service Award at last night's meeting of the Smallwood Chamber of Commerce. She was selected from a group of seven nominees, according to Paul Duggan, president of the association.

Owner of Smallwood Travel, Inc., Ms. Tellman was the organizer of the first annual Smallwood Crafts Festival. This event brought thousands of tourists to the area. As a result, income from tourism doubled this summer over the same period last year.

The winner of the Public Service Award will be honored at an awards dinner. This will take place on June 10 at 8 P.M. at Jan's Restaurant and Lounge. Tickets are on sale for $25 a plate.

After hearing of her award, Ms. Tellman remarked, "I was happy to do it."

2.
SENTENCE COMPLETERS

Adjectives

As we saw in the last chapter, a participle can be used to *describe* another word.

> The **exhausted** stenographer dropped her pad.
> PARTICIPLE   SUBJECT   VERB

> The **answering** machine was out of order.
> PARTICIPLE SUBJECT VERB

In these examples, the participles are describing (or adding information to) the subjects. This means that the participles here are acting as ADJECTIVES.

> AN ADJECTIVE IS ANY WORD (OR GROUP OF WORDS)
> THAT ADDS INFORMATION TO A NOUN OR PRONOUN.

You will remember that not all nouns are subjects. Therefore, an adjective may describe a noun even if the noun is *not* the subject in a sentence:

> The executive fired the exhausted stenographer.
>   S   V

In this example, stenographer is NOT the subject. But it is being described (or modified) by the adjective/participle *exhausted.*

★ EXERCISE 1
In these sentences, underline each adjective and circle the noun it is describing.

1. A roving reporter phoned in her story.
2. It concerned a growing controversy.
3. The demanding editor wanted the details.
4. The reporter interviewed a politician accused of graft.
5. She asked provoking questions.
6. The alleged criminal did not evade the questions.
7. He had been offered a tempting bribe.
8. Refusing, he called the FBI.
9. They had been investigating the suspected politician.
10. He claimed to be an honest man.

You probably noticed that the adjective in the last sentence was *not* a participle. This is because participles are only one type of adjective.

There are many words in English that are ADJECTIVES BY DEFINITION:

The *big* boss
The *small* chair
The *slow* typist
The *bleak* weather

You can probably think of a lot more.

★ EXERCISE 2
Underline each adjective and circle the noun it is modifying.

1. A difficult job can be challenging.
2. But a good boss is an inspiration.
3. Sheila has a quiet boss.
4. He keeps a low profile.
5. Gary has a dynamic boss.
6. She works long hours.
7. Both employers earn high salaries.
8. This is a fair situation.
9. They are smart individuals.
10. Sheila and Gary appreciate their rare positions.

Still other adjectives can be formed by adding a word ending (or SUFFIX) to another word.

The *reasonable* employer (reason + able)
The *tactful* salesperson (tact + ful)
The *friendly* receptionist (friend + ly)
The *tireless* file clerk (tire + less)

Below is a list of ADJECTIVE-SUFFIXES. If you memorize them, you will be able to recognize them when they appear in your own writing.

ADJECTIVE-SUFFIXES

-able	understandable	-ful	beautiful	-ive	active
-ac	demoniac	-ible	sensible	-less	helpless
-al	musical	-ic	economic	-ly	lonely
-an	American	-ical	whimsical	-ory	trasitory
-ant	expectant	-il	civil	-ose	bellicose
-ar	molecular	-ile	senile	-ous	glamorous
-ary	revolutionary	-ish	foolish	-ulent	fraudulent
-ate	fortunate	-ite	erudite	-y	angry
-ent	confident				

★ EXERCISE 3
Turn each of these words into an adjective by providing an appropriate suffix.

1. care _____
2. express _____
3. love _____
4. luck _____
5. bible _____
6. boast _____

7. admit   _____

8. spine   _____

9. photograph   _____

10. infinity   _____

11. sense   _____

12. magic   _____

13. compare   _____

14. terror   _____

15. verb   _____

16. glory   _____

17. biology   _____

18. insist   _____

19. mood   _____

20. planet   _____

Another type of adjective must be mentioned here. It consists of more than one word and is called a PREPOSITIONAL PHRASE.

> The book *on my desk* belongs to Roger.
> The office *across the hall* is the President's suite.
> The flowers *in that vase* are dying.

First of all, you will notice that a PREPOSITIONAL PHRASE comes *after* the noun it describes. In the three examples, the modified nouns are *book, office,* and *flowers.*

The second important fact about prepositional phrases is that they always *begin with a preposition.* In the three examples, the prepositions are *on, across,* and *in.*

A PREPOSITION is a connecting word that shows the relationship between a noun and another word in the sentence. Sometimes this is a space relationship:

> The book *on* the desk
> The worm *under* the rock

Sometimes this is a time relationship:

> The day *before* yesterday
> The week *after* next

Here is a list of some of the more frequently used prepositions:

aboard	beside	off
about	between	on
above	by	outside
after	except	over
among	for	to
around	from	under
at	in	up
before	inside	upon
behind	into	until
below	like	with
beneath	of	within

The third thing you must know about a prepositional phrase concerns its NOUN.

> A NOUN THAT FOLLOWS A PREPOSITION IS <u>NEVER</u> THE SUBJECT OF A SENTENCE.

Consider this sentence:

> The rug on the floor is blue.

As you know, the verb is *is;* the subject is *rug. Floor* is a noun, but it is NOT the subject of the verb *is.* The meaning of the sentence supports this: the rug is blue, not the floor! *On the floor* is just a three-word adjective describing *rug.*

Technically, the noun that follows a preposition is called the OBJECT of the preposition. A noun cannot be an object and a subject at the same time.

★ EXERCISE 4
In each sentence, cross out the prepositional phrase. Then underline the subject and circle the verb.

1. The woman in charge is Ms. Skelton.
2. She is the president of the company.
3. The suite on the sixth floor is her office.
4. The telephones inside her office never stop ringing.
5. The people around her work hard.
6. The man by her side is her partner.
7. He is chairman of the board.
8. They work very closely at the office.
9. The success of her career took much effort.
10. She is a woman of determination.

Adverbs

Verbs can be modified in much the same way as nouns are. For example, consider this sentence:

> Margaret types slowly.

In this case, the verb is *types,* and the subject is *Margaret.* The adverb *slowly* explains *how* she types; it does not describe Margaret herself.

> AN ADVERB IS ANY WORD (OR GROUP OF WORDS) THAT ADDS INFORMATION TO A VERB.

In the following sentences, the ADVERBS are underlined:

> Ben speaks <u>well.</u>
> He looks <u>confidently</u> at his listeners.
> He expresses his ideas <u>smoothly.</u>
> He <u>clearly</u> articulates each word.

Notice that three of the four ADVERBS used end in *-ly.* In fact, most adverbs in English do end in *-ly;* they are formed by adding the *-ly* to an adjective.

slow	→	slowly
happy	→	happily
quiet	→	quietly
strong	→	strongly

Even many adjectives that are participles can be used as adverbs by adding an -ly ending:

exhausted	→	exhaustedly
alleged	→	allegedly
haunting	→	hauntingly
laughing	→	laughingly

★ EXERCISE 5
In each sentence, underline the verb and circle the adverb.

1. Greg desperately wanted a vacation.
2. So he cautiously asked his boss for time off.
3. She answered him regretfully.
4. She seriously needed his help.
5. He patiently explained his needs.
6. His mind had been wandering aimlessly.
7. His work was being done sloppily.
8. His boss looked at Greg hesitantly.
9. Then she calmly told him to go.
10. He politely thanked her.

★ EXERCISE 6
First change these adjectives into adverbs. Then use each new adverb in a sentence.

1. silent →

   _____

2. excited →

   _____

3. merry →

   _____

4. horrible →

   _____

5. weary →

   _____

6. patient →

   _____

7. studious →

   _____

8. correct →

   _____

9. joyful →

   _____

10. boasting →

   _____

You should also know that PREPOSITIONAL PHRASES can be used as ADVERBS, not just as ADJECTIVES.

I walked across the room.

In this sentence, the verb is *walked,* and the subject is *I.* You already know that *across the room* is a prepositional phrase; it consists of a preposition *(across)* followed by a noun *(the room).* But this time, the prepositional phrase is not adding information to another noun in the sentence. Instead, it is modifying the verb; it explains *where* or *how* I walked.

Here are some other examples of PREPOSITIONAL PHRASES being used as ADVERBS:

The treasurer signed *on the dotted line.*
The comet streaked *through the sky.*
The witness squirmed *in his chair.*
The manuscript slipped *from my hands.*

★ **EXERCISE 7**
In this letter, underline all of the prepositional phrases. See if you can decide whether each prepositional phrase is acting as an adjective or as an adverb.

Dear Sirs:

I would like to report an automobile accident. I am also making a claim for damages to my car.

The accident occurred on February 13. My car was parked on Elm Street. A snowstorm during the night had made the street quite icy. Mr. Kowalski's car skidded on the ice and hit my car. The left rear fender of my car was crushed. The damages are estimated at $950. Mr. Kowalski admits responsibility and has filed a police report (#003 726).

I would like restitution for the repair costs. My car may be viewed at Al's Auto Body Shop, 261 Hughes Avenue.

Thank you.

Sincerely yours,

You are probably familiar with words like *not* and *never.* But did you know that they are ADVERBS?

Gwen never leaves work early.

In this sentence, the verb is *leaves,* and the subject is *Gwen.* The word *never* is changing the verb in such a way as to make it NEGATIVE. *Never* is an ADVERB, not part of the verb.

Ken did *not* answer the telephone.

This time, the verb is a two-word verb: *did answer.* The subject is *Ken.* Here, the word *not* also makes the verb negative; it comes between the two words of the verb, but it is still an ADVERB, not part of the verb itself.

Not all adverbs that work this way are negative. Here are some other examples:

Norma *always* works hard.
Alice *sometimes* goofs off.
She can *also* concentrate on her job.

Notice that in the last of these examples the verb is *can concentrate*, split up by an adverb.

★ **EXERCISE 8**
In each of these sentences, circle the adverbs and underline the verbs. Watch out for split verbs!

1. Anita never asks questions.
2. She often makes mistakes.
3. Dennis will sometimes correct Anita's errors.
4. Anita always appreciates his help.
5. But she does not show it.
6. Anita always conceals her errors.
7. She should not hide her feelings.
8. Dennis can always perceive Anita's gratitude.
9. He also recognizes her shyness.
10. Anita should not neglect a good friend.

One last point must be made about adverbs. Consider this sentence:

The terribly exhausted stenographer dropped her pad.

We've already seen that *dropped* is the verb, *stenographer* is the subject, and *exhausted* is an adjective describing the subject. But what is *terribly*?

From the *-ly* ending, we can tell that *terribly* is an ADVERB. But it does not seem to be modifying a verb. In fact, the only verb in this sentence is *dropped*, which is not connected to *terribly* at all.

In this case, *terribly* is adding information to *exhausted*. That is, the adverb is modifying an adjective.

Similarly, an adverb can modify another adverb:

Mercedes reads very slowly.

Here, *slowly* is an adverb describing the verb *reads*. But *very* is another adverb describing the main adverb *slowly*.

Therefore, we must expand our definition of the adverb:

AN ADVERB IS ANY WORD (OR GROUP OF WORDS) THAT ADDS INFORMATION TO A VERB, AN ADJECTIVE, OR ANOTHER ADVERB.

★ **EXERCISE 9**
In each of these sentences, an adverb is underlined. Circle the word that the adverb is describing. Then, in the space at the right, indicate whether the described word is a verb, an adjective, or another adverb.

1. An organized resume is <u>extremely</u> important.   _____

2. It should market your talent <u>convincingly</u>.   _____

3. You must design your resume <u>very</u> carefully.   _____

4. It must <u>clearly</u> outline your work history.   _____

5. It should <u>also</u> include your educational background.   _____

6. Specialized skills will be <u>particularly</u> salable.   _____

7. Extracurricular activities help <u>surprisingly</u> well.   _____

8. The resume should be typed <u>accurately</u>.   ——————

9. A <u>crisply</u> worded cover letter should accompany the   ——————
resume.

10. Then an interview will be granted <u>more</u> readily.   ——————

Direct Objects

As you've probably noticed, many of the sentences we've studied contained more than one noun. But not all of these nouns acted as the subject in its sentence.

For example, when we first discussed prepositional phrases, we said that the noun that follows a preposition is called the OBJECT of the preposition.

In the sentence:

The rug on the floor is blue.

we said that the *floor* is the object of the preposition *on.* Together, the prepositional phrase *on the floor* is acting as a three-word adjective describing *rug.*

Another important kind of OBJECT is called the DIRECT OBJECT. This is a noun or pronoun that *receives* the action of the verb.

Consider this example:

Amina wrote the letter.

Here, the verb is *wrote,* and the subject is *Emily.* We find the subject by asking a question: Who or what *wrote the letter?*

To find the DIRECT OBJECT, we ask a different question: *Emily wrote what?* The answer (in this case the *letter*) is the direct object.

In the following sentences, the objects are underlined:

The lawyers argued the <u>case</u>.
The jury delivered its <u>verdict</u>.
The judge conferred the <u>sentence</u>.

★ EXERCISE 10
In each sentence, underline the direct object.

1. Greg was writing a memo.
2. He made it short and clear.
3. It concerned a specific topic.
4. It transmitted the necessary information.
5. He carefully retained a copy.
6. Greg's boss answered his memo.
7. She asked several questions.
8. Greg examined his copy.
9. He had omitted some details.
10. He quickly wrote another memo.

Predicate Nominatives and Adjectives

There is one more type of sentence completer we must discuss here. Sometimes a noun that comes after a verb is not an OBJECT.

Janice is a dentist.

In this sentence, the verb is *is,* and the subject is *Janice.* But *dentist* is not an object. Janice isn't doing something to a dentist; Janice and a dentist are one and the same. In other words, the sentence:

Janice is a dentist.

can be written as an equation:

Janice = a dentist

When a noun after a verb is the equivalent of the subject, it is called a PREDICATE NOMINATIVE. (*Predicate* simply means *verb; nominative* simply means *noun.* So this difficult label actually makes sense.)

In the following sentences, the PREDICATE NOMINATIVES are underlined:

Juanita was a <u>secretary</u>.
Now she is an <u>administrator</u>.
She may be the next company <u>president</u>.

Adjectives can also be used this way:

Janice is skillful.

As in our earlier example, *is* is the verb, and *Janice* is the subject. But this time, they are followed by an adjective, not a noun.

Still, we can set up an equation:

Janice = skillful

When an adjective after a verb is the equivalent of the subject, it is called a PREDICATE ADJECTIVE.

In the following sentences, the PREDICATE ADJECTIVES are underlined:

Juanita is <u>ambitious</u>.
She appears <u>inexhaustible</u>.
She will be <u>successful</u>.

★ **EXERCISE 11**
In each sentence, a completer is underlined. In the space at the right, indicate whether it is a predicate nominative (PN) or a predicate adjective (PA).

1. Insurance is a <u>means</u> of restoring financial stability after a loss.   _____

2. In everyday life, financial risk is always <u>possible</u>.   _____

3. Insurance, therefore, is <u>necessary</u> to reduce the chances of financial loss.   _____

4. Establishing a cash reserve is one <u>way</u> to control risk.   _____

5. Simply taking precautionary measures to minimize risk is also <u>important</u>.   _____

6. But the most common protection against financial loss is an insurance <u>policy</u>.   _____

7. An insurance policy is a legal <u>contract</u> between the policyholder and the insurance company.   _____

8. Under this contract, the insurance company becomes <u>responsible</u> for the potential financial burden in certain loss situations.   _____

9. A premium is the <u>fee</u> charged to the policyholder.   _____

10. Those policies are <u>best</u> that insure against risks of large financial loss with low probability of occurrence.   _____

★ REVIEW EXERCISES

A. Underline every adjective in this letter. Then draw an arrow to the noun it is describing.

Dear Mrs. Cochran:

Paying bills on time can save you money! High interest rates accumulate fast on overdue accounts. So why not send us a personal check today to clear your balance of $264.84.

Your current bill is now 60 days overdue. Two months are not a great lapse of time. But you have always been a prompt customer. And delayed payments have a troublesome way of being forgotten.

We look forward to hearing from you soon and keeping your sound credit rating intact.

Yours truly,

B. Underline every adverb in this memo. Then draw an arrow to the verb it is describing.

TO: Mr. Frank Doolittle, Supervisor

FROM: Liza Higgins, Assistant

DATE: October 12, 19--

SUBJECT: Mailroom delays

At your request, I have looked carefully into the problem of mailroom delays. Departments are receiving mail belatedly for a number of reasons:

1 Some mail is addressed improperly. So it is sent initially to the wrong department and must later be forwarded.

2 The mailroom is understaffed. The clerks handle mail as promptly as possible. But they get to each department slowly. They cannot cover all the departments efficiently.

This problem must be dealt with immediately. Complaints are mounting daily.

LH

C. Cross out all the prepositional phrases in these minutes.

AD HOC COMPUTER COMMITTEE OF ESCO, INC.
MINUTES OF THE MEETING OF DECEMBER 13, 19--

Presiding: Seymour Griffen

Present: Jack Rosenthal
Jean Russo
Fred Kurtz

Absent: Rose Schwartz

The meeting was called to order at 1:45 P.M. by Mr. Griffen. The main discussion of the meeting concerned the decision to purchase a computer.

Among the proposals were these:

Mr. Rosenthal observed that the present system of time-sharing was resulting in a slow turnaround time. He delineated the problems that arise when data are not available.

Ms. Russo presented a cost analysis: within two years, the purchase of a computer can be anticipated to have paid for itself in savings to the company.

It was agreed to recommend the purchase of a computer. Mr. Kurtz is to prepare a report.

The meeting adjourned at 3:00 P.M.

Respectfully submitted,

D. In each sentence, identify the underlined word as either a direct object (DO), a predicate adjective (PA), or a predicate nominative (PN).

1. Mr. Gleason is a supermarket manager.   DO PA PN
2. He is good at his job.   DO PA PN
3. He runs the store efficiently.   DO PA PN
4. He is responsible for purchasing stock.   DO PA PN
5. He handles customer complaints calmly.   DO PA PN
6. He rarely gets upset.   DO PA PN
7. Shoppers appreciate Mr. Gleason's pleasant manner.   DO PA PN
8. As a result, they are satisfied customers.   DO PA PN
9. The company acknowledges Mr. Gleason's fine work.   DO PA PN
10. He is a valuable employee.   DO PA PN
11. So they pay him a generous salary.   DO PA PN
12. This is a wise business practice.   DO PA PN
13. Mr. Gleason is a contented employee.   DO PA PN
14. He is dependable.   DO PA PN
15. And he is loyal to the company for which he works.   DO PA PN

3.
THE SENTENCE
vs.
FRAGMENTS
vs.
RUN-ONS

The Basic Sentence

One of the first things we discussed at the beginning of this book was that the CORE OF AN ENGLISH SENTENCE CONSISTS OF A SUBJECT AND A VERB:

> Sam sees the tree.

We have also examined sentences with one subject performing two verbs:

> Sam sees the tree and hears the birds.

And we have seen sentences with two subjects both of which perform the same verb:

> Sam and Willy golf.

It is even possible for a sentence to have two subjects each of which performs two verbs:

> Sam and Willy golf and swim.

Thus, we have already identified the four basic sentence patterns. If we use *S* to mean *subject* and *V* to mean *verb,* we can make a chart:

> S V.
> S V and V.
> S and S V.
> S and S V and V.

At this point, it might be wise to put aside the old definitions of sentences you have heard in the past. It is best, for example, *not* to think of a sentence as a "complete thought." Very few people beyond the age of five can express a whole thought in one sentence. Usually it takes several sentences, a paragraph, a page, even an entire book for an adult to finish a thought. (Of course, some thoughts are so simple that one sentence is enough to express them completely.)

The point is that thoughts and sentences are not equivalent. It is sort of like saying, "How many clocks make an hour?" A clock measures time; it can tell us what time of day it is. But it is not time itself. Similarly, sentences express a thought; they communicate one person's thought to another person. But a sentence itself is not a thought.

Therefore, the safest definition of a sentence is one that is based on grammar, not thoughts. After all, a sentence is a grammatical unit. For now, let us say that

> A SENTENCE IS A GROUP OF WORDS CONTAINING A
> SUBJECT AND A VERB.

More Complicated Sentences

Just as adults need more than one sentence to express a complete thought, so do they also need longer sentences than the four basic ones listed on page 29.

One of the easiest ways to write a longer sentence is to take two good basic sentences:

> Sam sees the tree.
> Willy hears the birds.

and combine them.

First of all, they can be combined with punctuation. Instead of keeping them as two basic sentences with a period between them, we can attach them with a semicolon:

> Sam sees the tree; Willy hears the birds.

A semicolon, we might say, is used much the way the period is used: it gets a subject-verb core on either side.

But a semicolon doesn't add much meaning. It suggests that the two parts are closely related, but it doesn't say how. A more meaningful way to combine sentences is to use a word.

There is a group of words you are already familiar with, called COORDINATORS. (You may also know them as "conjunctions.") Coordinators are another easy way to combine two short sentences into one longer one:

> Sam sees the tree, *and* Willy hears the birds.

Here, *and* is a COORDINATOR. It is used with a comma (*before* it) to combine two short sentences into one. There is a subject-verb core (Sam sees) to the left of the *comma-and,* and there is a subject-verb core (Willy hears) to the right.

There are seven coordinators that work just like *and:*

and	yet	for	nor
or	but	so	

You should memorize them so that you'll recognize them in your own writing. Here's a little trick, a mnemonic (or memory) device:

> Memorize the sentence, "An old yellow book feels so new." The
> first letter of each of these words is also the first letter of one of
> the coordinators.

> An old yellow book feels so new.
>
> **AND OR YET   BUT   FOR   SO NOR.**

Obviously, the difference between the COORDINATORS is in their meanings. But grammatically, they all work the same way. Therefore, we can add two more complicated sentence patterns to our chart:

> S V ; S V.
> S V , [coordinator] S V.

The patterns hold up, too, if you want to attach any combination of the original four basic sentence patterns, for example:

S V and V, | coordinator | S V.

Sam sees and hears the birds, but Willy sleeps.

★ EXERCISE 1
Combine these pairs of sentences, using one of the seven coordinators.

1. Peter would like to be an accountant. He would like to be a computer programmer.

2. He wants an interesting job. He hopes for a good salary.

3. He has planned his career carefully. He will probably reach his goal.

4. Sometimes he gets discouraged. He never gives up.

5. Megan didn't like her job. She simply quit.

6. At first she felt relieved. She hadn't considered her alternatives.

7. Now she is unemployed. She doesn't know what to do.

8. She hasn't found a new job. She has very little experience.

9. She could ask for her old job back. She could return to school.

10. Pam is a diligent lawyer. She hasn't received a promotion.

11. She is eager to advance. She thrives on new challenges.

12. She should speak to her boss. He may not be aware of her ambitions.

13. He may discourage her plans. She will be disappointed.

14. He may also encourage her. She should try the direct approach.

15. Women and men must take charge of their own careers. Nothing will happen.

16. They must prepare for their chosen jobs. They must accumulate experience.

17. They must be patient. They must also assert themselves.

18. Some companies are very large. You will have to attract your boss's attention.

19. Employers regard good workers. First they must be aware of the workers' merits.

20. Do your best. You will succeed.

The Fragment

There is yet another way to combine two short sentences into one longer one. This requires another kind of conjunction called a SUBORDINATOR.

We have defined the sentence as A GROUP OF WORDS CONTAINING A SUBJECT AND A VERB. But now we must point out an exception.

It is possible for a group of words to contain a subject and its verb and still not be a complete sentence. Our original example is a perfectly good sentence:

Sam sees the tree.

It has a verb *(sees)* and a subject *(Sam)*. But suppose we add a word:

When Sam sees the tree.

This new version still has a verb *(sees)* and a subject *(Sam)*. But it's no longer a complete sentence. By adding the word *when,* we have turned a perfectly good sentence into a FRAGMENT.

This is because *when* is one of a group of words called SUBORDINATORS. These words, when attached to a good basic sentence, turn that sentence into a FRAGMENT, an *incomplete* sentence.

Here is a list of subordinators. Memorize them so that you will always recognize them when you see them:

SUBORDINATORS

W who, what, where, when, why, which, whether, while
I if
S since, so that
H how

A as, after, although
B before, because
O once
U unless, until
T than, that, though

Did you notice the mnemonic device in the chart? Every letter in the words WISH ABOUT is also the first letter of some of the subordinators. There are 23 subordinators in all, but, this way, you only have to memorize one letter at a time.

Now we can define a FRAGMENT, which is a serious error in sentence structure. A sentence may be incomplete (a FRAGMENT) for three different reasons:

(1) NO VERB:
Ruth, a public relations writer.

(2) NO SUBJECT:
Wrote the article.

(3) A SUBORDINATOR ATTACHED TO THE ONLY SUBJECT AND VERB:
When Ruth, a public relations writer, wrote the article.

★ **EXERCISE 2**
Some of these are correct sentences. Others are fragments. For each item, find any verbs, subjects, and subordinators. Then decide whether the item is a sentence (S) or a fragment (F).

1. You must prepare carefully.   S F
2. Before you go on a job interview.   S F
3. You should anticipate questions.   S F
4. That you may be asked.   S F
5. About items on your resume.   S F
6. You should dress conservatively.   S F
7. But feel comfortable about your appearance.   S F
8. You should take with you a pen, a pad, and your re-   S F
   sume.
9. You should be sure to arrive on time.   S F
10. To make a good first impression.   S F

★ **EXERCISE 3**
Identify each of the following as either a good sentence (S) or a fragment (F).

1. Even before the American revolution.   S F
2. The American labor movement had begun.   S F
3. The first unions were associations of skilled artisans.   S F
4. Whose aim was to provide each other with mutual   S F
   financial assistance in the event of misfortune.
5. As unions grew in the early nineteenth century.   S F
6. Small locals, isolated within their communities.   S F
7. Gradually began to unite, forming national associa-   S F
   tions.
8. More than thirty-two national unions were formed by   S F
   the end of the Civil War.
9. Some of them are still in existence.   S F
10. Their original purpose, to improve working conditions   S F
    and wages, continues to exist as well.

Still More Complicated Sentences

As you may have suspected, many of the sentences and fragments in the preceding exercises can be combined to form a single, long complete sentence. For example, the fragment:

> But feel comfortable about your appearance.

may be attached to the sentence before it:

> You should dress conservatively.

The resulting sentence:

> You should dress conservatively but feel comfortable about your
> appearance.

would follow the second of our basic sentence patterns (S V and V)—one subject *(you)* doing two verbs *(should dress* and *feel).*

Therefore, combining the sentences in this way would eliminate the error of the fragment.

But what about a fragment that has both a subject and a verb?

> Before you go on a job interview.

In this fragment from Exercise 2, there are a verb *(go)* and a subject *(you).* It is a fragment because the subordinator *before* is attached to the subject-verb core.

Prior to this fragment came a sentence:

> You must prepare carefully.

This sentence has one verb *(must prepare)* and one subject *(you).* If we combine the sentence and the fragment, we will not be forming one of our basic sentence patterns.

Nevertheless, attaching the fragment to the good sentence before it would correct the error:

> You must prepare carefully before you go on a job interview.

This is because SUBORDINATORS may be used much as COORDINATORS are. Here is the sentence pattern to add to our chart:

S V | subordinator | S V.

Notice, however, that no comma is used before the SUBORDINATOR.

★ EXERCISE 4
Combine the pairs of sentences by using a subordinator *between* them.

1. Some businesses are growing substantially. The economy as a whole is suffering from recession.

2. They are prospering. They benefit from the recessionary situation.

3. Employment agencies are busy. More unemployed people are looking for jobs.

4. Repair services do well. The stock market goes up or down.

5. People try to repair their old possessions. They spend money on new ones.

6. Discount stores show increased sales. Department store sales drop.

7. People want to get more for their money now. They are worried about the future.

8. Clever entrepreneurs discover. Recession can work to their advantage.

9. They provide goods and services. People in a recessionary economy demand.

10. These businesspersons use a difficult situation. Other people complain and wait.

★ EXERCISE 5
Combine the pairs of sentences by using a subordinator *between* them.

1. You should plan your wardrobe. You go on a job interview.

2. Your outfit deserves careful thought. First impressions are important.

3. Conservative garments are best. You want to appear competent and sensible.

4. They should also be comfortable. You don't want to be distracted.

5. For a woman, a simple skirt and blouse are a good choice. A dress is also acceptable.

6. Pants are not a good idea. They are appropriate to the particular job.

7. A man should wear a jacket and tie. The position is an office job or not.

8. Unpolished shoes or excessive makeup could ruin your chances. You answer any questions.

9. You should scrutinize yourself in a mirror. You leave for the interview.

10. You want to look your best. You can be your best.

SUBORDINATORS are a bit more flexible than COORDINATORS, for we can use them in an additional way. With a SUBORDINATOR, we can also attach a fragment to a good sentence *after* it:

FRAGMENT: After Mary composed the letter.
SENTENCE: She transmitted it.
LONGER SENTENCE: After Mary composed the letter, she transmitted it.

Thus, our fourth complicated sentence pattern can be charted like this:

subordinator S V, S V.

Notice that when a subordinator comes at the beginning of a sentence, a comma is used between the two subject-verb cores.

★ EXERCISE 6
Combine the pairs of sentences by using a subordinator at the beginning.

1. James did not intend to look for a job immediately. He set up his resume before graduation.

2. He did not want to risk being forgotten. He asked three teachers for letters of reference.

3. He could get practice. He went on a few job interviews.

4. He was ready to look for a job. He was prepared.

5. Judy wanted to start work right after school. She contacted the placement office a month before graduation.

6. That gave her several weeks. She knew she needed as much time as possible to look for a job.

7. She went on more and more interviews. She learned to relax.

8. The ideal job came along. She handled the interview impressively.

9. She had had practice. Nervousness didn't get in her way.

10. James and Judy planned ahead. Their job hunts were successful.

★ EXERCISE 7
Combine the pairs of sentences by using a subordinator at the beginning.

1. Some people get a great deal done in a given amount of time. Others do not.

2. You want to get more done. Effective scheduling is essential.

3. You set aside some time each day for planning. You will have trouble getting organized.

4. You allow time for planning. You should cross all other committed time off your calendar.

5. You set deadlines. You will be more likely to achieve your goals.

6. You schedule an activity. You should estimate its required time.

7. You schedule time for relaxation. You will not be as effective on the job.

8. Overcommitment is one of the major causes of ineffectiveness. You must decide what not to do.

9. You work best in the morning. Schedule important tasks for that time of day.

10. You capitalize on your time. You can become a more effective person.

The Run-On

In addition to FRAGMENTS, you must be aware of another possible sentence structure error. Just as a fragment is *not enough* to be a complete sentence, so it is possible to put *too much* into a sentence. The result is called a RUN-ON.

A RUN-ON occurs when two sentences are combined without using one of the four complicated sentence patterns. This is a run-on:

Mr. Nguyen dictated a letter Frank transcribed it.

As you know, this so-called sentence contains two subject-verb cores: Mr. Levitt (subject)–dictated (verb) and Frank (subject)–transcribed (verb). Therefore, we have enough material here for two separate sentences.

Putting a comma between the sentences will *not* help:

Mr. Nguyen dictated the letter, Frank transcribed it.

What we have written still doesn't conform to any of our sentence patterns.

Therefore, a RUN-ON occurs when we try to combine two sentences into one by just sticking them together:

S V S V.

Or a RUN-ON may occur when we combine two sentences into one by using just a comma:

S V, S V.

To correct the run-on, we have several choices:

Mr. Nguyen dictated the letter; Frank transcribed it.
S V; S V.

or:

Mr. Nguyen dictated the letter, and Frank transcribed it.
S V, | coordinator | S V.

or:

Mr. Nguyen dictated the letter before Frank transcribed it.
S V | subordinator | S V.

or:

After Mr. Nguyen dictated the letter, Frank transcribed it.
| subordinator | S V, S V.

★ **EXERCISE 8**
Some of these are good sentences (S), and others are run-ons (RO). Identify them accordingly.

1. Your salary indicates your value to the company.	S RO
2. When you want a raise, you must be well prepared.	S RO
3. Before your salary review, you should find out the average salaries in your field.	S RO
4. You should also find out the salaries of the jobs just above yours, this will indicate your ambition.	S RO
5. You should inform your boss of your expectations you should not be too subtle.	S RO
6. To get a raise, you must be doing more than your basic duties, they merit no extra reward.	S RO
7. You must be doing something extra, special reports and projects are good examples.	S RO
8. When your salary is reviewed, you should remind your boss of what you have done.	S RO
9. When bargaining, you should not threaten to resign, you may have to follow through.	S RO
10. Instead, you should ask for more than you want and then compromise.	S RO

★ **EXERCISE 9**
Some of these are good sentences (S), and others are run-ons (RO). Identify them accordingly.

1. Marlboro's manufacturing business had grown, she decided to change her accountant.	S RO
2. To find a new accountant, she began by soliciting recommendations from people in her industry.	S RO
3. She also spoke with bankers and lawyers in her community and then narrowed her list to six strong candidates.	S RO
4. She wanted an accounting firm with impeccable credentials, experience with businesses like hers was also a priority.	S RO
5. Her business must not be too big for the accountant to handle, it must not be too small to be important to the accountant.	S RO
6. Marlboro met personally with a partner from each accounting firm, she wanted to weed out personality conflicts.	S RO
7. Next she requested written estimates from each accountant in order to compare the costs and services that each would provide.	S RO
8. Marlboro involved her own management team in the final decision, the finance manager's opinion was especially valuable.	S RO
9. When the new accountant was chosen, Marlboro and her staff felt confident about their choice.	S RO
10. They had found a compatible professional who could handle the company's growth.	S RO

Words of Transition

WARNING: There is a group of words that look a lot like subordinators and often have the same meanings. They are called WORDS OF TRANSITION.

But words of transition may not be used to combine two short sentences into one long one. To use them this way results in a RUN-ON.

I felt sick. I stayed home.
RUN-ON: I felt sick therefore I stayed home.
OR
I felt sick, therefore I stayed home.
CORRECT: I felt sick. Therefore I stayed home.
OR
I felt sick; therefore I stayed home.

Therefore is NOT a subordinator or coordinator, so it CANNOT be used to combine two sentences into one. When *therefore* is used, a period or a semicolon is still required between the two subject-verb cores.

If you have memorized the coordinators and subordinators, there should be no problem. But here is a list of WORDS OF TRANSITION so that you'll know them when you see them.

WORDS OF TRANSITION

accordingly	henceforth	nevertheless
also	however	on the contrary
anyhow	in addition	on the other hand
as a result	indeed	otherwise
at the same time	in fact	still
besides	in other words	that is
consequently	instead	then
for example	likewise	therefore
furthermore	meanwhile	thus
hence	moreover	

Summary

SENTENCE STRUCTURE

Basic Sentences

S V.
S V and V.
S and S V.
S and S V and V.

More Complicated Sentences

S V; S V.
S V, [coordinator] S V.
S V [subordinator] S V.
[subordinator] S V, S V.

Fragment

[subordinator] S V.

Run-On

S V S V.
S V, S V.

★ REVIEW EXERCISES

A. Identify each of these as either a good sentence (S), a fragment (F), or a run-on (RO). Circle your choice.

		S	F	RO
1.	Most of the best jobs are never advertised.	S	F	RO
2.	Some are filled through employment agencies, many of the very best are filled through the grapevine.	S	F	RO
3.	When people in an organization know the job will be open and tell friends.	S	F	RO
4.	The friends tell friends, and applications pour in.	S	F	RO
5.	Placing a job-wanted ad in your local newspaper describing the kind of employment that you are seeking.	S	F	RO
6.	This wastes money, however, adding a reward to the ad makes a difference.	S	F	RO
7.	An ad that offers payment to anyone who knows about a good unadvertised position.	S	F	RO
8.	The reward is promised only if the information leads to the applicant's accepting the position.	S	F	RO
9.	You will have to pay just one person, the reward will probably be less than an agency fee would be.	S	F	RO
10.	You will be breaking into the whole network of grapevine news about the good jobs that are available in your locale.	S	F	RO
11.	Networking, or making contacts, is a way to achieve your goals.	S	F	RO
12.	Having lunch with persons of value to your career.	S	F	RO
13.	Good networking also means talking about your job with these persons, you must let them know how well you do it.	S	F	RO
14.	Registering your keen interest in career advancement.	S	F	RO
15.	You should make a list of everyone whom you know or know of, you should include your relatives and friends and their own networks.	S	F	RO
16.	Another list of the network that you want, the contacts that you need to achieve your goals.	S	F	RO
17.	On a third list, you should consider how to meet the contacts that you need.	S	F	RO
18.	Trade organizations as well as volunteer organizations.	S	F	RO
19.	It helps, too, to have a schedule to keep from "letting things happen," networking is "making things happen."	S	F	RO
20.	Networking works best when you know what you want from each person and what you can give back in return.	S	F	RO

B. This letter contains a number of fragments. Using the techniques you have learned in this chapter, revise the letter, correcting the errors.

Dear Mr. Fritz:

Along with the many other employees of Rome Industries. I would like to offer you my sincere good wishes. On the occasion of your retirement. We will truly miss you.

Because of your outstanding performance. As assistant public relations director. We would like to express our appreciation with a small gift. You will find a check for $1000 enclosed.

In addition, you will be cordially invited. To the annual executive banquet. At which you will be presented with a gold watch. Symbolizing your many years of loyal service.

I hope that your retirement. Will be healthy and rewarding. And that you will visit us whenever you have a chance. It will not be easy. To replace a colleague as amiable and efficient as you have been these nineteen years.

Sincerely yours,

C. This letter contains a number of run-ons. Revise the letter, correcting the errors.

Dear Ms. Lauren:

Thank you for inviting Dr. Marcus to speak at your health club, physical fitness through psychotherapy is a topic in which he is very interested.

Unfortunately, Dr. Marcus will be out of town through the month of August, therefore he will be unable to speak to your members until the fall. Moreover, he will be traveling through southern Italy, consequently, I will not be able to inform him of your invitation for several weeks.

Nevertheless, I am sure Dr. Marcus would appreciate your invitation, I will convey it to him as soon as he returns. Our office will get in touch with you at that time, I hope we will be able to arrange a date for the lecture then.

Sincerely yours,

D. This letter contains a number of run-ons and fragments. Revise the letter, correcting the errors.

Dear Mr. Woolf:

In reply to your inquiry of July 31, 19--, regarding Ms. Ruby R. Hood. I am pleased to supply the information you requested.

Ms. Hood was in our employ for three years, she was a visiting nurse in our midtown district. Her principal responsibility was to tend to a number of elderly patients. Whose needs included domestic assistance as well as medical attention and bedside care.

Ms. Hood was an outstanding nurse, many of her patients looked upon her with grandmotherly affection. She related well to even the most crotchety of them. And was capable of performing under the most difficult, even dangerous, of conditions.

It is entirely without hesitation. That I recommend Ms. Hood for the position of Head Nurse at your institution.

Very sincerely yours,

E. Without changing the order, rewrite these groups of words as a single paragraph. To do this, decide whether a period, a comma, or no punctuation at all is needed at the end of each line. Do not change the order of the lines, and remember to capitalize the first word of your new sentences.

1. Public relations letters
   a highly specialized mode of business communications
   are written to influence public opinion
   a public relations writer prepares news releases
   as well as advertisements, speeches
   and other written forms
   that promote an organization's positive image
   to become a public relations writer
   one must be clever with words
   but a knowledge of sales technique
   and a sense of timing
   are further requirements
   a persistent competitive spirit will also help
   for public relations is a difficult field
   to break into

   _____

   _____

   _____

   _____

   _____

   _____

   _____

   _____

   _____

   _____

   _____

   _____

   _____

   _____

   _____

   _____

   _____

2. Experiencing rapid growth in the past decade
the paralegal profession offers many opportunities
to become a paralegal can take
as little as three months
in one of the hundreds of paralegal training programs
across the country
paralegals are legal assistants
who work with lawyers and other legal professionals
the paralegal's duties include legal research
as well as drafting and indexing legal documents
and assisting in trial preparation
employed by local, state, and federal governments
by private law firms
and by corporations
there are over 80,000 paralegals in the United States
nearly 80 percent of them are women

_____

_____

_____

_____

_____

_____

_____

_____

_____

_____

_____

_____

_____

_____

_____

4.
SUBJECT-VERB AGREEMENT

The rules of SUBJECT-VERB AGREEMENT are all based on the use of S-endings. That's why, before we begin to discuss agreement, we must dispel a few myths about the S.

The main point is that, despite what you may have been told, the S-ending does *not* always make a word plural. Actually, the S-ending has several different uses, depending upon the kind of word it's attached to.

The Natural S

Many words in English have an S as their final letter. But these S's are *not* endings. They are part of the basic spelling of the word.

kiss   bus   miss   Paris

Such words end in S the way other words may end in T or N or R, and so on.

★ **EXERCISE 1**
Here is a list of words that end in S. Put a check next to those whose final letter is a natural S.

dismiss ___	wants ___	pens ___
glasses ___	bliss ___	discuss ___
happiness ___	tries ___	boss ___
moss ___	cross ___	toss ___
trusts ___	class ___	roses ___
abuses ___	sees ___	sadness ___
dress ___	address ___	asks ___
diets ___	amuses ___	helpless ___
factories ___	readiness ___	fixes ___
fuss ___	boxes ___	dishes ___

The Noun S

This is the PLURAL S. By adding an S to the end of a singular noun, the noun becomes plural:

1 book   2 book<u>s</u>
1 hat   several hat<u>s</u>

By adding this S-ending, we go from one to more than one.

However, if a noun already ends in a NATURAL S, we add an ES-ending to make it plural.

1 kiss   10 kisses
1 bus   many buses

ES is also used if a noun ends in CH, SH, X, or Z:

watch	watches
dish	dishes
tax	taxes
quiz	quizzes

Also, nouns that end in Y form plurals in one of two ways:

1. If the letter before the Y is a consonant, the plural is formed by changing the Y to I and adding ES.

company	companies
secretary	secretaries

2. If the letter before the Y is a vowel, just add an S.

attorney	attorneys
essay	essays

Since there are so many irregular nouns in English, it is difficult to come up with other rules. For example, some nouns that end in F or FE become plural by changing the F to V and adding ES:

half	halves
wife	wives

But others become plural by simply adding an S:

chief	chiefs
proof	proofs

Similarly, some nouns that end in O are made plural with an S:

radio	radios
piano	pianos

But other nouns that end in O need an ES to become plural:

tomato	tomatoes
hero	heroes

Special kinds of irregular nouns will be discussed later in this chapter. But you should always consult a dictionary whenever you aren't sure of a plural form.

★ **EXERCISE 2**
This chart should contain both the singular and plural form of each noun. Fill in the blanks.

SINGULAR	PLURAL	SINGULAR	PLURAL
cost			factories
journey		safe	
	buzzes	life	
	inquiries		foxes
	monies	banana	
anniversary		loss	
	requests		cargoes
	finances		trustees
success			phonies
ax		banjo	

The Possessive S ('s or s')

This S-ending is also attached to nouns. But it does *not* turn a singular noun into a plural noun. In fact, the POSSESSIVE S turns a noun into a kind of adjective!

> One girl has a pen.
> The girl's pen is green.
> (The pen of the girl is green.)

In the first sentence, the verb is *has,* and the subject is *girl.* Therefore, *girl* is being used as a noun.

But in the second sentence, the verb is *is,* and the subject is *pen.* The word *girl's* is describing the word *pen.* That means that by adding the *'s,* we turned an ordinary noun into an adjective.

As you can see, the difference between the NOUN S and the POSSESSIVE S is the use of a punctuation mark. This mark is called an APOSTROPHE.

Note: To make a *plural noun* possessive, *do not* add *'s.* Just add an apostrophe. (The S is already there!)

> The girls' pens are blue.
> (The pens of the girls are blue.)

For other uses of the APOSTROPHE, see the chapter on punctuation.

★ **EXERCISE 3**
Rephrase each of these by using a possessive S-ending.

Example:
The responsibilities of the supervisors are distributed equally.
The supervisors' responsibilities are distributed equally.

1. The policy of this company is to review salaries every six months.

   _____

   _____

2. The salaries of all employees are evaluated carefully.

   _____

   _____

3. The performance of an employee, of course, is most important.

   _____

   _____

4. The opinion of an immediate superior is also a major consideration.

   _____

   _____

5. The objectivity of the administration is reasonably high.

   _____

   _____

6. The loyal service of an employee is usually recognized.

   _____

   _____

7. The merit of a raise is usually acknowledged.

_____

_____

8. A reward often follows the outstanding performance of someone.

_____

_____

9. The employees of this company find the system fair.

_____

_____

10. The bosses know how to maintain the satisfaction of their workers.

_____

_____

The Verb S

Note: The VERB S is only used in the PRESENT TENSE. That means the verb must be happening RIGHT NOW.

This is the difficult S-ending. It is the reverse of the way we usually think of S-endings. First, it is added to VERBS, not nouns. Second, it makes a verb, in a sense, SINGULAR!

The basic rule is this: When the subject of a PRESENT TENSE VERB is a SINGULAR noun, the verb needs an S-ending.

> The stenographer takes dictation.
> The secretary types the letter.

If the PRESENT TENSE VERB has a PLURAL noun for a subject, the verb gets NO S-ending.

> Stenographers take dictation.
> Secretaries type letters.

Notice that this means that between a verb and its subject there is really only one S-ending to go around. Either there is an S on the verb, _or_ there is an S on the subject.

> My vacation seems short.
> Our vacations seem short.

If a singular noun has a NATURAL S at the end, it doesn't really have an S-ending. So its verb would still need an S-ending:

> The boss yells.
> The bosses yell.

★ **EXERCISE 4**
In each sentence, if the subject is singular, make it plural. If the subject is plural, make it singular. Then change the verb to agree with the new subject.

Example:
The new file clerk appears to be doing well.
The new file clerks appear to be doing well.

1. An airport employs many people.

_____

2. The pilot flies jets all over the world.

_____

3. The navigator keeps track of direction.

_____

4. The flight attendants take care of the passengers.

_____

5. The ground crew checks the plane's condition.

_____

6. The baggage handlers toss the luggage.

_____

7. The ticket agents arrange the seating.

_____

8. The customs official opens bags.

_____

9. Tower controls direct the planes.

_____

10. The security agents watch for terrorists.

_____

★ **EXERCISE 5**
In these sentences, find the subjects. Then decide whether the verb should have an S-ending or not. Circle the correct verb form.

1. Local government (offer, offers) many job opportunities.
2. Cities (hire, hires) policemen.
3. Citizens (need, needs) fire protection.
4. Sanitation workers (clean, cleans) the streets.
5. Town Hall (employ, employs) many clerks and secretaries.
6. Politicians (have, has) government jobs, too.
7. The mayor's salary (come, comes) from the government.
8. Taxes (pay, pays) all these wages.
9. So taxpayers really (employ, employs) all these people.
10. Each citizen (are, is) actually an employer.

In the last sentence of the preceding exercise, the verbs were a bit different from the others. Yet *is* and *are* are verbs that you have already seen. You know that they are part of the verb TO BE. You may not know that TO BE presents special problems in subject-verb agreement.

First of all, TO BE is irregular. So we can't just add an S-ending or not. The S-forms and the non-S-forms are completely different words (as in the case of *is* and *are*).

Also, unlike any other verb in English, TO BE has an S-form and a non-S form in the PAST TENSE, too.

	PRESENT	PAST
SINGULAR	is	was
PLURAL	are	were

Here are a few examples:

One bookkeeper is not enough.
Two bookkeepers are enough.

One executive was working on the deal.
Several executives were working on the deal.

Am, the fifth form of the verb TO BE, is of course used only when the subject is *I.*

I am busy.

★ EXERCISE 6
In each sentence, find the subject. Then circle the correct form of the verb.

1. Recession (is, are) a serious economic problem.
2. Because of it, companies (is, are) closing down.
3. Workers (is, are) being laid off.
4. Consumers (is, are) buying fewer goods and services.
5. As a result, stores (is, are) going out of business.
6. Homeowners (is, are) having difficulty meeting mortgage payments.
7. Real estate prices (was, were) high.
8. Now, however, real estate values (is, are) falling.
9. Banks (was, were) paying higher interest rates than they are now.
10. Americans (is, are) worried about the future.

Using *am* when the subject is *I* brings up another important point about SUBJECT-VERB AGREEMENT. What happens to the verb when its subject is a pronoun?

Since pronouns don't get S-endings to make them plural, and since some pronouns (like *you*) can be used as either singular or plural, the rules we've learned so far won't help us when a pronoun is the subject of a present tense verb.

But the problem is not difficult:

WHEN THE SUBJECT IS *HE, SHE, IT, THIS,* OR *THAT,* THE VERB NEEDS AN S-ENDING. WHEN THE SUBJECT IS *I, YOU, WE, THEY, THESE,* OR *THOSE,* THE VERB GETS NO S-ENDING.

For example:

He travel<u>s</u> on business quite often.
They travel on business occasionally.

This idea <u>is</u> interesting.
Those are not interesting.

★ EXERCISE 7
Identify the subject of each sentence; then circle the correct form of the verb.

1. It (are, is) easy to get to our office.
2. We (travel, travels) by various means.
3. I (take, takes) the bus to work every day.
4. You usually (drive, drives).
5. She (have, has) to take a bus and then a train.
6. They (walk, walks) together.
7. When it (rain, rains), they don't walk.

8. Then they (take, takes) a cab.
9. It (are, is) most expensive to drive to work.
10. You (have, has) to pay for gas as well as parking.

Although the basic rules of subject-verb agreement are straightforward, there are situations in which the rules are not easy to apply. Looking for an S-ending on the subject to decide whether the verb needs an S-ending will not always work.

COMPOUND SUBJECTS

In our last unit, you will remember, one of our basic sentence patterns included a COMPOUND SUBJECT:

> S and S V.
> Sam and Willy talk.

That is, the whole subject consists of two nouns (at least) connected by the word *and.*

In terms of subject-verb agreement, compound subjects (nouns connected by *and*) are considered plural. That means their present tense verbs *do not* take S-endings.

> The desk *is* mine.
> The chair *is* mine.
>   BUT
> The desk and chair *are* mine.

In this example, neither noun in the subject has an S-ending on it. Still, we give the verb no S-ending either. By connecting the nouns with *and,* we are in effect adding them together; the subject is now two things.

Of course, sometimes one or more nouns in a compound subject will have an S-ending.

> The treasurer and her two assistants work hard.
> The typewriters and adding machine need repair.
> All sales representatives and their families are invited to the company picnic.

But these S-endings are just an extra clue. The *and* alone tells us *not* to put an S-ending on the verb.

⋆ **EXERCISE 8**
After finding the subject (Watch out for compounds!), circle the correct verb in each of these sentences.

1. My salary and benefits (satisfy, satisfies) me.
2. Ten vacation days and twelve holidays (are, is) allowed off.
3. My insurance (cover, covers) all kinds of emergencies.
4. Medical bills and dental expenses (are, is) included.
5. I even (have, has) life insurance.
6. Profit sharing and incentives (augment, augments) my income.
7. A pension plan and savings program (help, helps) me prepare for retirement.
8. My expense account (meet, meets) my business needs.
9. Business trips and conventions occasionally (break, breaks) the routine.
10. My work and its returns (are, is) quite rewarding.

OR AND *NOR*

When the nouns in a subject are connected by *or,* the rules change. Let's look at some variations:

> My secretary or my assistant *screens* my calls.
> My secretaries or my assistant *screens* my calls.
> BUT
> My secretary or my assistants *screen* my calls.
> My secretaries or my assistants *screen* my calls.

Can you see the pattern? The word *secretary* has no effect on the verb; whether it has an S-ending or not doesn't matter.

The word *assistant* is what counts here. When *assistant* has no S-ending (the first two examples), the verb gets an S-ending. When *assistants* is used with an S-ending (the second two examples), the verb gets *no* S-ending.

This is because *assistant* is the noun closest to the verb.

> WHEN THE NOUNS IN A SUBJECT ARE CONNECTED BY <u>OR</u>, THE NOUN CLOSEST TO THE VERB DETERMINES WHETHER THE VERB GETS AN S-ENDING.

This rule applies with the expression "either . . . or . . ." also:

> Either your bill or our records *are* in error.

The noun *records* is closest to the verb; because *records* has an S-ending, we use a verb with no S-ending, *are.*

The rule holds true, as well, with *nor* and the expression "neither . . . nor . . .":

> Neither I nor my partner *recalls* your order.

Here, *partner* is closest to the verb, so *recalls* gets an S-ending.

★ **EXERCISE 9**
In each sentence, examine the subject; then circle the correct form of the verb.

1. Neither good connections nor a wealthy father (are, is) enough to get ahead.
2. Friends or parents (are, is) of course helpful.
3. But your career choice or specialization (do, does) not necessarily coincide with theirs.
4. An ambitious self-starter (make, makes) his or her own contacts.
5. A liberal arts college or vocational training (provide, provides) a good start.
6. Either a sound education or solid work experience (are, is) essential.
7. Related courses or apprentice work (prepare, prepares) you for your first real job.
8. Good grades or favorable references (say, says) much about your work habits.
9. Summertime or after-school jobs (help, helps) build up resumes.
10. Your own ambition and determination (are, is) what ultimately count.

INDEFINITE PRONOUNS

INDEFINITE PRONOUNS are a group of pronouns that do not point out a specific person or thing. When used as the subject of a present tense verb, an INDEFINITE PRONOUN presents a problem because it doesn't have an S-ending to let us know whether it is singular or plural.

Fortunately, INDEFINITE PRONOUNS can be divided into three smaller groups, according to whether they are singular or plural. This means that there is some memorizing involved, but the effort will pay off in fewer errors.

1. Singular Indefinite Pronouns

Singular indefinite pronouns require an S-ending on their verbs.

> another   little   every
> each   much

These words (except *every*) can be used alone:

> <u>Little</u> <u>remains</u> to be done.

Or they may be used with a real noun right after them:

> <u>Little work</u> <u>remains</u> to be done.

(Of course, in the second situation, the S-ending on the verb is obviously needed because *work* has no S-ending. Right?)

Some of these words *seem* to mean something plural. For instance, when we say "every person in the room" we are referring to a lot of people. However, what we *mean* is "every single person in the room considered individually." The same thing is true of *each*: it implies "each *one*."

Much is similar. It suggests a large quantity of something. But think of it as a single quantity, very big but only one. "Much money" could mean many dollars, but it is *one* amount altogether.

There is also a group of "combination" indefinite pronouns that are singular, too (and so need an S-ending on their verbs). These can be learned by studying a chart. Attach any one word on the left to any one word on the right, and you come up with a SINGULAR INDEFINITE PRONOUN.

> some
> every
>   one
>   body
> any
>   thing
> no

For example:

> Someone <u>has</u> borrowed my slide rule.
> Nothing <u>is</u> impossible.

Some of these combinations "sound" plural, like the other singular indefinite pronouns mentioned before. Here, though, we have an extra clue: *One, body,* and *thing* are all singular. Neither has an S-ending. So their verbs (in the present tense) must take an S-ending.

---

1. Everyone (want, wants) to join the committee.
2. Each (pay, pays) a membership fee.
3. Much (are, is) collected.
4. Another problem (remain, remains).
5. Somebody (have, has) to be elected chairperson.
6. No one (seem, seems) willing to take the post.
7. Finally, two members (volunteer, volunteers).
8. Little (are, is) said before the vote.

9. Someone (move, moves) to end the meeting.
10. Another (are, is) scheduled before adjournment.

---

2. Plural Indefinite Pronouns

Five indefinite pronouns are always plural. Therefore, when used as a subject of a present tense verb, they require *no* S-ending on the verb.

both   few   many   several   others

For example:

Few recognize the importance of perseverance.
Many give up too readily.

Notice that the *meaning* of these words is plural, which should help when you memorize them.

★ **EXERCISE 11**
Circle the correct verb for each sentence.

1. Many (have, has) applied for the job.
2. Several (are, is) being interviewed.
3. Few actually (qualify, qualifies).
4. Two applicants (seem, seems) most experienced.
5. Both (have, has) done similar work in the past.
6. Each (are, is) well trained.
7. Many questions (are, is) put to them.
8. Several points (contribute, contributes) to the final decision.
9. Both (are, is) eventually hired.
10. The others (are, is) turned away.

---

3. Variable Indefinite Pronouns

The last group of indefinite pronouns is tricky because they are variable.

all   most   none   some

These pronouns can be singular or plural depending upon the "real" noun to which they refer.
When the "real" noun is used, this is clear:

Some coffee *is* left.
Some employees *are* leaving.

Because *coffee* has no S-ending, we know to use *is;* because *employees* has an S-ending, we know to use *are.*
But it is possible to have a sentence in which the "real" noun is omitted —in response to a question, for example, or in a paragraph when the noun has been mentioned previously:

The responsibility is all yours.
None is mine.

These books belong to you.
None are mine.

It is essential, therefore, that when you use a variable indefinite pronoun, you keep in mind the "real" noun it is referring to.
Here's a trick you can use to help you decide whether or not the verb gets an S-ending:

—If you can *count* the real noun that an indefinite pronoun is referring to, *do not* give the verb an S-ending.

—If you must *measure* the real noun, *do* give the verb an S-ending.

Look back at our first example. *Coffee* must be measured, so it is singular and requires an S-ending on its verb. But *employees* can be counted, so the subject is plural and the verb needs no S-ending.

Similarly, we must measure *responsibility,* but we can count *books.*

⋆ **EXERCISE 12**
In each sentence, circle the correct verb form after considering the subject.

1. Some of the ink (have, has) spilled.
2. Some of the letters (were, was) ruined.
3. None of the blotters (are, is) helping.
4. None of the work (are, is) salvageable.
5. Most of the mess (have, has) been cleaned up.
6. Most of the papers (are, is) being retyped.
7. All of the damage (were, was) unnecessary.
8. All of us (need, needs) to be more careful.
9. One of us (are, is) responsible.
10. Some (are, is) still angry.

THERE

The important point to remember about *there* is that, although it may be the first word of a sentence, it is *not* the subject.

There goes my boss.

You may have recognized that *there* is actually an adverb. In the above example, the verb is *goes;* the subject (who goes?) is *my boss.*

Sentences that begin with *there* are called INVERTED SENTENCES because in such situations the subject is the noun *after* the verb. Many inverted sentences can be reversed and put back into normal subject-verb order:

There is a calculator on the desk.
A calculator is on the desk.

There are four documents relevant to this case.
Four documents are relevant to this case.

Reversing an inverted sentence (at least mentally) can help you decide if the verb needs an S-ending.

In any case, remember: When a sentence begins with *there,* the subject comes *after* the verb. So you have to look or think ahead when deciding whether or not to put an S-ending on the verb.

⋆ **EXERCISE 13**
Find the subject in each of these sentences. Then circle the correct verb form.

1. There (seem, seems) to be a lack of organization in this office.
2. There (are, is) papers strewn all about.
3. There (are, is) an excess of noise.
4. There (appear, appears) to be no one answering the telephones.
5. There (are, is) too many people taking coffee breaks at once.
6. There (are, is) coffee spilled on the floor.
7. There (have, has) been an audit done by the company.

8. There (seem, seems) to be no solution.
9. There (are, is) no recommendations.
10. There (are, is) too much work getting done.

IRREGULAR NOUNS

As with other parts of speech, many English nouns are irregular. That is, they don't form their plural by the addition of an S-ending. Therefore, when an irregular noun is the subject of a present tense verb, the decision to put an S-ending on the verb is not simple to make.

Take, for example, these three "people" nouns:

> man
> woman
> child

Each noun is used to refer to a single individual.

> The man seems tired.
> The woman is concerned.
> The child sleeps.

There is no S at the end of the noun, so when it is the subject of a present tense verb, we use an S-ending on the verb.

But think of the plural forms of these nouns:

> man   men
> woman   women
> child   children

All three plurals end in EN. (By the way, this should make it easier for you to remember which is which.) So, when used as a subject of a present tense verb, there is no S-ending to remind us *not* to use an S-ending on the verb.

> The men work hard.
> The women contribute equally.
> The children learn.

What you must remember (and this is true for all irregular nouns) is that *a present tense verb gets no S-ending when its subject is a plural noun.*

Another such group of tricky nouns are those that form the plural with a vowel change:

> foot   feet
> mouse   mice

There is also a group of words that are difficult for the opposite reason: these are nouns that indicate fields of study or branches of knowledge. For example:

> mathematics
> linguistics
> economics

These words are the names of *single* subjects. So, even though the nouns have S-endings, the verb must get an S-ending, too.

> Economics confuses me.

If you think of such nouns as having a natural S-ending, it should be easier for you.

The names of several diseases work this way. They end in S, but they are still *one* disease:

> Tuberculosis ha<u>s</u> become less common.

Notice that some words that fall into this category are actually variable. When used to indicate a subject area, they are considered singular; when used in some other sense, they are considered plural:

> Politics *is* a fascinating subject.
> A person's politics *change* as circumstances change.

In the second sentence, *politics* is used to mean "political views."

Then there are those words that end in S and are usually considered plural, although their *meaning* is actually singular.

> <u>Pants</u> <u>are</u> acceptable office wear for women nowadays.
> The <u>scissors</u> <u>are</u> in my desk drawer.

Finally, you must keep in mind that many English words are derived from foreign languages. While most such words are anglicized (that is, adapted to English grammatical forms), some retain their foreign form for the plural. Again, this means that a final S may not be a guide to whether or not the verb needs an S-ending.

The following list illustrates some typical foreign endings to watch out for:

SINGULAR	PLURAL
crisis	crises
analysis	analyses
stimulus	stimuli
cactus	cacti
medium	media
datum	data
criterion	criteria
phenomenon	phenomena
larva	larvae
vertebra	vertebrae

As pointed out earlier in this chapter, always consult a dictionary whenever you are unsure of a noun's plural form.

★ EXERCISE 14
In each of these sentences, decide whether the subject is singular or plural. (Don't be fooled by final S-endings!) Then circle the required verb form.

1. Five women (have, has) conducted a scientific experiment.
2. The data (were, was) collected in a laboratory.
3. Mice (were, was) used in the experiment.
4. Measles (were, was) the main topic of the scientists' investigation.
5. Their thesis (appear, appears) in the introduction of their report.
6. Their analysis (have, has) sparked a controversy.
7. Their research tactics (are, is) being questioned.
8. The phenomenon (are, is) not unusual in the scientific community.
9. The media (are, is) not covering the story.
10. News (have, has) to be more earthshaking.

COLLECTIVE NOUNS

COLLECTIVE NOUNS are words that refer to a *group* of things or people but that act as a single unit.

For instance, a *class* may contain 25 students, but there is only one class.

Therefore, collective nouns are singular; used as the subject of a present tense verb, they require an S-ending on the verb.

The class listens attentively.

There are many such nouns in English; here are a few examples:

army	family	orchestra
committee	group	series
crowd	jury	team

Of course, a collective noun can be made plural when referring to two or more such units.

The football teams confront each other in the stadium.

Also, a collective noun may occasionally be used to refer, not to the group, but to the individual members of the group. In this special case, the collective noun would be considered plural, and the verb would get no S-ending.

The team remove their uniforms right after each game.

Team here implies "the members of the team," which is plural, with an S-ending on *members*.

This may be a good place to raise the problem of the word *number*. Sometimes *number* is a kind of collective noun:

The number of desks in this office is inadequate.

The number, considered as a single unit or figure, requires an S-ending on the verb.

At other times, *number* is plural:

A number of new desks have been ordered.

A number, considered as a total, is plural and requires *no* S-ending on the verb.

★ EXERCISE 15
Find the subject in each of these sentences; consider whether it is a collective noun. Then circle the correct form of the verb.

1. Our program director believes that the Navy (offer, offers) good opportunity.
2. Many (feel, feels) that military training is good experience for anyone.
3. Her staff (disagree, disagrees) with her.
4. A series of opinions (have, has) been expressed.
5. Some (feel, feels) that military training is good experience.
6. The majority (are, is) less certain.
7. Sometimes, a team (provide, provides) important support for an individual.
8. Other times, a group (obstruct, obstructs) individual growth.
9. Nevertheless, the director (want, wants) to find a new career.
10. Military life (are, is) one of her options.

PREPOSITIONAL PHRASES

As you have already learned, a PREPOSITIONAL PHRASE that is attached to a subject is actually a long adjective. It adds information to the subject, but it does not change whether the noun is singular or plural.

> The engineer is working hard.
> The engineer *at the controls* is working hard.

In the first sentence, *engineer* is the subject, so *is* (a verb with an S-ending) is needed. In the second sentence, *engineer* is still the subject, so *is* is still the correct verb. *Controls* is plural, but because it is not the subject, its S-ending doesn't affect the verb.

In the following examples, the reverse occurs:

> The secretaries do a lot of typing.
> The secretaries *in the pool* do a lot of typing.

In the first sentence, the verb *do* (with no S-ending) is used because the subject *secretaries* is plural (with an S-ending). In the second sentence, the verb remains *do* because the subject has remained *secretaries*. *Pool* is part of the prepositional phrase; it is not the subject and so has no effect on the verb.

Let's look at this matter another way:

> These ledgers are inaccurate.
> One *of these ledgers* is inaccurate.

In the first sentence, the verb *are* has no S-ending because the subject *ledgers* does have an S-ending. But in the second sentence, the verb *is*, with an S-ending, is needed because *ledgers* is no longer the subject; this time, *one* is the subject and *ledgers* is part of a prepositional phrase.

Note: Words like *kind, part, portion,* and *type* are always singular, even when followed by a prepositional phrase containing a plural noun:

A portion of the responsibilities is mine.

★ **EXERCISE 16**
Circle the correct form of the verb after identifying the subject. (Watch out for prepositional phrases.)

1. The effects of corporate policies on the environment (have, has) come under close scrutiny in recent years.
2. Paper recycling in the office (are, is) being encouraged.
3. The use of styrofoam by fast food chains (have, has) come under vocal attack.
4. Excessive layers of packaging (induce, induces) consumers to buy another company's product.
5. Guidelines for the safe disposal of industrial waste (are, is) being more carefully enforced.
6. However, more work in this area (need, needs) to be done.
7. Not surprisingly, most companies in America (put, puts) financial concerns ahead of the environment.
8. Fear of increased production costs (lead, leads) to reluctance to comply with environmental regulations.
9. Shortages of enforcement staff (encourage, encourages) scofflaws.
10. The survival of our planet (depend, depends) on the willingness of consumers to insist that companies become environmentally responsible.

PARENTHETICAL EXPRESSIONS

Parentheses, as you know, are punctuation marks used to set off extra or interrupting comments in a sentence. For example:

> Knowledge of office machines (especially the dictaphone and the word processor) is valuable nowadays.

A PARENTHETICAL EXPRESSION, like a comment enclosed in parentheses, is an extra bit of information inserted into a sentence.

A parenthetical expression may be used to describe the subject of a sentence. Much like prepositional phrases, therefore, parenthetical expressions act as adjectives and do not affect whether the subject is singular or plural.

Look at these examples:

> The dictaphone and the headset *cost* $400.
> The dictaphone including the headset *costs* $400.

In the first sentence, the verb *cost* needs no S-ending because the subject is compound *(the dictaphone AND the headset)*. In the second sentence, the verb *costs* does need an S-ending because the subject is simply *the dictaphone; including the headset* is a parenthetical expression, an adjective describing the subject but not part of the subject itself.

Sometimes a parenthetical expression is set off by two commas:

> My boss, like her predecessor, is hard to please.

Often, parenthetical expressions are introduced by words such as:

as well as	like
in addition to	together with
including	with

★ EXERCISE 17
In each sentence, identify the subject. (Be sure to eliminate parenthetical expressions.) Then circle the correct form of the verb.

1. Social work, including case work, group work, and community organization, (are, is) a twentieth-century development.
2. Churches along with philanthropic groups (were, was) the original sources of public relief.
3. The availability of government resources, in addition to private funds, (have, has) added greatly to the number of jobs for social workers.
4. Psychology, along with sociology, (are, is) an important requirement for the would-be social worker to study.
5. College departments as well as specialized graduate schools (provide, provides) training for social workers.
6. A troubled economy with its accompanying social problems (increase, increases) the need for social work.
7. Social ills including unemployment, drug addiction, alcoholism, and broken families (grow, grows) in hard times.
8. Individuals along with their families (require, requires) greater help in adjusting to society.
9. Social workers, with the aid of other professionals like physicians and psychiatrists, (are, is) trained to help these people.
10. Social work, together with other kinds of counseling, (make, makes) a good career choice for the future.

WHO, WHICH, AND *THAT*

When the subordinators *who, which,* and *that* are used in one of our basic sentence patterns,

S V | subordinator | S V.

they often serve both as the SUBORDINATOR *and* as the SUBJECT of a verb.

> I am studying accounting, which I find difficult.
> I am studying accounting, which is difficult for me.

In the first sentence, *which* is connecting two subject-verb cores, I am studying and I find. But look carefully at the second sentence. We still have I am studying to the left of *which,* yet to the right we have only the verb is. This is because which is the subject of is as well as the sub-ordinator. It is a kind of PRONOUN standing for *accounting.*

Now, the point to remember for subject-verb agreement is that *which, who,* and *that* are neither singular nor plural. When they are the subject of a present tense verb, the S-ending depends upon the "real" noun to which the SUBORDINATOR/PRONOUN refers. Therefore, in our example, we need *is* with an S-ending because *which* is referring to a singular noun, *accounting,* with no S-ending.

Sometimes our basic sentence patterns can be rearranged. The first subject and verb can be split up by the subordinator and the second subject and verb.

> S V | subordinator | S V.
> S | subordinator | S V V.

It is basically the same sentence pattern, but with a slightly rearranged order.

> The receptionist whom I hired expresses herself clearly.

Here, *receptionist* is the subject of the verb *expresses.* I is the subject of the verb *hired.* They are connected by the subordinator *whom.*

Now look at this example:

> A receptionist who expresses herself clearly pleases the customer.

This time, *receptionist* is the subject of the verb *pleases;* the other verb *expresses* has the subordinator *who* for its subject. Because *who* is standing for *receptionist,* we need an S-ending on the verb *expresses.*

Again, the rule to follow is this: when *who, which,* or *that* is used as the subject of a present tense verb, check the real noun the subordinator is standing for before you decide whether or not the verb needs an S-ending.

★ EXERCISE 18
In each sentence, circle the correct form of the verb in parentheses.

1. Accounting is one of the major fields which (offer, offers) many opportunities.
2. The many factors that have led to the growth of accounting (include, includes) the expansion of corporate activity and the complex tax structure.
3. Accounting, which (were, was) developed in the nineteenth century, involves the classification and analysis of financial records.

4. The professional who (supply, supplies) these services is called an accountant.
5. She evaluates bookkeeping records, which (show, shows) the progress or decline of a business.
6. She also establishes the financial records and chooses the system of accounts that best (provide, provides) the needed information.
7. Individuals who meet educational and experiential requirements (are, is) eligible for the title Certified Public Accountant.
8. Such certification, which (are, is) government controlled, requires the passing of an examination.
9. People who (meet, meets) the requirements join such organizations as the American Institute of Accountants and the American Accounting Association.
10. A career in accounting (are, is) challenging and rewarding.

★ **REVIEW EXERCISES**

A. Circle the correct form of the verb in each sentence.

1. Two-thirds of total U.S. economic activity (consist, consists) of consumer spending.
2. There (are, is) a direct correlation between a strong economy and what consumers spend.
3. Bleak news reports, along with local talk of sagging business, (frighten, frightens) consumers.
4. Similarly, high unemployment statistics and the fear of losing one's own job (discourage, discourages) a person from spending.
5. People (prefer, prefers) to buy expensive items when they are hopeful about the future.
6. Neither optimistic government reports nor stock market gains (are, is) enough to convince people to spend.
7. Few (make, makes) purchases when they see neighbors losing their jobs.
8. Everyone (worry, worries) when local businesses close.
9. Most (wait, waits) for signs that the economy is looking up.
10. Much (depend, depends) on sales in major industries.
11. A steady rise in auto sales (are, is) one encouraging factor.
12. Another sign that consumers can look for (are, is) improved real estate sales.
13. Stable wholesale prices (have, has) an effect on the economy, too, by minimizing inflation.
14. American industry (realize, realizes) that the American consumer is the key to the economy.
15. Economics (are, is) a subject fascinating to explore.

B. For each of these, underline the correct verb form.

1. Preparing for retirement (is, are) an important aspect of personal finance.
2. Financial goals and the means to achieve them (is, are) necessary considerations when planning a successful retirement.
3. Individuals who plan early (is, are) likely to enjoy a secure and satisfying retirement.
4. Yet many (puts, put) off planning for retirement until relatively late in life.
5. There (is, are) several concerns when planning for retirement.
6. For example, upon retirement, income from salary or wages (ceases, cease).
7. Usually, neither Social Security benefits nor a pension plan (provides, provide) equivalent income.
8. Therefore, the accumulation of income-producing resources (is, are) an important long-range goal.

9. Moreover, living on a fixed income, together with the effects of inflation, (reduces, reduce) an individual's purchasing power after retirement.
10. Thus, an emotional crisis sometimes (compounds, compound) financial difficulties.
11. A wise individual (plans, plan) for both the additional leisure time and the reduced income brought about by retirement.
12. On the one hand, regular savings and thoughtful investment (alleviates, alleviate) the financial difficulties of retirement.
13. On the other hand, developing hobbies and interests (enriches, enrich) the retirement years with rewarding experiences.
14. Retirement (does, do) not have to be a dreaded time of financial deprivation.
15. With forethought and effort, it (becomes, become) a well-earned and pleasurable rest.

C. There are a number of S-ending errors in this letter. Find and correct them.

Dear Mr. Hyman:

As you know, job hunting in this day and age are a difficult proposition. With the economy down and competition up, we need all the help we can get to land that dream job.

Now, Integrity Careers, Inc., have the help you need. Our career guidance kit, "Know Thyself," provide the answers to your biggest questions: What job do I really want? What are my most marketable skill? What factors has kept me from reaching my goals up to now? What do I do to finally land the job of my dream?

This kit, including job lists and model resumes, are not available in any store. You can get it only through Integrity Careers, Inc. That's right! Only those who receives this letter even know the kit exist.

So why not send us $50 postage paid to receives your Integrity Career Guidance Kit? And start today toward a successful tomorrow.

Yours truly,

D. This invitation contains a number of S-ending errors. Find and correct them.

Corro Communications are pleased to announce the promotion of Augusta Samuels to assistant vice president of marketing. The former advertising director of our south and midwest divisions bring to her new job a wealth of dedication and experience.

Ms. Samuels new office will be located in the New York headquarters building at 1 Sixth Avenue.

To mark the occasion, Corro request the pleasure of your company at a reception honoring Ms. Samuel. The reception will be held on May 24 at 4:30 P.M. in the Executive Lounge of the headquarters building.

R.S.V.P.   David Nathan, Ext. 222

E. Proofread the letter for S-ending errors.

Dear Mr. Mitchell:

Thank you for submitting your resume and application to the Du-Rite Corporation. We appreciate your interests in a position with our company.

Although we received over 200 responseses to our advertisement for an administrative assistant, we have given each applicants resume careful consideration. Because your background and experience meets our companys criteria, we would like to invite you to come in for an interview.

Interviews will be held the week of September 4. Please call us at (921) 664-0932 for an appointment.

Sincerely yours,

5.
VERB FORMS

The last chapter focused mainly on the problem of knowing when to use S-endings on verbs, or how to use the present tense. In this chapter, we will look at the other verb tenses—how to form them and use them—for verbs, unfortunately, are the most changeable part of speech in English.

Tense Recognition

If you recall, in Chapter 1 we mentioned the PRINCIPAL PARTS OF THE VERB. We stressed that the simple present and the simple past are the only parts that act as verbs on their own; the other parts need helping verbs.

INFINITIVE:	to sing
PRESENT TENSE:	sing, sings
PAST TENSE:	sang
PRESENT PARTICIPLE:	singing
PAST PARTICIPLE:	sung

Basically, the other tenses in English are formed by using one of the participles with a helping verb. For instance, the PRESENT PARTICIPLE (the -ING part) is often used with parts of the verb *to be,* and the PAST PARTICIPLE is often used with parts of the verb *to have.* Different combinations of helping verbs and participles result in different tenses.

★ **EXERCISE 1**
Here is a list of verbs in a variety of different tenses. Following the list is a chart in which you are to sort out all the verbs. That is, you are to put each verb in the box with the others of the same tense. The first verb in each category has been done for you.

was falling	sing
will have sung	have sung
had spoken	is going
will walk	has been driving
answered	had been going
is talking	will have eaten
will have been studying	has been saying
have worked	will be studying
will type	will be typing
wrote	had been laughing
type	is trying
was holding	have wanted
has been going	had smelled
will have been typing	will file
will be filing	worked
was walking	will have gone

are	try
will have been filing	had worked
had been crying	is typing
danced	was saying
had remembered	had been doing
will study	will be walking
will have talked	will have been walking
have fallen	has been asking

type	is talking	have worked	has been going
answered	was saying	had spoken	had been doing
will walk	will be typing	will have gone	will have been walking

Tense Formation

As you may have gathered from Exercise 1, *have worked* and *had worked* are in two different tenses. Each uses the PAST PARTICIPLE *worked* (from the verb *to work*), but the first uses the PRESENT TENSE of *to have (have)* while the second uses the PAST TENSE of *to have (had)*. Therefore, the "combination" tenses that result are *not* the same.

This takes us to the second point about verb tenses. Like other verbs, the two major helping verbs have five principal parts. That is what allows us so many different combinations of helping verbs and participles.

INFINITIVE:	to be	to have
PRESENT TENSE:	are, is, am	have, has
PAST TENSE:	were, was	had
PRESENT PARTICIPLE:	being	having
PAST PARTICIPLE:	been	had

Let's look at our model verb *to sing*. The past participle *sung* may be used with the present and past tenses of *to have:*

has sung
have sung
had sung

All three are perfectly good two-word verbs and may be used with a subject to form a sentence:

The soprano has sung that aria many times.

Similarly, the present participle of *to sing (singing)* may be used with the present or past tense of *to be:*

are singing
is singing

am singing
were singing
was singing

All five of these two-word verbs may be used with a subject to form a complete sentence:

Today, she is singing with the Metropolitan Opera.

The present participle may also be used with the past participle of *to be:*

been singing

However, as you know, a participle cannot be used with a subject unless it has a helping verb. Although *singing* has a helping verb *(been), been* itself needs a helping verb. Since *been* is a past participle, we need part of the verb *to have:*

has been singing
have been singing
had been singing

All of these three-word verbs may now be used with a subject to form a complete sentence:

She has been singing with the Met for six years.

On the basis of these various combinations, we can form a little chart:

VERB FORMATION

has
have } sung
had

are
is
am   } singing
were

has } was
have } been
had }

★ **EXERCISE 2**
A verb form has been omitted from each of these sentences. Following each sentence is a list of verbs, some of which will correctly fill in the blank in the sentence. First, decide which of the principal parts of the verb is needed. Then, put a check next to each verb that can be correctly inserted into the sentence.

1. My employer had _____.

spoken ___	went ___	forgotten ___
say ___	done ___	take ___
written ___	did ___	go ___
been ___	took ___	gone ___
do ___	said ___	taken ___

2. Right now, his assistant _____.

laughed ___	typing ___	argues ___
types ___	laughs ___	speaks ___
speaking ___	spoke ___	worked ___
works ___	argue ___	said ___
says ___	knows ___	known ___

3. He is _____.

types ___	typing ___	speaking ___
answering ___	spoke ___	laughed ___
works ___	filing ___	wastes ___
laughing ___	try ___	working ___
filed ___	loafs ___	trying ___

4. Yesterday, he _____.

typed ___	rests ___	transcribes ___
filed ___	worked ___	correcting ___
forgot ___	typing ___	transcribed ___
resting ___	decided ___	files ___
works ___	work ___	corrected ___

5. For years, they have _____.

work ___	argue ___	cooperated ___
fought ___	argued ___	conferring ___
bicker ___	confides ___	disagreed ___
disagree ___	fighting ___	conferred ___
arguing ___	bickered ___	cooperate ___

Irregular Verbs

Just as nouns can be irregular in the way they form the plural, so verbs can be irregular in the way they form the PAST TENSE and the PAST PARTICIPLE. Consider these two model verbs:

INFINITIVE:	to talk	to speak
PRESENT TENSE:	talk, talks	speak, speaks
PAST TENSE:	talked	spoke
PRESENT PARTICIPLE:	talking	speaking
PAST PARTICIPLE:	talked	spoken

The PRESENT TENSE and the PRESENT PARTICIPLE are not really problems. We have already studied the rules for using S-endings on present tense verbs. And the present participle is formed by simply adding an ING-ending to the infinitive without the *to.*

With REGULAR VERBS, the PAST TENSE and the PAST PARTICIPLE are rather simple, too. In fact, both are formed by adding an ED-ending to the infinitive without the *to.* This means that for regular verbs the past tense and the past participle are spelled exactly alike. One of our model verbs, *to talk,* is an example of this.

Problems arise, though, with IRREGULAR VERBS. First of all, the PAST TENSE and the PAST PARTICIPLE of irregular verbs are *not* formed by adding an ED-ending to the infinitive. Secondly, the PAST TENSE and the PAST PARTICIPLE of many irregular verbs are two completely different words. Our other model verb, *to speak,* is an example of this.

To make matters worse, there are no rules to help us determine the past tense and past participle of irregular verbs. (That, logically enough, is why they are called "irregular.") However, they do fall into groups from which we can see *spelling patterns.* These are of some help.

I. For example, there is a group of verbs whose past tense and past participle are the same as the present tense. That is, the verb undergoes *no* change. Here is a partial list of them:

Present Tense	Past Tense	Past Participle
cast	cast	cast
cost	cost	cost
cut	cut	cut
hit	hit	hit
quit	quit	quit
split	split	split
bet	bet	bet
let	let	let
set	set	set
bid	bid	bid

rid	rid	rid
shed	shed	shed
spread	spread	spread
burst	burst	burst
hurt	hurt	hurt
put	put	put

Thus, no matter what tense you wish to form, the "meaning" verb is always the same:

> I hit my head on that shelf quite often.
> I hit my head on it yesterday.
> I have hit my head on it every day this week.

II. A second group of verbs has only two forms; almost like regular verbs, the PAST TENSE and the PAST PARTICIPLE are alike:

Present Tense	Past Tense	Past Participle
have	had	had
make	made	made
build	built	built
bend	bent	bent
lend	lent	lent
send	sent	sent
spend	spent	spent

For example:

> Sue spends too much money on shoes.
> Last Friday, she spent her whole paycheck on shoes.
> She had spent the check before that on shoes, too.

III. Then there is a group of verbs that, again, are alike in the past tense and past participle. But what makes them unique is that the past forms are constructed by changing a vowel in the present tense:

Present Tense	Past Tense	Past Participle
bleed	bled	bled
feed	fed	fed
lead	led	led
read*	read	read
speed	sped	sped
meet	met	met
win	won	won
dig	dug	dug
stick	stuck	stuck
sit	sat	sat
hold	held	held
shoot	shot	shot
hang	hung	hung
swing	swung	swung
slide	slid	slid
light	lit	lit
shine	shone	shone
bind	bound	bound
fight	fought	fought
find	found	found
wind	wound	wound

---

*Notice that, although *read* is spelled the same in all three parts, it is pronounced as if a vowel has been changed.

For example:

> David reads a book every week.
> Last week, he read *The Sun Also Rises* by Ernest Hemingway.
> He has read all of Hemingway's other novels, too.

IV. In yet another group of verbs, the past tense and past participles are alike. But this time there is the addition of a T- or D-ending as well as a vowel change:

Present Tense	Past Tense	Past Participle
feel	felt	felt
creep	crept	crept
keep	kept	kept
sleep	slept	slept
sweep	swept	swept
weep	wept	wept
tell	told	told
sell	sold	sold
lose*	lost	lost
hear*	heard	heard
mean*	meant	meant
say	said	said
flee	fled	fled
stand	stood	stood
think	thought	thought
seek	sought	sought
buy	bought	bought
bring	brought	brought
catch	caught	caught
teach	taught	taught

For example:

> I stand on the bus every morning.
> I stood all the way to work today.
> I have stood the whole way each morning this week.

V. As we have seen, some irregular verbs are different in all three parts:

Present Tense	Past Tense	Past Participle
is, are, am	was, were	been
go	went	gone
do	did	done

We have already seen examples of these verbs in use; here are a few more:

> I go to the movies at least once a week.
> I went to the movies last Saturday.
> I have gone to the movies every Saturday this month.

---

*Notice that the vowel sound changes, although its spelling does not.

VI. Some verbs are different in all three parts as a result of two separate vowel changes:

Present Tense	Past Tense	Past Participle
begin	began	begun
drink	drank	drunk
ring	rang	rung
sing	sang	sung
swim	swam	swum
come	came	come
run	ran	run

Notice that the last two of these verbs *(come* and *run)* have a past participle that is just like the present tense:

> For exercise, I run every afternoon.
> I ran yesterday for one hour.
> I have run in several marathons.

VII. Some verbs form the past tense by changing the vowel in the present and form the past participle by adding an N to the present:

Present Tense	Past Tense	Past Participle
arise	arose	arisen
drive	drove	driven
ride	rode	ridden
rise	rose	risen
take	took	taken
write	wrote	written
give	gave	given
shake	shook	shaken
blow	blew	blown
know	knew	known
grow	grew	grown
throw	threw	thrown
draw	drew	drawn
eat	ate	eaten
see	saw	seen

For example:

> I usually take the train to work.
> But yesterday I took the bus.
> I have taken the bus twice this week.

VIII. A similar group of words forms the past tense by changing the vowel in the present and forms the past participle by adding an N to the past tense:

Present Tense	Past Tense	Past Participle
bear	bore	born
tear	tore	torn
swear	swore	sworn
get	got	gotten
break	broke	broken
choose	chose	chosen
speak	spoke	spoken
steal	stole	stolen

For example:

> Mandy <u>tears</u> her stockings too often.
> She <u>tore</u> a pair this morning.
> She <u>has torn</u> three pairs this week.

Also in this last category is that especially tricky verb *to lie*, meaning *to recline*. It is often confused with *to lie*, meaning *to tell a falsehood*, and *to lay*, meaning *to set out* (as in "laying out a picnic blanket"). But each verb has its own distinct set of verb forms:

Present Tense	Past Tense	Past Participle
lie (to tell a falsehood)	lied	lied
lie (to recline)	lay	lain
lay (to set out)	laid	laid

The first verb, you'll notice, is REGULAR; it simply needs an ED-ending for both the past tense and the past participle. The last verb is almost regular, but instead of an ED-ending, the Y is changed to I and just a D is added. This is patterned just like the verb *to pay*:

> pay   paid   paid

The difficult verb is the middle one, and there's nothing to do but memorize it. (Notice that *not one* of its parts has a *D* in it!)

★ **EXERCISE 3**
Referring to the preceding pages as little as possible, fill in the blanks in this chart. When it is complete, you will be able to use the chart as a quick reference.

PRESENT TENSE	PAST TENSE	PAST PARTICIPLE
arise		
		born
	began	
	bent	
bet		
bid		
		bound
	bled	
		blown
break		
bring		
	burst	
		bought
	cast	
catch		
		chosen
come		
cost		

PRESENT TENSE	PAST TENSE	PAST PARTICIPLE
	crept	
		cut
dig		
	did	
		drawn
drink		
	drove	
	ate	
		fed
feel		
fight		
	found	
		fled
		flown
forget		
get		
		given
	went	
grow		
hang		
	had	
		heard
	hit	
hold		
		hurt
		kept
	knew	
lay		
	led	
	lent	
		lain
	lied	
light		
		lost
make		
mean		

PRESENT TENSE	PAST TENSE	PAST PARTICIPLE
	met	
pay		
		put
		quit
	read	
		rid
	rode	
ring		
rise		
	ran	
say		
	saw	
		sought
		sold
		sent
	set	
	shook	
shed		
shine		
shoot		
	sang	
		sat
sleep		
	slid	
	spoke	
	sped	
spend		
	split	
		spread
stand		
steal		
stick		
		sworn
	swept	
swim		
swing		

PRESENT TENSE	PAST TENSE	PAST PARTICIPLE
	took	
		taught
		torn
tell		
throw		
	won	
	wound	
		written

★ **EXERCISE 4**
In each sentence, there is an infinitive in parentheses. On the line at the right, fill in the correct form of the verb.

1. All her life, Audrey has (to want) to become a nurse. _____

2. As a child, she (to love) to play nurse with her dolls. _____

3. She also (to read) all the *Cherry Ames* books. _____

4. Whenever she went to the doctor, she (to ask) the nurse dozens of questions. _____

5. When Audrey started college, she naturally (to major) in nursing. _____

6. But as she studied, she realized her enthusiasm had (to change). _____

7. Audrey's career goal was not what she thought it had (to be). _____

8. When she finished college, she immediately (to continue) her education. _____

9. Audrey now (to attend) medical school. _____

10. She is (to study) to become a doctor. _____

The Future Tense

You may have noticed that one category of tenses has not been discussed yet. All of the verbs that we've looked at so far are variations of the present tense or variations of the past tense. But what about the FUTURE TENSE?

The future tense is formed a bit differently. In English, we indicate an action that has not yet happened by using the helping verb *will*. But unlike the other helping verbs, *will* is NOT used with a participle.

Will is a special kind of helping verb called a MODAL, which is used with an infinitive to form a whole verb. To do this, take the infinitive of the verb that signifies the action:

    to sing

Then, drop the *to* and replace it with the modal:

    to̶ sing
    will sing

The resulting combination verb may be used with a subject to form a complete sentence:

> The soprano *will sing* the aria tonight.

The future tense, of course, gets as complicated as the past and present tenses. The future modal *will* may be used along with the other helping verbs and the participles of the verb you use for meaning. For instance, if you use *singing* (the present participle), you'll need a form of *to be* in front of it:

> will (to be) singing

The use of *will* requires the infinitive without the *to,* so the correct verb form is:

> will be singing

Or, we may use the past participle *sung,* which will need a form of *to have* in front of it:

> will (to have) sung

Again, the modal *will* requires an infinitive without the *to,* so the correct verb form is:

> will have sung

Finally, we may use the present participle *singing* with the past participle of *to be (been),* which needs part of *to have* in front of it:

> will *(to have)* been singing

And this time, too, *will* requires the infinitive without the *to.* The correct verb form is:

> will have been singing

Naturally, all of these variations of the future tense may be used with a subject to form a complete sentence:

> By the time the curtain falls, she *will have been singing* for three
> hours.

Note that, like *will,* other helping verbs fall into the category of modals. The most common modals are:

can	could
may	should
might	would
must	would rather
shall	had better

When used as helping verbs, the modals alter the meaning of the main verb:

> I *should type* this letter before I make any phone calls.
> I *may leave* early today if my boss permits me to.

★ EXERCISE 5
A verb form has been omitted from each of these sentences. Following each sentence is a list of verbs, some of which will correctly fill in the blank in the sentence. Put a check next to each verb that can be correctly inserted into the sentence.

1. Tomorrow, they will _____.

work ____	tries ____	studying ____
apologizing ____	meet ____	prepare ____
rest ____	study ____	rested ____
try ____	thought ____	apologize ____
prepared ____	working ____	met ____

2. I will be _____ when you arrive.

sleeping ____	works ____	planned ____
study ____	typing ____	worked ____
types ____	slept ____	writing ____
planning ____	cooking ____	studying ____
cooked ____	written ____	working ____

3. She will have _____ by next Sunday.

resting ____	finished ____	try ____
gone ____	graduating ____	recovering ____
tried ____	goes ____	graduated ____
learning ____	learned ____	rested ____
recovered ____	went ____	finishes ____

4. By one o'clock, he will have been _____ for an hour.

talking ____	studies ____	writing ____
works ____	walking ____	typed ____
typing ____	slept ____	studying ____
sleeping ____	written ____	talked ____
walked ____	working ____	trying ____

★ EXERCISE 6
For each of these sentences, fill in the blank with one of the modals listed on page 74. (There may be more than one possible answer for each sentence.)

1. With sufficient self-confidence and capital, you _____ start your own business.

2. Without these two crucial ingredients, you _____ be better off working for someone else.

3. A business-owner _____ be completely self-assured, about his personality as well as his goods or services.

4. A business-owner _____ also be optimistic and genuinely believe in his business's potential.

5. If you are at all hesitant about starting a business, you _____ keep your present job.

6. In addition, to start a business, you _____ have at least a year's expenses in addition to start-up costs.

7. In all likelihood, your business _____ not show a profit the first year.

8. At the beginning, a successful business _____ barely break even.

9. But you _____ not give up.

10. If your business survives its first few years, yours _____ be a true success story.

Tense Use

Up to now, we have discussed only tense FORMATION; we have said nothing about how to USE the tenses. Although there are so many tenses in English, their use is not as tricky as it may at first seem.

Essentially, VERB TENSES are used to express ideas about TIME. Tenses enable us to communicate information about things that happen in time. But, of course, tense and time are not the same thing; a verb tense won't tell us the hour of day it is or the day of the week.

Still, because tense is used to talk about time, the relationship between the tenses is temporal (that is, based on time). Therefore, it is possible to arrange the various tenses on a TIME LINE in order for us to see the differences among them. We could call the center of the line "present" and number it 0:

−3	−2	−1	0	+1	+2	+3
PAST			PRESENT			FUTURE

Anything to the left of 0 would be considered in the "past" and be numbered negative. Anything to the right of 0 would be considered in the "future" and be numbered positive.

First of all, let's set up a model verb for reference:

> TO TALK
>
> Future
> (1) will talk
> (2) will be talking
> (3) will have talked
> (4) will have been talking
>
> Present
> (5) talk, talks
> (6) is, are, am talking
> (7) has, have talked
> (8) has, have been talking
>
> Past
> (9) talked
> (10) was, were talking
> (11) had talked
> (12) had been talking

Tenses 1, 5, and 9 are our "base" tenses; they are the SIMPLE FUTURE, the SIMPLE PRESENT, and the SIMPLE PAST. When we write an essay or letter, our main action is usually based in one of these tenses—past, present, or future. For example:

> Today, Mr. Lewis *talks* to the Rotary Club.
> Last week, he *talked* to the Town Council.
> Next week, he *will talk* to the Elks.

On a time line, the SIMPLE TENSES may be arranged this way:

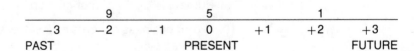

	9		5		1	
−3	−2	−1	0	+1	+2	+3
PAST			PRESENT			FUTURE

Sometimes, though, we mention secondary actions that happen before or after our main action. That's when we have to use the more complicated tenses.

Tenses 2, 6, and 10 are called the FUTURE CONTINUOUS, the PRESENT CONTINUOUS, and the PAST CONTINUOUS. This is because using the present participle (the ING-ending) implies that the action happened over a stretch of time. The continuous tenses refer to the same time as the simple tenses, but the action of a continuous tense goes on longer. For example:

> Today, Mr. Lewis *talks* to the Rotary Club.
> He *is talking* about the problem of local pollution.
>
> Next week, he *will talk* to the Elks.
> He *will be talking* about another public issue.

On the time line, the CONTINUOUS TENSES may be indicated with arrows:

	10→		6→		2→	
	9		5		1	
−3	−2	−1	0	+1	+2	+3
PAST			PRESENT			FUTURE

Tenses 3, 7, and 11 are called the FUTURE PERFECT, the PRESENT PERFECT, and the PAST PERFECT. They all use the helping verb *to have* plus a past participle. The PERFECT TENSES are used for actions that don't coincide in time with the main action in the SIMPLE or CONTINUOUS TENSES.

For example, Tense 11 is used for actions that happened even *more in the past* than Tense 9:

> Last week, Mr. Lewis *talked* to the Town Council.
> The week before, he *had talked* to the mayor about his speech.

Therefore, on the time line, Tense 11 would be to the left of Tense 9.

Similarly, Tense 7 is used for actions that happened sometime *between* the simple past and the simple present:

> Last week, Mr. Lewis *talked* to the Town Council.
> Since then, he *has talked* privately to several council members.
> Today, he *talks* to the Rotary Club.

Therefore, on the time line, Tense 7 would go between Tense 9 and Tense 5.

Finally, Tense 3 is used for actions that will happen between the present and some time in the future:

> Mr. Lewis *will talk* to the Elks next week.
> Before then, he *will have talked* to the mayor again.

On the time line, Tense 3 should go between Tense 5 and Tense 1. Our time line should now look like this:

	10→		6→		2→	
11	9	7	5	3	1	
−3	−2	−1	0	+1	+2	+3
PAST			PRESENT			FUTURE

The last tenses, Tenses 4, 8, and 12, are called the FUTURE PERFECT CONTINUOUS, the PRESENT PERFECT CONTINUOUS, and the PAST PERFECT CONTINUOUS. And, as you may have guessed, they are used to express actions that happen at approximately the same time as the perfect tenses (Tenses 3, 7, and 11), but they continue for a longer period.

For example, Tense 12 is used for actions that happen more in the past than Tense 9 and that continue longer than Tense 11:

> Last week, Mr. Lewis *talked* to the Town Council.
> He *had been talking* individually to different council members the
>   week before.

Tense 8 is used for actions that happen between the simple past and the simple present but that continue longer than Tense 7:

> Today, he *talks* to the Rotary Club.
> He *has been talking* about his speech for days.

Lastly, Tense 4 is used for actions that will happen between the present and some point in the future but will continue longer than Tense 3:

> He *will talk* to the Elks next week.
> By then, he *will have been talking* to local organizations for over
>   a month.

Therefore, on the time line, Tenses 4, 8, and 12 coincide with Tenses 3, 7, and 11 but are indicated with arrows:

12→	10→	8→	6→	4→	2→	
11	9	7	5	3	1	
−3	−2	−1	0	+1	+2	+3
PAST			PRESENT			FUTURE

What the time line and the preceding examples suggest is that the tenses are used in combinations with each other. That is, the perfect tenses are usually used when the simple tenses have already been assigned to an action at a different time. Some examples may make this more clear:

> Past + Past Perfect
> She *went* to lunch after she *had finished* the filing.
> (The action that occurred first is *more in the past.*)
>
> Present + Present Perfect
> She *is* a stenographer now, but she *has held* many jobs since
> graduating from high school.
> (Between the present and some point in the past, a third action
> took place.)
>
> Future + Future Perfect
> He *will have caught* up on all his work before he *leaves* on vacation.
> (Neither action has occurred yet, but one will happen first.)

In the last example, note the use of the simple present (*leaves*) to express an idea in the simple future. This phenomenon in English is exemplified also by the use of *to be going to* (the present continuous tense):

> I <u>am going</u> to answer the mail this afternoon.

The perfect continuous tenses are used in similar combinations to the perfect tenses:

> Past Perfect Continuous
> She *had been waiting* for an hour before I *noticed* her.
> Present Perfect Continuous
> She *started* to wait at noon. It *is* now one o'clock.
> She *has been waiting* for an hour.

Future Perfect Continuous
She *will have been waiting* for two hours by 2 P.M.

★ **EXERCISE 7**
The following pairs of sentences are almost the same; only the tenses are different. The questions test your ability to interpret the meanings of the different tenses. Be prepared to explain your answers.

1. Eileen will take the subway to school today.
   Sylvia took the subway to school today.
   Who is already sitting in class? _____

2. Mrs. Hartman washed her kitchen floor.
   Mrs. Ortiz has washed her kitchen floor.
   Whose floor is more likely to still be wet? _____

3. May spends her weekly paycheck on new shoes.
   June spent her weekly paycheck on new shoes.
   Who has purchased more pairs of shoes? _____

4. Sue was late for work every day.
   Max is late for work every day.
   Who is more likely to get fired? _____

5. Amy had the flu when Easter vacation started.
   Dan had had the flu when Easter vacation started.
   Who was sick during vacation? _____

6. Ann decided she didn't like her blind date when she met him.
   Rose had decided she didn't like her blind date when she met him.
   Who made up her mind because of what the man was really like?
   _____

7. Henry will have reached the restaurant when we get there.
   Norma will reach the restaurant when we get there.
   Who will reach the restaurant first, Henry or Norma? _____

8. Lois will be getting dressed when her date arrives.
   Judy will have gotten dressed when her date arrives.
   Who will be ready when her date arrives? _____

9. Mr. Toshiro has been president for five years.
   Mr. Svensen was president for five years.
   Who is now the company's president? _____

10. Lisa has been talking on the phone for hours.
    Steve talks on the phone for hours.
    Who makes a regular practice of talking on the phone for hours?
    _____

★ **EXERCISE 8**
These sentences are written in the present tense. First, underline the verb in each sentence. Then rewrite the sentence in the past tense. (You may have to change more than the verb.)

Example:
I have to type too many letters this week.
I had to type too many letters last week.

1. Foreign investors in China face many difficulties.

   _____

   _____

2. Bureaucratic delays frequently snarl their investments.

   _____

   _____

3. The eventual death of Den Xiaoping threatens future instability.

_____

_____

4. American trade sanctions also jeopardize investments.

_____

_____

5. American companies fear negative publicity.

_____

_____

6. They do not wish to be seen as profiting from Chinese repression.

_____

_____

7. Still, many foreign companies consider China an attractive market.

_____

_____

8. China has a large literate workforce willing to work for low wages.

_____

_____

9. China's domestic market offers a huge pool of consumers.

_____

_____

10. Underlying this investment boom is China's renewed rapid economic growth.

_____

_____

Passive Voice

In addition to TENSE, verbs in English also have what is known as VOICE. Voice can be either ACTIVE or PASSIVE.

In most of the sentences we have seen so far, the verbs have been ACTIVE. That is, the subjects have been *doing* the action expressed by the verbs. In our old example:

Sam sees the tree.

the subject *Sam* is doing the action of seeing. The object *tree* is what he sees.

In a sentence with a passive verb, the subject does NOT do the action. Rather, the subject *receives* the action, which is done by a different noun. The passive version of our example would look like this:

The tree is seen by Sam.

In this sentence, the verb is *is seen;* the subject is *the tree.* However, the subject is not doing anything. (Obviously, trees can't see!) Another noun *(Sam)* is doing the action, and the tree is being acted upon.

The subject of an ACTIVE VERB *acts. The subject of a* PASSIVE VERB *does not act.*

★ **EXERCISE 9**
After identifying the verb and the subject in each sentence, decide whether the verb is in the active voice (A) or the passive voice (P).

1. Burt was hired as a salesperson.   A   P
2. Recently, he has been asked to take on extra duties.   A   P
3. He used to spend his day dealing with customers.   A   P
4. Now he is expected to fill in for his busy boss.   A   P
5. He helps with the inventory and purchasing.   A   P
6. He visits dealer showrooms and factories.   A   P
7. Sometimes a major decision must be made in his   A   P
   boss's absence.
8. Burt is authorized to make such decisions.   A   P
9. Because of his additional responsibilities, his title   A   P
   should be changed to Assistant Manager.
10. That way, he will earn more money.   A   P

A passive verb always consists of a form of the verb *to be* followed by a past participle. Therefore, a passive verb can have as many tenses as an active verb; this is indicated by using the appropriate tense of *to be.*

ACTIVE	PASSIVE
He will see	He *will be* seen
He will be seeing	(He *will be being* seen)
He will have seen	He *will have been* seen
He will have been seeing	(He *will have been being* seen)
He sees	He *is* seen
He is seeing	He *is being* seen
He has seen	He *has been* seen
He has been seeing	(He *has been being* seen)
He saw	He *was* seen
He was seeing	He *was being* seen
He had seen	He *had been* seen
He had been seeing	(He *had been being* seen)

Note: The passive verbs in parentheses are rarely used because the meaning is so convoluted. For example, instead of saying:

He will be being seen by us.

it is much more clear to use the active voice:

We will be seeing him.

To convert a sentence from ACTIVE VOICE to PASSIVE VOICE is a four-step process.

Mrs. Miller hired Richard.

First, the object of the active sentence becomes the subject of the passive sentence:

Richard _____ _____.

Secondly, the subject of the active sentence becomes the AGENT (or the *doer*) of the passive sentence. Note that the agent is preceded by the word *by:*

Richard _____ by Mrs. Miller.

Thirdly, the verb *to be* is put into the tense of the active verb. (In this case, *hired* is in the simple past tense.)

Richard was _____ by Mrs. Miller.

Finally, the past participle of the active verb is inserted after the form of *to be:*

Richard was hired by Mrs. Miller.

★ **EXERCISE 10**
Change each sentence from active voice to passive voice. (Be sure that you use the right tense!)

1. Allbright Enterprises ordered a new copier on Tuesday.

   _____

   _____

2. The Allied Trucking Company delivered it on Thursday.

   _____

   _____

3. The manufacturer immediately sent the bill.

   _____

   _____

4. Allbright received the bill on Friday.

   _____

   _____

5. They paid it promptly.

   _____

   _____

6. However, a secretary discovered a malfunction in the machine on Monday.

   _____

   _____

7. Paper was jamming the mechanism.

   _____

   _____

8. Allbright considered stopping payment on their check.

   _____

   _____

9. But the manufacturer guarantees its merchandise.

   _____

   _____

10. They repaired the copier Tuesday afternoon.

   _____

   _____

To convert a sentence from PASSIVE VOICE to ACTIVE VOICE, we just reverse the process.

Mrs. Miller was thanked by Richard.

First, the agent of the passive sentence becomes the subject of the active sentence. (Remember to eliminate the *by*.)

Richard _____ _____.

Next, the subject of the passive sentence becomes the object of the active sentence:

Richard _____ Mrs. Miller.

Finally, the past participle of the passive sentence is put into the tense of the *to be* verb, which is not used in the active sentence. (Here, *was* is simple past.)

Richard thanked Mrs. Miller.

⋆ **EXERCISE 11**
Change each sentence from passive voice to active voice, being careful to use the right tense.

1. That porch was constructed by Harold Dawson.

   _____

   _____

2. He was contracted by Emma Hobbs to build it.

   _____

   _____

3. Mr. Dawson had been taught carpentry by his father.

   _____

   _____

4. So the porch was expertly crafted by him.

   _____

   _____

5. The floorboards were evenly laid by him.

   _____

   _____

6. The railings were hand-notched by him.

   _____

   _____

7. Even the molding was hand-carved by him.

   _____

   _____

8. Mrs. Hobbs was pleased by his final product.

   _____

   _____

9. He was paid handsomely by her.

_____

_____

10. The work of a fine craftsperson cannot be matched by a machine.

_____

_____

It is important to be able to convert from PASSIVE VOICE to ACTIVE VOICE (and vice versa) because, in business writing especially, the active voice is often more effective. It is more direct and emphatic than the passive voice.

For example, when writing a collection letter, one might say:

Your bill *has not been paid* in over 90 days.

But an active version of this sentence would be stronger:

You *have not paid* your bill in over 90 days.

Putting the verb in the active voice means that the subject is acting. In this case, the emphasis is therefore placed on the person who owes the money. The recipient of the letter *(you)* is made responsible for paying the bill.

On the other hand, sometimes receivers of the action may be more important than the doer. In such an instance, the passive voice would be effective. Consider these two examples from a claims letter:

ACTIVE: You made an error on invoice 7625.
PASSIVE: An error was made on invoice 7625.

The first sentence is *accusatory;* it places blame for the error directly upon the recipient of the letter. However, in a situation like this, rectifying the error is more important than knowing who committed it. Therefore, the second sentence may be more effective because the recipient would not be on the defensive.

The choice to use passive voice rather than active voice, clearly, depends upon the circumstances. Business judgment and a bit of insight into human psychology can help.

★ **EXERCISE 12**
Find the verbs in this letter and decide whether they are active or passive. Then, on another sheet of paper rewrite the letter, changing the voice wherever you feel a change would make the letter more effective.

Dear Mrs. Franklin:

Your credit reputation is in danger!

The balance of $319.19 on your account has not been paid. It is now 90 days past due.

Two statements and three letters regarding your balance have been sent to you by us. Yet they have been ignored.

We know that you have been a reliable customer for many years although your bills have been paid slowly on occasion. This time, however, your payment is much later than usual.

Please do not force your account to be closed by us or this matter to be turned over to our attorneys. Send us your check for $319.19 today.

Sincerely yours,

★ REVIEW EXERCISES

A. In each of these sentences, there is an infinitive in parentheses. Change the infinitive to the appropriate verb form and write your answer in the space provided.

1. Employment opportunities for health-care professionals are (to expect) to increase dramatically over the next decade. _____
2. For this reason, many people have (to pursue) careers as paraprofessionals in the health-care field. _____
3. These people participate in life-and-death situations, for which they are (to pay) well. _____
4. Some have (to become) emergency medical technicians. _____
5. These people are the ambulance staff who, if (to train) as paramedics, can administer first-line treatment. _____
6. Other paraprofessionals (to work) as cardiopulmonary technicians. _____
7. In high demand, these people conduct and monitor the various tests (to perform) on patients' hearts and lungs. _____
8. A third paraprofessional, the respiratory therapist, works with patients whose breathing has been (to obstruct). _____
9. Special training is (to require) of all three types of health-care paraprofessionals. _____
10. Such organizations as the National Association of Emergency Medical Technicians, the National Society for Cardiopulmonary Technology, and the American Association for Respiratory Therapy can (to provide) additional information on training and career opportunities. _____

B. In the space provided, supply the correct verb form of the infinitives in parentheses.

1. Nydia has always (to want) to be a gym teacher. _____
2. As a child, she had (to be) very athletic. _____
3. She (to learn) how to swim before she was four years old. _____
4. In high school, she (to serve) as captain of the girls' basketball team. _____
5. She has always (to take) sports, as well as her own physical fitness, very seriously. _____
6. When she was on a team, she (to train) hard every day. _____
7. While growing up, she was (to advise) to become a teacher. _____
8. Physical Education (to seem) to be the only choice for an athletic young woman's career in those days. _____
9. So, in college, she (to combine) sports with education courses. _____

10. While playing basketball, she was also (to prepare) to   _____
take the teachers' licensing examination in her state.

11. In her senior year, she (to begin) to send her resume   _____
to high schools in her home town.

12. One day, however, a scout from the New York Stars   _____
(to arrive) at Nydia's campus.

13. The New York Stars (to be) a women's professional   _____
basketball team.

14. After watching Nydia play, the scout (to offer) her a   _____
contract with the team.

15. Nydia realized that, since her childhood, the world of   _____
professional athletics had (to begin) to open up to
women.

C. 1. This paragraph is in the present tense. In the space provided, rewrite it in the past tense, changing the verbs and any other necessary words.

Example:

I want to go home early today.
I wanted to go home early yesterday.

Justin wants to become an airlines reservations agent. He enjoys working with the public, and he has the necessary qualifications. He is a high school graduate, speaks two foreign languages, types 55 words per minute, and has worked with computers. He has been a salesperson for the past two years, which is also helpful. Most importantly, he relates well to people.

_____

_____

_____

_____

_____

_____

_____

_____

_____

2. This paragraph is in the past tense. In the space provided, rewrite it in the present tense, changing the verbs and any other necessary words.

Example:

I felt confident about the interview yesterday afternoon.
I feel confident about the interview this afternoon.

Alicia was a flight attendant, a job which involved serving others. Her position required patience and tact since she dealt with potentially irritable passengers. She had to keep passengers calm as well as serve them food and beverages. She not only catered to their needs, but also maintained their safety. Because she performed her duties well and was often complimented by passengers, she has been promoted to Supervisor of Flight Training.

_____
_____
_____
_____
_____
_____
_____
_____
_____
_____
_____

3. This paragraph is in the past tense although many of the verbs are in the past perfect tense. To change the meaning of the paragraph to the present tense, shift all the verbs and write your new version in the space provided.

Example:

Keisha had dropped out of college but then decided to return to school.
Keisha dropped out of college but now has decided to return to school.

Donna had entered corporate management immediately after finishing college. She had started as a product manager and moved up to assistant vice president for finance. Then she wanted to open her own business. She was considering cosmetics, a traditionally "women's field," but she preferred to invest in a "mainstream" industry. So she investigated computer software. She found the field attractive and so was planning to quit her job in the near future.

_____
_____
_____
_____
_____
_____
_____
_____
_____

D. Proofread this letter for errors in verb forms. Then correct all the errors.

Dear Mr. Temple:

It is my great honor to informed you that you have been name Employee of the Month by the administrators of the Union Bank of Freeport.

Words cannot expressed our deep appreciation of your valiant behavior during the holdup on April 22. We feel strongly that your fast thinking and good judgment save the lives of your fellow employees as well as our customers, not to mention the thousands of dollars that would have been losted had the robbers escape.

In recognition of your heroism and the stress it must have create for you, we would like you to spent, as our guest, a weekend of your choice at Todman's Mountain Resort. In addition, we will be please to present you with a plaque commemorating the occasion at the staff luncheon to be helded on Friday, May 10, at 1 p.m.

Thank you, Mr. Temple. You're a very special man.

Sincerely yours,

E. This news release contains a number of errors in verb forms. Find and correct the errors.

For Immediate Release   July 16, 19--

FIRST NATIONAL BANK SPONSORS SENIORS EMPLOYMENT PROGRAM

Anso, California. July 16, 19--. The First National Bank of Anso has announce plans to sponsor an employment program for local senior citizens. The program is schedule to begin August 1, according to Mr. Robert Delaney, bank manager.

Many senior citizens, including retire persons with many years of work experience, have trouble matching their skills to the current job market. Mr. Delaney explain: "Job descriptions change along with the times. We intend to help senior citizens rethink what they can do and convinced local employers they can do it."

Interviews with local companies are been schedule for the first two weeks of August. Any Anso senior seeking full- or part-time employment is urge to register at one of the bank's five branches. Applicants need not be experience but must be 60 years or older.

Local employers interest in hiring an Anso senior should call Mr. Delaney at 292-3334.

6.
PRONOUNS

Pronouns are, basically, substitutes for nouns. They are mainly used to avoid repetition. For example, the following sentence repeats a word unnecessarily:

Sam enjoys Sam's work.

Instead of using *Sam* a second time, we may use a pronoun in its place:

Sam enjoys *his* work.

Choice of the pronoun *his* is determined by many factors. *Sam's*, the original noun for which *his* stands, is a *masculine, singular, possessive* noun. We therefore replace *Sam's* with *his*, which is a *masculine, singular, possessive* pronoun.

Case

The first consideration when selecting a pronoun should be its CASE. Case is the form of a noun or pronoun, and it is determined by the function of the noun or pronoun in the sentence. That is, a pronoun used as the subject in a sentence requires one form while a pronoun used as the object in a sentence requires a different form.

Sam sees the tree.
He sees the tree.

Howard admires Sam.
Howard admires him.

In the first pair of sentences, *Sam* is the subject of the verb *sees* so that the pronoun *he* must be used in its place. In the second pair of sentences, *Sam* is the object of the verb *admires* (*Howard* is the subject here), so the pronoun *him* must be used to replace it.

There are three pronoun cases in English—subjective, objective, and possessive. Let's consider the subjective and objective cases first.

	SUBJECTIVE CASE	OBJECTIVE CASE
SINGULAR	I you he she it	me you him her it
PLURAL	we you they	us you them

The two principal uses of SUBJECTIVE PRONOUNS are as SUBJECTS and as PREDICATE NOMINATIVES. (See pages 8–10 and 24–26.)

> *Frances* prepares all the paychecks.
> *She* prepares all the paychecks.
>
> It may have been *Kay* who took the message.
> It may have been *she* who took the message.

If the pronoun is *not* working as a SUBJECT or as a PREDICATE NOMINATIVE, then the OBJECTIVE CASE should be used.

For example, use the OBJECTIVE CASE when the pronoun is the OBJECT of the VERB:

> I saw *Julio* at the meeting.
> I saw *him* at the meeting.

Also, use the OBJECTIVE CASE when the pronoun is the OBJECT of a PREPOSITION:

> This letter is from *Gary.*
> This letter is from *him.*

And use the OBJECTIVE CASE when the pronoun is the OBJECT of an INFINITIVE:

> My boss asked me to help *Faizal.*
> My boss asked me to help *him.*

★ **EXERCISE 1**
In each of these sentences, choose the correct form of the pronoun in parentheses and write your answer in the space provided.

1. Augusta explained to (we, us) how to operate the switchboard.   _____

2. The telephone system has dozens of extensions, and (they, them) can be very confusing.   _____

3. Sometimes (I, me) have trouble remembering each salesperson's extension number.   _____

4. Other times, several calls come in at once, which upsets (I, me).   _____

5. But the salespeople are patient with (I, me).   _____

6. (They, Them) are nice to the other operators, too.   _____

7. The only thing that angers (they, them) is a disconnected call.   _____

8. This can cost (they, them) a sale.   _____

9. Augusta thinks that being a switchboard operator doesn't suit (I, me).   _____

10. Yet it was (she, her) who gave me the job.   _____

Sometimes the choice between SUBJECTIVE and OBJECTIVE is not so straightforward.

For instance, a pronoun may be part of a compound subject or object:

> Marc and (I, me) will prepare the advertising.

In this sentence, the verb is *will prepare,* and the subject includes both the name *Marc* and the pronoun. Therefore, since we need a SUBJECT, the correct pronoun here would be *I:*

> Marc and <u>I</u> <u>will prepare</u> the advertising.

Let's consider another example:

> The task was assigned to Marc and (I, me).

This time, the verb is *was assigned,* and the subject is *the task.* That means the pronoun form we need is not a subject but an OBJECT. The correct pronoun here would be *me:*

> <u>The task</u> <u>was assigned</u> to Marc and **me.**

The same principle applies when the compound subject or object contains *or* instead of *and:*

> <u>Ms. Hoeung</u> or <u>I</u> <u>will help</u> with your order.
> <u>Joy</u> <u>prefers</u> to work with Nora or **him.**

There is a simple method for determining the correct pronoun in a compound subject or object: IN YOUR MIND, SAY THE SENTENCE USING ONLY THE PRONOUN (LEAVE OUT THE REAL NOUN AND THE <u>OR</u> OR <u>AND</u>). You will, in all likelihood, *hear* the correct choice.

> Neither Sam nor (he, him) saw the tree.
> (Leave out *Neither Sam nor* and say to yourself, *"He* saw the tree.")

> The supervisor recommended raises for Alex and (she, her).
> (Leave out *Alex and* and say to yourself, "The supervisor recommended raises for *her.")*

⋆ **EXERCISE 2**
In each sentence, choose the correct form of the pronoun in parentheses and write your answer in the space provided.

1. On Tuesday, Mr. Fielding asked Sophia to work with Tom and (I, me) on the new project. _____

2. I had my first meeting with (she, her) and Tom Wednesday morning. _____

3. She told Tom and (I, me) she had had little experience with computers. _____

4. But between Tom and (I, me), I knew we could train her quickly. _____

5. As Tom began organizing the data, Sophia and (I, me) discussed how to operate the equipment. _____

6. Then, (he, him) and I began to program the computer while Sophia watched. _____

7. Soon she was asking Tom and (I, me) questions. _____

8. Gradually catching on, she was able to alternate with (I, me) and Tom before too long. _____

9. Now it is (she, her) and Tom who do all the input. _____

10. But she still always works with either Tom or (I, me) nearby. _____

Another difficult situation arises when using the subordinators *than* and *as,* for they are often used incompletely. To understand this, let's consider an example:

I like Bobby better than Johnny.

This sentence may mean, "I like Bobby better than I like Johnny." Or it may mean, "I like Bobby better than Johnny likes Bobby."

According to our first possible meaning, *Johnny* is an OBJECT. If we wanted to use a pronoun, we would need *him:*

I like Bobby better than **him.**

The second possible meaning uses *Johnny* as a subject. If we wanted to use a pronoun, we'd need *he:*

I like Bobby better than **he.**

Sentences using *than* and *as* are not always as ambiguous as the preceding example. Nevertheless, when the *than* or *as* is followed by a pronoun, it is wise to complete the idea (at least in your mind) by filling in the "understood" words. This will help determine the case of the pronoun.

Doris is more efficient than (I, me).

Say to yourself, "Doris is more efficient than **I** am." By inserting the verb *am,* you will more readily see the need for a subject *(I).*

So Mr. Garcia pays Doris more than (I, me).

Say to yourself, "So Mr. Garcia pays Doris more than he pays **me.**" Inserting the subject and verb *he pays* makes clear the need for an objective pronoun *(me).*

★ **EXERCISE 3**
Complete each sentence by supplying the understood words. Then write your pronoun choice in the space to the left.

Example:

<u>she</u>   No one in the office is friendlier than (she, her).
        No one in the office is friendlier than she is.

_____ 1. Juanita is much more productive than (I, me).

_____

_____ 2. I can't seem to get as much done as (she, her).

_____

_____ 3. I have been on the job as long as (she, her).

_____

_____ 4. The company even gave me more training than (she, her).

_____

_____ 5. Yet tasks seem to be more difficult for me than (she, her).

_____

_____ 6. I always need more time to complete them than (she, her).

_____

_____ 7. On the other hand, I am more accurate and careful than (she, her).

_____

_____ 8. The supervisor must correct Juanita more frequently than (I, me).

_____ 9. Yet I'm sure he will recommend Juanita for the next available promotion rather than (I, me).

_____ 10. Because he'll consider quantity rather than quality, she will seem more deserving than (I, me).

The difference between WHO and WHOM is confusing to many people, but it needn't be. For the difference between *who* and *whom* is the same as the difference between *he* and *him*. WHO IS THE SUBJECTIVE FORM, AND WHOM IS THE OBJECTIVE FORM. The fact that *him* and *whom* both end in *m* should make the difference even easier to remember.

For example:

We hired the applicant (who, whom) was most qualified for the job.

The pronoun here will serve as the subject of the verb *was qualified*. Therefore, the correct pronoun is *who:*

We hired the applicant who was most qualified for the job.

Consider another example:

The director did not care (who, whom) we hired.

This time, we do *not* need a subject. *(Director* is the subject of the verb *did care; we* is the subject of the verb *hired.)* Actually, the pronoun will be the OBJECT of the verb *hired,* which makes *whom* the correct choice:

The director did not care **whom** we hired.

The same principles apply to *whoever* and *whomever*. *Whoever* is the subjective form; *whomever* (with the *m*) is the objective form.

Whoever is hired must prove himself on the job.
Assign the job to **whomever** you choose.

★ **EXERCISE 4**
In each of these sentences, choose the correct form of the pronoun in parentheses and write your answer in the space provided.

_____ 1. (Whoever, Whomever) becomes chairperson of the board will have a lot of responsibility.

_____ 2. The chairperson is the one (who, whom) the board members look to for leadership.

_____ 3. She is the person (who, whom) must maintain order at meetings.

_____ 4. She is the person (who, whom) must arbitrate when the board cannot arrive at a decision.

_____ 5. She is the person (who, whom) employees consider responsible for company policy.

_____ 6. (Whoever, Whomever) is chairperson has a strong, direct influence on profits and dividends.

_____ 7. That is why stockholders take great interest in (who, whom) is made chairperson.

_____ 8. The president may recommend (whoever, whomever) he or she prefers for the post.

_____ 9. But all of the directors on the board are the ones (who, whom) make the final choice.

_____ 10. (Who, Whom) should be given so much power is determined by vote of the majority.

★ **EXERCISE 5**
Proofread this letter for errors in pronoun case. Then on another sheet of paper revise the letter, making all necessary corrections.

Dear Evan:

Both the staff and me would like to congratulate you on your recent promotion to regional sales manager. No one could be happier than us that your years of hard work have been recognized.

At the same time, we will truly miss your cheerful presence. How could we not regret losing a colleague whom has been as helpful and friendly as you?

Please accept our sincere good wishes for you continued success. We hope you will visit us whenever you can.

Sincerely yours,

The POSSESSIVE CASE poses a set of entirely different problems. To begin with, POSSESSIVE PRONOUNS can be divided into two subcategories—those used with a noun and those used alone.

POSSESSIVE CASE

	With a Noun	Without a Noun
Singular	my	mine
	your	yours
	his	his
	her	hers
	its	its
Plural	our	ours
	your	yours
	their	theirs

The first thing you should notice is that NO POSSESSIVE PRONOUN TAKES AN APOSTROPHE. There is no need for the possessive *'s* ending because the idea of possession is already built into the pronoun form itself.

Your selection of one form of possessive pronoun over the other will depend upon whether or not you intend to mention the noun being possessed. For example:

This book belongs to Maria.
It is *her* book.
It is *hers*.

Note that the possessive case of nouns and pronouns is required before present participles that are used as nouns.

Jay is chattering.
Jay's chattering bothers us.
His chattering bothers us.

In the first sentence, the verb is *is chattering*, and its subject is *Jay*. But in the second and third sentences, the verb is *bothers*, and the subject is *chattering*; that means *chattering* is being used as a noun. Therefore, the POSSESSIVE FORM is used (*Jay's* in sentence 2; *His* in sentence 3).

One last point about possessives: THE ONLY POSSESSIVE FORM OF <u>WHO</u> IS <u>WHOSE</u>, whether it is used with a real noun or not. Like the other possessive pronouns, it takes *no* apostrophe.

I will find out *whose* fault this is.

★ **EXERCISE 6**
Each of these sentences is followed by two revisions that require pronouns. Fill in the blanks with the appropriate pronoun form.

Example:
This is Adele's phone number.
This is *her* phone number.
This is *hers*.

1. This is Mr. Doyle's office.
This is _____ office.
This is _____.
2. Next door is Ms. Kraus's office.
Next door is _____ office.
Next door is _____.
3. Down the hall is the receptionist's desk.
Down the hall is _____ desk.
Down the hall is _____.
4. The secretaries' area is on the second floor.
_____ area is on the second floor.
_____ is on the second floor.
5. The vice president's suite is very plush.
_____ suite is very plush.
_____ is very plush.
6. The executives' lounge is also quite comfortable.
_____ lounge is also quite comfortable.
_____ is also quite comfortable.
7. The employees' entrance is around back.
_____ entrance is around back.
_____ is around back.
8. The president's elevator is off limits.
_____ elevator is off limits.
_____ is off limits.
9. This is the department we are assigned to.
This is _____ department.
This is _____.
10. This office will belong to you.
This will be _____ office.
This will be _____.

★ **EXERCISE 7**
Proofread this letter for pronoun errors. Then on another sheet of paper rewrite the letter, making all necessary corrections.

Dear Ms. Teasdale:

It is with pleasure that Trumbel's Department Store welcomes you as a new charge customer. We hope that are association will be a long and satisfying one.

A Trumbel's account makes you shopping more convenient. It entitles you to copies of all our seasonal catalogs as well as advance notice of every sale. It enables you to charge all your purchases, not only at our main store, but at all suburban branches, too. And it makes it possible for you to shop by both phone and mail.

Every month, you will receive a statement of all purchases made the preceding month. It's clear, itemized format enables you to verify all purchases against your sales receipts. Theirs never a finance charge on accounts paid within thirty days.

Enclosed is you're Trumbel's credit card. Please sign it immediately and carry it with you on you next visit to a Trumbel's store.

Yours truly,

Before we leave the topic of CASE, there is one last matter to be discussed: REFLEXIVE PRONOUNS.

REFLEXIVE PRONOUNS

Singular	Plural
myself	ourselves
yourself	yourselves
himself	themselves
herself	
itself	

A reflexive pronoun is used when the object of a verb is the same person, place, or thing as the subject. The reflexive pronoun indicates that the verb's action is "reflected" back upon the subject. For example:

Mrs. Sterne blames herself for the billing error.

In this sentence, the verb is *blames,* and the subject is *Mrs. Sterne.* Because the action of the verb is done both by and to Mrs. Sterne, a reflexive pronoun *(herself)* is used as the object.

The same principle applies for the object of a preposition or the object of an infinitive:

We will keep the good news to *ourselves* for a few days.
Ms. Pacheco told me to help *myself* to a cup of coffee.

Reflexive pronouns have one other use. They may be used for emphasis, to intensify the meaning of a sentence:

The vice-president apologized for the error.
The vice-president *himself* apologized for the error.

The director must make the decision.
The director *herself* must make the decision.

★ **EXERCISE 8**
In each of these sentences, circle the correct form of the pronoun.

1. Between you and (me, myself), I don't really like the new supervisor.
2. She seems to think too much of (her, herself).
3. Yet she has no more experience than you or (I, myself).
4. Still, the director has delegated much authority to (her, herself).
5. I think we should be accountable only to the director and (us, ourselves).
6. An intermediary will not make (us, ourselves) more efficient.
7. But we must resign (us, ourselves) to the new hierarchy.
8. The supervisor will be watching over (us, ourselves) very closely.
9. She will know our grumbling is directed at (her, herself).
10. After all, (she, herself) is our new boss.

Reference

Since pronouns are used to avoid repetition, they are only used when the real noun to which they refer has already been mentioned.

> Hedy told Herb that she had gotten a job.

In this example, the pronoun *she* refers to *Hedy.* We could say, "Hedy had gotten a job," but we use a pronoun to avoid repetition.
Here is another example:

> If Mr. Edwards were less volatile, the employees would like him better.

This time, the pronoun is *him,* and it is referring to *Mr. Edwards.*

★ **EXERCISE 9**
In each sentence, circle the pronoun and draw an arrow to the noun to which it refers.

Example:
Zoraida bought (herself) a new suit for the interview.

1. The national economy has taken its toll on small businesses.
2. This company is finding itself in financial trouble.
3. Several accounts have not paid their bills in over six months.
4. Yet the billing department has tried its best to secure payment.
5. In addition, sales are off from their level of last year.
6. Yet the sales manager has used numerous techniques to motivate his staff.
7. Despite poor cash flow, the company must meet its payroll every month.
8. Suppliers must be paid regularly for their merchandise.
9. The accountant has presented her report to the board of directors.
10. The board members will confront the crisis at their next meeting.

A number of reference errors are common when using pronouns. Consider this example:

> Annette met Lisa right after she left work.

The pronoun in this sentence is *she.* The problem is that *Annette* and *Lisa* may each be referred to as *she,* and we have no way of knowing which is intended. As a result, the meaning of the sentence is unclear. To correct the error, we must rewrite the sentence.
If the pronoun in the original sentence is meant to refer to *Annette,* one possible solution would be:

> Right after Annette left work, she met Lisa.

Here the pronoun *she* can only be referring to *Annette: Lisa* is not mentioned until after the pronoun is used, and it would make no sense to say, "Lisa met Lisa."

If the pronoun in the original sentence refers to *Lisa,* we might choose this revision:

> Right after Lisa left work, Annette met her.

Again, *her* can only be referring to *Lisa*—it would be ridiculous to say, "Annette met Annette."

Here is another similar example:

> When Mr. Orsini hired Gregory, he was very happy.

As in the previous example, the pronoun *he* may be referring to either *Mr. Orsini* or *Gregory.* Because we cannot tell which noun is intended, the sentence must be revised:

> Mr. Orsini was very happy when he hired Gregory.
> OR
> Gregory was very happy when Mr. Orsini hired him.

Sometimes faulty pronoun reference occurs, not because there are too many nouns possibly being referred to, but because there is none. That is, a pronoun is misused when the real noun to which it refers has not actually been mentioned.

> Since the legal profession is highly valued by the public, they are
> very well paid.

The pronoun in this example is *they.* When we look for the noun to which *they* refers, we find two possibilities, *the legal profession* and *the public.* However, both these real nouns are singular and would be referred to by *it.* So *they* cannot mean either *the legal profession* or *the public.*

As you may have surmised, *they* is meant to refer to *lawyers,* a noun which never appears in the sentence. The pronoun, therefore, is faulty; it is not avoiding repetition of a noun because the noun hasn't even appeared once. The best way to revise such an error is to use the real noun instead of the pronoun:

> Since the legal profession is highly valued by the public, lawyers
> are very well paid.

Let's consider another example:

> When I signed up with the employment agency, they didn't tell me
> about the placement fee.

There are, in fact, three pronouns in this sentence: *I, they,* and *me. I* and *me,* of course, refer to the person who wrote the sentence. The problem pronoun is *they.*

Since *employment agency* is singular, we would use *it* to refer to it. *They,* therefore, is referring to a noun that doesn't appear in the sentence —probably to the *people* who work for the employment agency. Among the possible corrections, one way to revise the sentence smoothly would be to omit both the pronoun *and* the real noun:

> When I signed up with the employment agency, I wasn't told about
> the placement fee.

Remember, when you discover a pronoun reference error in your writing, there may be more than one way to revise the sentence.

★ EXERCISE 10
Each sentence contains an instance of faulty pronoun reference. In the space provided, rewrite the sentence to eliminate the error and clarify the meaning.

1. As I walked into the office, my foot hit against the glass door, and I broke it.

2. Wendy enjoyed working in the publicity department because they were so patient.

3. Although the merchants are accused of cheating a group of tourists, they say they are not guilty.

4. After searching through the files all morning, Laura realized that she would never find it.

5. The president and his assistant studied the reports carefully because they are concerned with cutting costs and increasing productivity.

6. A desk-top copier would be more economical for this office than a larger one.

7. I tried very hard to relax, but once the interview began it didn't help me.

8. Mr. Douglas had worked for Mr. Lancaster for ten years before he retired.

9. If you are well trained, it will be easier to get a well-paying job.

10. Amelia worked part-time for a pediatrician and enjoyed it very much.

★ **EXERCISE 11**
Proofread this letter for errors in pronoun reference. Then on another sheet of paper rewrite the letter, making all necessary corrections.

Ms. Hester Prynne
The Hawthorne Company
1650 Pearl Street
Salem, MA 02121

Dear Ms. Prynne:

Please be informed that Mr. Ethan Brand has been an employee of the Molineaux Corporation for the past eight years.

Mr. Brand began with our firm as assistant to the vice president in charge of marketing, Mr. Goodman, until his promotion nine months later. At that point, Mr. Brand served under the new vice president, Mr. Brown. When he retired three years later, he himself was made vice president.

As you can see, Mr. Brand moved up with the company quite fast. His knack for seeking out new markets and expanding old ones proved its value many times over. As vice president for the past two years, Mr. Brand has been responsible for a sales increase of nearly 300 percent.

Although we are sorry to be losing Mr. Brand as a permanent full-time employee, we intend to retain him on a consultant basis in the future. I can therefore wholeheartedly recommend him as a consultant for your company, for it is a skill at which he outshines all competition.

Yours truly,

THE MOLINEAUX CORPORATION

Alberto Rappaccini
President

Agreement

Pronoun agreement is similar to subject-verb agreement. It, too, involves matching plurals with plurals and singulars with singulars.

> A SINGULAR PRONOUN MUST BE USED TO REFER TO A SINGULAR NOUN; A PLURAL PRONOUN MUST BE USED TO REFER TO A PLURAL NOUN.

Thus, the following sentence contains an example of faulty pronoun agreement:

> The latest copying *machine* is very complex, and they are always breaking down.

The pronoun *they* is plural, but it is referring to *the latest copying machine*, which is singular. Therefore, noun and pronoun do not agree. Two corrections are possible.
The pronoun may be made singular to match the singular noun:

> The latest copying *machine* is very complex, and *it* is always breaking down.

Or the noun may be made plural to match the plural pronoun (this solution will not be possible in every situation):

> The latest copying machine*s* are very complex, and *they* are always breaking down.

Note that, in either case, a verb must be changed to maintain subject-verb agreement as well.

The rules for subject-verb agreement will be helpful here in determining whether a noun is singular or plural:

> Everyone has some job that (she, they) can do well.

The pronoun here refers to *everyone,* which you will remember is singular. Therefore, the correct choice must be *she.*

> Everyone has some job that *she* can do well.

Here is a similar example:

> Both Ross and Myra have *their* assignments.

Remember collective nouns?

> The more money a group has, the more projects (it, they) can undertake.

The pronoun here refers to *group,* which is singular and therefore requires *it. They* may imply the *members* of the group, but the plural *members* doesn't appear in the sentence. So the correct choice reads:

> The more money a group has, the more projects *it* can undertake.

★ **EXERCISE 12**
In each of these sentences, select the correct pronoun form and write your answers in the space provided.

_____ 1. No one can be sure what (his, their) future will hold.

_____ 2. But people can determine the direction that (her, their) life will take.

_____ 3. When one makes a career choice, (you, one) will narrow down the possibilities.

_____ 4. But if the choice is based on self-awareness, (it, they) will facilitate the most rewarding possibilities.

_____ 5. When a person is looking for a job, (he, they) should consider likes and dislikes as well as skills and experience.

_____ 6. We should also try to have realistic expectations of what a job will provide for (you, us).

_____ 7. A satisfying job won't necessarily make you happy for the rest of (one's, your) life.

_____ 8. But wisely choosing that job for yourself will give (one, you) a sense of control.

_____ 9. A person who feels in control of (her, their) life will also feel good about herself.

_____ 10. Such a person can be more confident about (her, your) future.

★ **EXERCISE 13**
Proofread this letter for errors in pronoun agreement. Then on another sheet of paper rewrite the letter, making all necessary corrections.

Dear Dr. Barnes:

Because you have been our family's physician for many years, I am taking the liberty of writing to you for advice.

As you know, I have been a clerk-typist since graduating from high school. Now I am considering a career as a medical secretary. People have told me that a medical secretary will start at a good salary and that their working conditions are pleasant.

However, I would like to learn more about the duties of a medical secretary. Could you tell me about it or suggest a book or magazine that would have the information I need?

I would also like to know whether I will need additional training. My typing and shorthand are good, but I may need specialized skills. If so, would a business school provide me with it? Or can I learn these skills on the job?

I would appreciate your guidance very much, Dr. Barnes. You were always there for me and our brothers in the past. So you seemed the best place to start thinking about my future.

Thank you.

Sincerely yours,

"SEXIST" PRONOUNS

As women have assumed a larger and larger role in the work place, the words used to describe business roles have been reexamined. Since, for example, a "businessman" often turns out to be a woman, more and more people are opting for the sexually neutral term "businessperson."

The third person singular pronouns in English *(he/she, him/her, his/hers)* are still divided by gender, and so pronoun use presents a problem for the writer wishing to avoid "sexist" language. Traditionally, masculine pronouns have been used to refer to abstract, singular human nouns:

> *An employer* must be able to rely on *his* secretary.

But this is no longer considered acceptable.

To avoid the problem, several solutions are possible. A common approach, if an awkward one, is to use both third person singular pronouns:

> An employer must be able to rely on *his or her* secretary.

This, however, can become extremely cumbersome, especially when a passage contains several pronouns. Some writers, therefore, revise their sentence to avoid singular human nouns in the first place; that way, a third person plural pronoun (with no gender reference) may be used:

> *Employers* must be able to rely on *their* secretaries.

Yet another way to handle the problem, perhaps the simplest, is to alternate the masculine and feminine pronouns throughout your writing.

Keep in mind, though, that many companies have policies regarding "sexist" language. Some, for instance, still forbid the use of the term *Ms.* on company correspondence; some retain old forms such as *chairman* or *congressman*. Similarly, a company may have a policy regarding pronoun use; before you revise your boss's or your own letters to eliminate all the "sexist" pronouns, find out how your company stands on the issue.

★ REVIEW EXERCISES

A. In each sentence, select the correct pronoun form and write your answer in the space provided.

_____ 1. Between you and (I, me), I don't like sharing an office with Lenny.

_____ 2. Lenny and (I, me) just don't get along.

_____ 3. He is the kind of person (who, whom) will take any excuse to goof off.

_____ 4. No one is as lazy as (he, him).

_____ 5. (He, Him) and his friends talk on the phone all day.

_____ 6. While (his, he's) working, he whistles and taps his pencil.

_____ 7. I find (him, his) whistling particularly annoying.

_____ 8. Whenever he sees that I'm busy, he tries to engage in conversation with (I, me).

_____ 9. (Its, It's) hard to get my work done with so many distractions.

_____ 10. I'd rather share an office with someone (who, whom) takes his job more seriously.

B. Some of these sentences are correct. Others contain errors in pronoun use. If the sentence is incorrect, revise it and write your new sentence in the space provided. Indicate a correct sentence with a *C.*

1. Ralph has not seen his friend Calvin since he finished technical school.

_____

_____

2. Their jobs took them to different parts of the country.

_____

_____

3. Ralph's job took his family and he to Cincinnati.

_____

_____

4. Calvin was saddened by him leaving.

_____

_____

5. But then Calvin hisself got a job in Boston.

_____

_____

6. Both men are computer programmers, and each enjoys their work.

_____

_____

7. Now Ralph is being transferred, and him and his family will be moving to Boston.

_____

_____

8. So Ralph and Calvin are looking forward to there reunion.

_____

_____

9. They know they have both changed over the years.

_____

_____

10. But they hope to resume they're friendship where it left off.

_____

_____

C. Proofread this memorandum for errors in pronoun use. Then on another sheet of paper rewrite the memo, making all necessary corrections.

TO: Laura McCall

FROM: Eve Post

DATE: August 29, 19—

SUBJECT: Employee Complaints

I have reviewed the recent employee complaints and found that they are primarily unhappy with office conditions. The most frequently mentioned complaints are:

1 The air conditioning and heating systems are inadequate, and it is usually out of order.

2 Carpeting in the main reception area is badly frayed and has caused many people to trip.

3 Larger offices are not assigned by merit or seniority; rather, their assigned by favoritism.

4 Secretaries are not permitted to reorder supplies until they are exhausted.

The first two complaints involve capital repairs, so they will require authorization. The second two complaints concern policy, which I am currently investigating. I will get back to you as soon as possible with suggestions for possible action.

D. Proofread this letter for errors in pronoun use. Then on another sheet of paper rewrite the letter, making all necessary corrections.

Dear Mr. Wilson:

When a person has made an expensive purchase, they are right to be angry when their order is mishandled. Please accept our sincere apology for our error in the delivery of your Persian rug.

I have checked your purchase order and confirmed you're complaint. You did, indeed, order a 10' × 14' Bukhara at $6000, not the $5000 9' × 12' Kirman which we delivered. If you call this department for an appointment, our delivery team will pick it up and lay the correct rug for you at no extra charge.

To show you how sorry us at Van Dyke's Carpets are, we would like to offer you a gift of a 2' × 3' Bukhara. This area rug, a $250 value, will make a lovely complement to your new rug when it is placed in an entryway or foyer.

I am sure, Mr. Wilson, that you will enjoy many years of function and beauty from your new Bukhara. Thank you for your patience and understanding.

Sincerely yours,

VAN DYKE'S CARPETS, INC.

Allen Van Dyke
Vice President

E. This letter contains a number of errors in pronoun use. Find the errors and then on another sheet of paper rewrite the letter, making all necessary corrections.

Dear Mr. Taft:

Only an idiot would leave their car unlocked in New York City. Yet thousands of cars are stolen every year because drivers not only fail to lock their cars—they even leave the keys in the ignition!

We know, Mr. Taft, that you would not ignore such a simple precaution. That is why we'd like to take this opportunity to advise you of another simple means of protecting you're car—the Crookproof Cutoff Switch.

For only $19.95 you can now <u>guarantee</u> the safety of your automobile. By installing a Crookproof Cutoff Switch on your car, it will make theft virtually impossible. Because only you know where the switch is installed, you and only you can start your engine. Even a thief with a key will be stopped dead in their tracks.

So don't delay, Mr. Taft. Lock your car, take your keys, and install a Crookproof Cutoff Switch today. For only $19.95, you'll protect it for a long, long time.

Yours truly,

7.
ADVANCED SENTENCE STRUCTURE

Parallelism

A PARALLEL SENTENCE is one in which elements of equal (or "parallel") weight are expressed in equal (or "parallel") grammatical forms.

This principle of sentence structure can be illustrated most easily with a LIST. PARALLELISM dictates that items in a list (whether they are verbs, nouns, or any other part of speech) must be expressed in *parallel grammatical forms.* Consider this example:

> Rosemary *types, files,* and *takes* dictation.

This sentence lists three things that Rosemary, the subject, can do. Each of Rosemary's skills is listed as a verb. (The basic sentence pattern here is S V, V, and V.) And because all three skills are given equal weight (or importance) in the sentence, all are expressed in the same verb form, the simple PRESENT TENSE.

Not all lists, of course, consist of verbs. Look at this example:

> *Typing, filing,* and *taking* dictation are Rosemary's strongest skills.

This time, Rosemary's skills are listed as subjects of the verb *are.* (Sentence pattern: S, S, and S V.) Again, all three are of equal importance, so all are expressed in the same form: the PRESENT PARTICIPLE.

Sometimes, the parallelism of a sentence is begun but not carried through.

> This project is tedious, difficult, and makes me very tired.

In this sentence (verb: *is;* subject: *project*), a list of adjectives is begun: *tedious, difficult,* and _____. But after the *and,* when the reader expects a third and final adjective, there is a new *verb* instead! This sentence, therefore, demonstrates *faulty parallelism* and must be corrected:

> This project is tedious, difficult, and tiring.

This time, the list is completed with a third adjective, not a verb. The long section "makes me very tired" is replaced with one word: *tiring.*

★ EXERCISE 1
These sentences are cases of faulty parallelism. Find and correct each error, and write your revised sentences in the space provided.

1. Finding a job in today's economy requires ingenuity, perseverance, and it helps to be flexible.

   _____

   _____

2. Traditional ways to get a job included mailing resumes, using a school placement counselor, or employment agencies.

   _____

   _____

3. These methods don't always work in the face of a weak economy, high unemployment, and lots of people are competing with you.

_____

_____

4. With experience in sales, public relations, and the ability to supervise others, Lewis sought a position as a store sales manager.

_____

_____

5. Instead of using resumes, agencies, or even answering help-wanted ads, he personally visited every major store in his community.

_____

_____

6. One store owner was impressed by Lewis's assertiveness, determination, and she liked his personality.

_____

_____

7. Due to her present business volume, staff size, and the costs of her overhead, she didn't need a sales manager.

_____

_____

8. Instead, she offered Lewis a job as salesperson, with a reasonable starting salary, commission structure, and the benefits were also good.

_____

_____

9. Lewis was concerned about income, security, and to be able to advance on the job.

_____

_____

10. He accepted the job, confident he could impress his employer, increase her sales, and achieving his own career goals would come in time.

_____

_____

Sometimes parallel sentence structure involves more than single parts of speech. Longer sections of a sentence must also be set up in parallel forms when the meaning of those sections is balanced. The following sentence contains faulty parallelism:

Reading an annual report is not as laborious as to write one.

The correct version of this sentence should express the two activities *(reading* and *to write)* in parallel forms, for the two activities are being "balanced," held up for comparison. Therefore, there are two solutions. We may use a present participle for both activities:

Reading an annual report is not as laborious as *writing* one.

Or we may use infinitives:

> *To read* an annual report is not as laborious as *to write* one.

Parallelism may also be disrupted by the slightest change in wording:

> Paul got his information reading books and by talking to people.

In this example, parallel verb forms are used *(reading* and *talking).* However, the second present participle is preceded by a preposition *(by),* which unbalances the sentence. This can be corrected in a number of ways. First of all, the *by* may be omitted:

> Paul got his information *reading* books and *talking* to people.

Or, *by* may be used before both verb forms:

> Paul got his information *by reading* books and *by talking* to people.

Finally, the *by* may be inserted before the first participle but omitted before the second:

> Paul got his information by *reading* books and *talking* to people.

In this last solution, the *by* is not actually part of the parallel sections, but rather commences them.

Consider yet another example:

> Mrs. Grey is a boss whom employees respect but is a little frightening.

The solution here depends upon where we see the parallelism beginning. If we see the parallelism as including *whom:*

> Mrs. Grey is a boss *whom employees respect* but *is a little frightening.*

we may correct the error by inserting another pronoun:

> Mrs. Grey is a boss whom employees respect but *who* is a little frightening.

On the other hand, if we see the parallelism as beginning after *whom,* we must completely rewrite the second section:

> Mrs. Grey is a boss whom employees respect but *fear.*

By balancing the verb *respect* with another verb, *fear,* we not only restore the parallelism; we have also made the sentence more concise without changing the meaning.

⋆ EXERCISE 2
These sentences contain instances of faulty parallelism. Correct the errors and write your revised sentences in the space provided.

1. Having started a family and able to finish school at the same time, Beth was prepared for the pressures of her new job.

   _____

   _____

2. Still, holding a job and to try to raise her family were difficult.

   _____

3. Her ambitions were to nurture her children, her career, and remain sensitive to her husband's needs.

_____

_____

4. Beth succeeded because of her children's understanding, her husband's support, and due to the fact that the family respected what she was doing.

_____

_____

5. Sometimes Beth's husband was the housekeeper, dishwasher, babysitter, and he also cooked the meals.

_____

_____

6. Beth reciprocated by doing the shopping, the laundry, and made time to be alone with her husband.

_____

_____

7. The children learned to clean their own room, make their own lunch, and the value of independence.

_____

_____

8. On weekends, they all made a point of spending time together and to discuss their feelings.

_____

_____

9. Beth had explained her hopes for the family, her goals for her career, and why she had wanted to work in the first place.

_____

_____

10. As a result of Beth's working, the family has benefited socially, financially, and they feel better about each other, too.

_____

_____

A number of idiomatic expressions also demand parallel sentence structure. Consider this example using the expression "_____ than _____":

He was more willing *to make* his boss coffee than *to run* errands for him.

The word *than,* here, is both preceded and followed by an infinitive *(to make* and *to run).* Similarly, the expression "_____ rather than _____" requires parallel structure:

I decided to *get* a job after high school rather than *begin* college immediately.

Although *rather than* is preceded and followed by an infinitive *(to get* and *to begin),* we may omit the second *to* with the understanding that the parallelism begins with the word *get.*

Another idiom that requires parallel structure is found in the following example:

Maria is *not only* clever *but* efficient.

With the expression "not only _____ but _____," we must use parallel forms to fill in the blanks. Therefore, we may rewrite this sentence in a variety of ways:

Maria not only *is clever* but *is efficient.*

or:

Not only *is Maria clever,* but *she is efficient.*

The more words we include between *not only* and *but,* the more words we must insert after *but.*

Note: In the preceding examples, use of the word *also* would NOT disrupt the parallelism:
Maria not only *is clever* but also *is efficient.*

"Both _____ and _____" works in a similar way:

My boss explained *both* how to operate the computer *and* how to process orders.

By moving the *both,* we can eliminate repeating the words *how to:*

My boss explained how to *both* operate the computer and process orders.

Finally, "either _____ or _____" and "neither _____ nor _____" require parallel structure:

Raises were given *neither* to the secretaries *nor* to the junior executives.
Either we work together, *or* we fail separately.

Again, each of these can be revised to avoid repetition as long as the parallelism is maintained:

Raises were given **to** *neither* the secretaries *nor* the junior executives.
We *either* work together *or* fail separately.

★ **EXERCISE 3**
In the space provided, rewrite the sentences, correcting any faulty parallelism.

1. Many small investors would rather save their money than risking it in the stock market.

2. They are more interested in financial security than to make a large profit.

3. They think they must either jeopardize all they own in the stock market or must settle for 3½% interest.

_____

_____

4. Actually, small investors can afford neither low interest rates nor to risk all their money in the stock market.

_____

_____

5. So, both recession and the fact that savings accounts yield low interest have led many people to other areas of investment.

_____

_____

6. These people are looking not only for security but a high return.

_____

_____

7. Many, therefore, have put their money into mutual funds rather than depositing it in a savings account.

_____

_____

8. Mutual funds not only provide high yield but they offer reasonable security.

_____

_____

9. They provide the investor not only with professional management but also diversification.

_____

_____

10. Thus, the investor is taking neither an enormous risk nor giving up to recession.

_____

_____

Misplaced Modifiers

A modifier should be placed as close as possible to the word it modifies. A MISPLACED MODIFIER, as you would expect, is one that has been incorrectly placed in the sentence. The following sentence contains an example:

> When only a small child, my mother inspired me to become a nurse.

The expression "When only a small child" is clearly not modifying *mother* (a woman is not a mother at the same time that she is a small child). It is intended to modify *me*, yet it is placed closer to *mother* than to *me*. The sentence may be revised by moving the expression closer to the noun actually being modified:

> My mother inspired me, when only a small child, to become a nurse.

Sometimes, as in the preceding example, a reader will know anyway which word a misplaced modifier is actually modifying. But more often, a misplaced modifier will make a sentence ridiculous, confusing, or both.

> I bought the gift at a large department store which cost only $10.99.

Clearly, an entire department store cannot cost $10.99. But according to the principles of sentence structure, the modifier "which cost only $10.99" is modifying *store,* the nearest noun. Revised, this sentence should read:

> I bought the gift, which cost only $10.99, at a large department store.

Consider the meaning of this sentence:

> Curtis found a memo inserted in a file that had been prepared by his boss.

If it was indeed the file that was prepared by Curtis's boss, then this sentence is correct. But if the boss actually prepared the memo, not the file, revision is called for:

> Curtis found, inserted in a file, a memo that had been prepared by his boss.

Even more unclear is this example:

> People who ride the subway on a daily basis witness its continuing deterioration.

The problem here is that the adverb, *on a daily basis,* is placed between two verbs, *ride* and *witness.* The reader has no way of knowing which verb is in fact being modified. If the writer intended to modify *ride,* the modifier must be placed *before* the verb:

> People who, on a daily basis, ride the subway witness its continuing deterioration.

On the other hand, if the modifier is meant for *witness,* it must come *after* the verb:

> People who ride the subway witness on a daily basis its continuing deterioration.

★ **EXERCISE 4**
In the space provided, rewrite each of these sentences, correcting any misplaced modifiers.

1. Employees were curious about the executive board meeting all through the company.

   _____

   _____

2. Secretaries could not figure out why the president had been so nervous around the water cooler.

   _____

   _____

3. He had explained to his assistant why the company was in trouble on Monday.

_____

_____

4. He began the meeting by saying, "Customers who buy our products frequently are discovering defects."

_____

_____

5. The meeting was attended by all executive personnel that stretched on for hours.

_____

_____

6. An assistant delivered cold dinners to hungry board members in cardboard boxes.

_____

_____

7. After much discussion, they pinpointed the source of the problem behind locked doors.

_____

_____

8. They agreed on the following day to institute new procedures.

_____

_____

9. After going through the assembly line, the board decided that each product would be inspected by an expert.

_____

_____

10. They are trying to devise a set of standards for employees that are foolproof.

_____

_____

★ **EXERCISE 5**
Some of these sentences are fine; others contain misplaced modifiers. If the sentence is correct, write a *C* in the space provided. If it is incorrect, rewrite the sentence.

1. Acme Typewriter Repair provides prompt service, which greatly pleases its customers.

_____

_____

2. All one must do is call their number, which is listed in the Yellow Pages.

_____

_____

3. They fixed the typewriter in our reception area, which is only six months old but already unreliable.

_____

_____

4. We had called them Monday morning, and their serviceman arrived before noon.

_____

_____

5. The precision of this man greatly impressed our office manager, who seemed to know exactly what he was doing.

_____

_____

6. In less than ten minutes, we watched as he returned the machine to perfect working order.

_____

_____

7. So, due to a broken typewriter, little company time was lost.

_____

_____

8. The receptionist was back at her keyboard by 12:15 P.M.

_____

_____

9. Of course, Acme is as prompt in its billing as in its service.

_____

_____

10. Tuesday, their bill was on our office manager's desk, which was very reasonable.

_____

_____

Dangling Modifiers

While a modifier may go astray by being placed too far from the word it modifies, a modifier will also be incorrect if there is *no* word at all being modified in the sentence. Such a modifier is called a DANGLING MODIFIER; it has no word to attach itself to and so is not in fact properly part of the sentence. Consider this example:

Walking down the street, a limousine caught my attention.

"Walking down the street" should be modifying a noun somewhere else in the sentence. However, the rest of the sentence follows a simple pattern

(Subject-Verb-Object) and contains only two nouns *(limousine* and *attention).* Neither of these nouns can walk.

The problem is that the modifier is describing a pronoun *(I)* that does not actually appear in the sentence. To correct the error, the pronoun must be inserted:

> *While I was* walking down the street, a limousine caught my attention.

or:

> Walking down the street, *I noticed* a limousine.

Present participles, like *walking* in the preceding example, are frequent causes of dangling modifiers. Infinitives are similar culprits.

> To get the order out on time, temporary help had to be hired.

Again, "to get the order out on time" should be modifying a noun. But the only noun elsewhere in the sentence is *temporary help.* But who had to get the order out on time? Certainly not the new employee, but the boss or the company itself, neither of which is mentioned in the sentence. To correct the error, an appropriate noun must be inserted:

> *For the company* to get the order out on time, temporary help had to be hired.

or:

> To get the order out on time, *Mr. Guzman had to hire* temporary help.

Dangling modifiers are a particular danger in writing instructions or making general statements about human behavior, when the doer of an action is left unspecified. For instance:

> To become a successful entrepreneur, self-confidence is essential.

"To become a successful entrepreneur" cannot be modifying *self-confidence,* the only noun in the rest of the sentence. Indeed, only a human being can become an entrepreneur, yet none is mentioned. A number of revisions are possible:

> *For a person* to become a successful entrepreneur, self-confidence is essential.

or:

> To become a successful entrepreneur, *one needs* self-confidence.

★ EXERCISE 6
In the space provided, rewrite these sentences, correcting any dangling modifiers.

1. Settling down at my desk, the day started.

   _____

   _____

2. The morning passed quietly, preparing reports and filing them away.

   _____

   _____

3. When nearly finished with the last report, the telephone rang.

_____

_____

4. Answering it promptly, a salesman walked in.

_____

_____

5. To run an office smoothly, tact is often necessary.

_____

_____

6. Asking the salesman to have a seat, the caller left a message.

_____

_____

7. About to give his sales pitch, two customers arrived.

_____

_____

8. Listening to one customer's complaint, the salesman continued pushing his products.

_____

_____

9. Wandering around the showroom, I tried to keep an eye on the second customer.

_____

_____

10. Finally handling each in turn, the day resumed its leisurely pace.

_____

_____

★ **EXERCISE 7**
Some of these sentences contain dangling modifiers; other sentences are correct. Rewrite, in the space provided, those sentences in need of revision; indicate with a _C_ those that are correct.

1. At the grand opening of his boutique, Al seemed relaxed and self-assured.

_____

_____

2. Walking in and out all day long, Al served dozens of customers single-handedly.

_____

_____

3. Though he intended to hire a salesperson, he knew that for now he could manage alone.

_____

_____

4. However, when first starting up the business, help was required.

_____

_____

5. Without any help, Al did all the buying.

_____

_____

6. Also, pricing and displaying the merchandise himself, the boutique was set up for opening day.

_____

_____

7. But, to incorporate the operation, legal assistance was necessary.

_____

_____

8. To set up his system of record keeping, an accountant's advice was relied on, too.

_____

_____

9. Even the layout of the store needed the work of a professional architect and designer.

_____

_____

10. To get a business going, the expense of a team of professionals should not be avoided.

_____

_____

Indirect Discourse

INDIRECT DISCOURSE refers to a sentence that relates, without the use of quotation marks, what another person has said or asked. (Thus, when quotation marks *are* used, and the speaker is quoted word for word, the mode is called DIRECT DISCOURSE; see page 138 for a discussion of quotation marks.) Indirect discourse falls into two subdivisions, INDIRECT QUOTATIONS and INDIRECT QUESTIONS.

INDIRECT QUOTATIONS

For the purpose of accuracy, it is often wise, when quoting another person's remarks, to cite those remarks word for word and put them in quotation marks. However, there are times when a full quotation is not necessary.

Only part of the quotation may be relevant to your own subject. Or an exact repetition of the speaker's words may disrupt the flow of your own writing. For such reasons, it is important to know how to transpose a direct quotation into an indirect quotation.

For example, suppose your boss, Ms. Fein, tells you, "I am angry." If you want to report her remark to someone else, you have a number of options. You may use direct quotation:

Ms. Fein says, "I am angry."

To avoid direct quotation, though, you may alter her remark slightly without becoming inaccurate.

1. First, you eliminate the quotation marks and the comma that preceeds the quotation.
2. Then, you insert the subordinator *that* before the quotation.
3. Finally, you may have to change the pronouns and verb forms in the quotation.

Therefore, our example could become:

Ms. Fein says *that she is* angry.

We have replaced the quotation marks with *that;* since only Ms. Fein would refer to herself as *I,* we have replaced *I* with *she;* and to agree with *she,* we have changed the verb to *is.*

One of the difficulties with indirect quotations involves the verb tense. The tense of the verb in the indirect quotation depends upon the tense of the original statement.

When the original statement is in the present tense (as in our example), then the tense of the verb in the indirect quotation should match the tense of the verb of saying:

Ms. Fein says, "I am angry."
Ms. Fein *says* that she *is* angry.

Ms. Fein said, "I am angry."
Ms. Fein *said* that she *was* angry.

When the verb in the original statement is in the past tense, it must be taken a step back on our tense "time line" (see Chapter 5) when quoted indirectly.

★ EXERCISE 8
In the space provided, re-write as an indirect quota-tion each of these direct quotations.

Example:
Herb told me, "You are the dumbest person I have ever known."
Herb told me that I was the dumbest person he had ever known.

1. Pat told the personnel officer, "I am applying for a position as an administrative assistant."

_____

_____

2. The personnel officer replied, "We have no such opening at this time."

_____

_____

3. Pat said, "I would like to make out an application for your waiting list anyway."

_____

_____

4. While she was writing, the man said, "We are looking for an executive secretary."

_____

_____

5. He continued, "The position is with the assistant vice president of marketing."

_____

_____

6. Pat said, "I am willing to begin as a secretary if there are opportunities for advancement."

_____

_____

7. The personnel officer assured her, "We fill most higher positions from within the company."

_____

_____

8. Then he added, "If your skills are appropriate, I will arrange an interview for you."

_____

_____

9. Pat informed him, "I can type 80 words a minute and take dictation at 120."

_____

_____

10. Now, she tells people, "Within an hour, I had the job."

_____

_____

INDIRECT QUESTIONS

When one is not asking a question but relating that someone else has asked a question, it is not always necessary to repeat the question word for word. That is, like any statement, the question may be repeated indirectly.

For instance, suppose your boss asks, "Are you angry?" If you repeat the question to a third person, you may do so directly:

Ms. Fein asks, "Are you angry?"

The process of transforming this DIRECT QUESTION into an INDIRECT QUESTION is fourfold:

1. Eliminate the punctuation: quotation marks, question mark, and comma before the question. *End the whole sentence with a period.*
2. Insert the word *if* or *whether* before the question. Or, if the original question already contains a subordinator, retain it. For example—

> Ms. Fein asks, *"What* are you doing?"
> Ms. Fein asks *what* you are doing.

3. Adjust all necessary tenses and pronouns.
4. Invert the subject and verb in the question back to normal sentence order —first subject, then verb.

Thus, our example becomes:

> Ms. Fein asks if you are angry.

Note that the indirect question ends with a period, not a question mark, because it is not actually a question but a statement.

The third step in the process requires further explanation, for the pronouns in the question itself will depend upon to whom the question is being put. For example, Ms. Fein may be questioning you yourself:

> Ms. Fein asks me, "Are <u>you</u> angry?"
> Ms. Fein asks me if <u>I am</u> angry.

On the other hand, she may be directing the question to the same person to whom you are speaking:

> Ms. Fein asks you, "Are <u>you</u> angry?"
> Ms. Fein asks you if <u>you are</u> angry.

Or, Ms. Fein may be questioning one person, and you are repeating it to yet another:

> Ms. Fein asks her, "Are <u>you</u> angry?"
> Ms. Fein asks her if <u>she is</u> angry.

The matter of tenses for indirect questions is the same as for indirect quotations. When the question is in the present tense, then the tense of the verb in the indirect question should match the tense of the verb of asking:

> Ms. Fein asks, "Are you angry?"
> Ms. Fein *asks* if you *are* angry.

> Ms. Fein asked, "Are you angry?"
> Ms. Fein *asked* if you *were* angry.

If the original question is in the past tense, then the verbs should *not* match when an indirect question is used:

> Ms. Fein asks, "Were you angry?"
> Ms. Fein *asks* if you *were* angry.

> Ms. Fein asked, "Were you angry?"
> Ms. Fein *asked* if you *had been* angry.

As with indirect quotations, when the original direct question is in the past tense, the verb in the indirect question must be more in the past than the verb of asking.

★ **EXERCISE 9**
In the space provided, rewrite as an indirect question each of these direct questions.

Example:

My mother asked me, "What questions did the panel pose at the interview?"

My mother asked me what questions the panel had posed at the interview.

1. The program director began by asking me, "Have you had any previous experience in an old age home?"

   _____

   _____

2. Then she asked, "Can you tell us about your relevant education?"

   _____

   _____

3. The director's assistant wanted to know, "How did you find working with people much older than yourself?"

   _____

   _____

4. A third person queried, "What special approaches are necessary when working with an elderly population?"

   _____

   _____

5. Next, the director again asked, "What would you do if you thought someone were having a heart attack?"

   _____

   _____

6. Another member of the panel inquired, "What musical instruments do you play?"

   _____

   _____

7. Then the assistant asked, "Do you feel you can work on your own?"

   _____

   _____

8. She further questioned, "Are you willing to work long hours?"

   _____

   _____

9. The director then asked, "What salary range would you consider acceptable?"

   _____

   _____

10. Finally, she inquired, "When can you start?"

_____

_____

★ REVIEW EXERCISES

Proofread these letters for faulty parallelism, misplaced modifiers, and dangling modifiers. Where direct discourse is used, determine whether indirect discourse would be more appropriate. Then, rewrite each letter, making all necessary changes.

A.
October 8, 19--

Trumbel's Furniture Center
4069 Lexington Avenue
New York, New York 10077

Dear Sirs:

As advertised in your fall catalog, I would like to order a desk. The model number is 15C-2J, solid oak, priced at $495.

Please send the desk to the following address and charge it to my account, number 7651-38-801, immediately:

  96 Lakeview Drive
  Riverdale, New York 11232

Thank you.

Yours truly,

_____

B.
April 28, 19--

Highpoint Tenants' Association
7272 Cliffside Drive
Baltimore, MD 12991

Dear Apartment Owner:

It is with great pleasure that your executive council has contracted our refrigeration and stove repair services. It is our intention to provide each apartment in Highpoint with the most prompt and efficient repair service possible.

For an annual fee of $150 per apartment, we have agreed to assume responsibility for all malfunctions of refrigerators, freezers, and gas ranges. There will be no additional charge for repairs to you, even if the cost of these services should exceed $150.

This contract is on an apartment-by-apartment basis. Therefore, please let us know, "Are you interested in securing our Kitchen Insurance for your home?" We have enclosed a handy, self-addressed reply card for your convenience. Or you may call us at 824-5200 during business hours.

We look forward to serving you.

Very truly yours,

_____

C.

Dear Mrs. Poirot:

Thank you for your letter of April 10 regarding the portable television you wish to return. In checking our records, you have indeed owned the set for only six weeks.

We can clearly understand your anger at having a television purchased so recently break down. Unfortunately, our terms of sale disallow return of merchandise beyond seven days of purchase.

However, your set is under warranty with the manufacturer for twelve months. We have contacted the factory repair service for you, who informed us, "We will get in touch with Mrs. Poirot immediately to arrange for the free repair of her set."

Thank you for understanding our position, Mrs. Poirot. We hope that we have been of some help in this matter and that you will enjoy your television for many years to come.

Sincerely yours,

D.

Dear Ms. MacIntosh:

Thank you for requesting credit privileges at Degnan's Department Store.

A standard review of credit applications includes checking accounts, savings accounts, and any debts that you may have outstanding. Having investigated your ability to assume such credit, it appears that your current obligations are substantial. We therefore feel that the extension of further credit would endanger your financial reputation.

We hope you will continue with Degnan's as a cash customer. Please be assured that our decision in no way reflects your integrity and that, should your current obligations be reduced, we will gladly reconsider your application in the future.

Cordially yours,

E.

TO: Mr. Buckheim

FROM: Ms. Brandes

DATE: October 18, 19—

SUBJECT: Telephone-Answering Machines

On Tuesday, October 12, you instructed me, "Find out which telephone-answering equipment will best suit our office needs." You asked me, "What are the three top models?" Here is the information I discovered:

1 Dictaphone, model 108B—equipped with 30-second announcement cartridge, 90-minute message cassette, and remote control
message receiver; available at Berkeley's Office Equipment, Inc.,
for $165

2 Ansaphone, model 26-60, comes equipped with 30-second announcement cartridge, 60-minute message cassette, fast-forward
device, and remote control message receiver and is available at
Audrey's Audio for $100

3 Quadraphone, model number XJ9, equipped with 20-second announcement cartridge, 90-minute message cassette, message
length switch, and remote control message receiver; at all Taylor
Discount Stores for $125

All three models use standard leaderless C-type cassettes, and all
operate only on 110 AC electrical outlets.

Please let me know if you require additional information.

RB

8.
MECHANICS

Punctuation

Although we haven't focused on punctuation directly, you have already learned a great deal about it, for many of the rules of punctuation are closely related to the principles of sentence structure. You should therefore be familiar with the use of periods and semicolons, for example, and with some of the uses of commas.

This chapter will look more closely at the various marks of punctuation. As you study their uses, you should keep in mind the principles of grammar and sentence structure that you have already mastered.

THE PERIOD

The two major uses of the period are to mark the end of a sentence and to indicate an abbreviation.

When you proofread your work for sentence completeness, be sure to mark the end of each sentence with a period:

> Lorna has gone on vacation.
> I will miss her help while she is gone.

Indirect questions (see Chapter 7) should also be ended with a period:

> Before she left, she asked me if I would water her plants.
> I asked her if she would send me a postcard.

Other types of sentences that should be ended with a period are *commands:*

> Please type this letter for me.
> Answer the phone.

and requests phrased as questions:

> Would you please type this letter as soon as possible.
> May we have your response by the end of the week.

Most abbreviations (see page 146) require the use of periods:

Mr.	Co.
Ms.	Inc.
Mrs.	Corp.

Nowadays, however, periods are often omitted in the abbreviation of organizational names:

ITT	FBI
IBM	CIA
UAW	NATO
AFL-CIO	OPEC

Also, you should be careful not to confuse *abbreviations,* such as the above, with *contractions* (see Apostrophes, page 135). A contraction, which is a combined form of more than one word, requires an apostrophe to indicate the omitted letters (for example, *don't* for *do not*).

One other use for the period is called an ELLIPSIS, which consists of three spaced periods (. . .). An ellipsis is used within a quotation to indicate an omitted word or words.

> President Ohashi began his address to the Board of Directors by saying, "The age of the personal computer has just begun. This company got started two years ago with just a quarter of a million dollars and ten thousand sales. Now, despite the birth of several competitors, our market is expanding phenomenally. Next year, we expect to sell 500,000 computers."

> President Ohashi began his address to the Board of Directors by saying, "The age of the personal computer has just begun....Next year, we expect to sell 500,000 computers."

If you restrict your use of periods to the situations just explained, you will not run into trouble. However, there are specific occasions when a period should NOT be used although you may be tempted:

- DO NOT use a period after a heading or a title.

> Chapter One: Recognizing Verbs and Subjects

- DO NOT use a period after a sentence ending in a punctuated abbreviation.

> Our guest speaker this evening is Marcus More, Ph.D.

- DO NOT use a period when the numbers or letters of a list have been enclosed in parentheses.

> The following factors will be considered: (a) attendance, (b) punctuality, and (c) performance.

But

> The following factors will be considered:
> 1. Attendance
> 2. Punctuality
> 3. Performance

- DO NOT use periods (or zeros) after even amounts of dollars.

> Your check for $40 has been received.
> Your check for $40.58 has been received.

- DO NOT use a period after a Roman numeral that is part of a name.

> Elizabeth II has been Queen of England since 1952.

THE EXCLAMATION POINT

An exclamation point, instead of a period, is used at the end of a sentence in order to indicate emphasis or strong emotion:

> Stop interrupting me!
> Unauthorized personnel are not to be admitted!

In addition, an exclamation point should be used after an *interjection,* a word or phrase inserted into a sentence to indicate emphasis or surprise:

> Boy! Was I angry.
> Stop! Do not read any further.

THE QUESTION MARK

The question mark is used after direct questions:

> Will my order be ready by Tuesday?
> Have you checked your records?

Note: Question marks and exclamation points should never be followed by a period or comma.

Similarly, when a question is being directly quoted, the sentence may contain a question mark:

> "Do you mind if I smoke?" asked the interviewer.
> He then asked, "How old are you?"

★ EXERCISE 1
Terminal punctuation has been omitted from these sentences. For each, decide whether a period, exclamation point, or question mark is needed and indicate your choice in the space provided.

1. Have you any idea what it takes to become a physician ____
2. The ordeal is almost beyond belief ____
3. The work actually begins in high school, where one must work hard to qualify for a top-notch college ____
4. Once in college, the pressure really mounts ____
5. Do you think a student with less than straight A's will be accepted by a medical school ____
6. Course work in medical school demands rigorous study and the suppression of any social life ____
7. Have you heard enough ____
8. Just wait until you're an intern ____
9. You'll learn, at this stage, how to function without sleep ____
10. But after these fifteen years, from high school through your residency, you'll have the satisfaction of being called "doctor" for the rest of your life ____

★ EXERCISE 2
Proofread this letter for errors in punctuation. Then on another sheet of paper, rewrite the letter, making all necessary corrections.

Dear Advertiser:

In response to your request, you will find enclosed our latest Secretary's World media kit. This kit contains all the materials you'll need to determine the appropriateness of Secretary's World to your product!

In addition to a rate card and a sample copy of our magazine. We have enclosed an editorial calendar that outlines upcoming articles and a readership profile which is based on a nationwide readership survey.

I hope the information contained in our media kit proves useful to you, should you decide to include <u>Secretary's World</u> in your advertising campaign, we would like to know if you'd be interested in our special money-saving rates? Our advertising sales representatives are available to help you set up the most cost-productive package for your needs.

Don't delay, call to reserve space now.

Sincerely,

THE SEMICOLON

As you know, a semicolon may be used to join two closely related sentences:

> Sam sees the tree. Willy hears the birds.
> Sam sees the tree; Willy hears the birds.

> I will arrange a guest speaker. Arlene will take care of refreshments.
> I will arrange a guest speaker; Arlene will take care of refreshments.

This is the reason, by the way, that a semicolon often appears before such words of transition as *however* and *therefore:*

> We have sent you three bills and two statements; however, we have not received your payment.

> I received your bill for consultant services performed in April; therefore, I am enclosing a check for $940.

<u>Remember</u>: The test for correct semicolon use is to see whether a period would be grammatically correct in its place. If not, the semicolon has been misused.

THE COLON

Colons are used after formal introductory statements. They alert the reader to what follows. Some of the main uses of colons follow.

• Use a colon before *a formal list:*

> When evaluating a credit application, consider the following: credit history, employment history, and current assets.

• Use a colon before *an explanation:*

> A letter refusing credit should be positive: you hope to continue business on a cash basis.

• Use a colon before *a quotation:*

> *Secretary's World* reports: "Secretaries are members of the fastest-growing occupational group (annual average job openings are now 300,000 and expected to expand to 325,000)."

Colons are also used in these situations:

1. After the salutation in a business letter

> Dear Sir:
> Gentlemen:

2. Between a title and a subtitle

> *Word Processing: An Introduction*

3. Between the hour and minute of a time reference

> 9:10 A.M.
> 11:15 P.M.

★ **EXERCISE 3**
Punctuate each sentence by inserting a semicolon or a colon.

1. My day begins at 6 45 A.M.
2. It takes me approximately 45 minutes to shower, dress, and have breakfast then I rush to catch the 7:45 bus.
3. I occupy myself during the bus ride in a number of ways reading a newspaper, writing a letter, or just getting a bit of extra sleep.
4. When I arrive at the office, I perform a daily routine I buy coffee and a donut and have a second breakfast at my desk.
5. I'm always ready to get started by nine o'clock that's when my boss arrives.
6. Everyday, he greets me with the same remark "Ready to get this show on the road?"
7. My first task is to open all the mail this is usually interrupted by the arrival of our first appointment.
8. Some mail requires an immediate response I take care of this before I do anything else.
9. Next I do the previous day's billing I try to get this done in time for the morning mail.
10. Before long, the best time of the morning arrives my coffee break!

THE COMMA

Commas are used to indicate a pause. Their use is determined by sentence structure and meaning. If you *limit* your use of commas to the situations explained below, you should have no trouble. Then, remember the old saying: "When in doubt, leave it out."

As you will recall, two of our basic sentence patterns (see Chapter 3) required commas:

> S V, ⌐coordinator⌐ S V.
> Sam speaks, and Willy listens.

The second basic sentence pattern looked like this:

> ⌐Subordinator⌐ S V, S V.
> When Sam speaks, Willy listens.

Note: Be careful *not* to use a comma when a coordinator is connecting two verbs—

S V and V.
Sam speaks and listens.

Basically, the rule is this: A SUBJECT SHOULD NEVER BE SEPARATED FROM ITS VERB WITH A SINGLE COMMA.

Remember: When the subordinator is in the *middle*, there is usually *no* comma—

S V ⟨subordinator⟩ S V.
Sam speaks as Willy listens.

A comma may also be used after an introductory expression, such as a word of transition (see page 38).

Indeed, Sam likes to dominate a conversation.
Nevertheless, Willy doesn't understand much of what he says.

Introductory *phrases* fall into this category, too.

In general, Sam makes little sense.
Trying to sound important, he tends to make a fool of himself.

A third use of commas is to separate items in a series or list.

Latasha has studied marketing, salesmanship, and advertising.
Your report must be either in the files, on my desk, or among my
    other mail.
To look your best, feel your best, and be your best require a
    personal program of sound diet and strenuous exercise.

Note that a comma precedes the coordinator at the end of the list. However, commas should NOT be used if a coordinator appears before each item:

I am tired and hungry and annoyed.

A special case arises when adjectives are listed before a noun:

All-City Video employs courteous, knowledgeable, helpful sales-
    people.
They offer the lowest retail prices in town.

A comma is needed when inserting *and* between the adjectives would sound all right (as in the first example). But if *and* cannot be inserted, then do NOT use a comma (as in the second example).

★ **EXERCISE 4**
In each of these sentences, insert commas where appropriate. (More than one may be needed per sentence.)

1. When Lydia got a job as assistant to a civil engineer she knew very little about the field.
2. Like most people she knew that civil engineers design and build such structures as bridges dams and highways.
3. After getting the job Lydia researched the field further.
4. She found that some civil engineers specialize in earthquake construction and she learned that nuclear waste disposal is another area of specialization.
5. However Lydia's new firm is involved in municipal improvement.
6. The company is at work on street improvement water quality and bridge construction projects.
7. Lydia's new boss is currently overseeing the construction of a subway system so she frequently must deal with public officials.
8. Lydia finds her work very exciting and her boss is pleased with her performance.
9. In fact she has offered to send Lydia to school to take courses in business management accounting and economics.
10. Confident about her future Lydia hopes to move up quickly with the firm.

Finally, commas should be used to set off an "interrupting" expression in a sentence. Such expressions are not essential to the structure or meaning of the sentence and are therefore separated from the rest. Interrupters fall into several categories:

1. Contrasted Elements

> The chairman of the board, not the stockholders, made the decision.
> I returned to school to improve my typing, not my English.

Note: When the interrupter appears in the middle of the sentence, it is both preceded *and* followed by a comma. An interrupter at the end (or beginning) of a sentence requires only one comma to separate it from the rest.

2. Parenthetical Expressions

> The affidavit, I think, is ready to be typed.

I think can be removed from the sentence without altering the meaning, so it is set off with commas.

> It is, in fact, a convincing legal document.

Similarly, *in fact* can be eliminated without changing the meaning of the sentence.

3. Appositives

> The president of this company, Rafa al-Habobi, started out as a sales trainee.

The president of this company and *Rafa al-Habobi* are one and the same person, so the name is set off with commas.

> A woman of humble origins, Mrs. Figueroa is now the owner of a large retail chain.

A woman of humble origins is just a way of describing Mrs. Figueroa, so the description is separated from the name with a comma.

4. Explanatory Expressions

> Linda Porter, M.D., performed the surgery.

Degrees and titles that follow a person's name are set off with commas.

> Batale Lusangu now works for Jericho Steel, Inc.

The abbreviations *Inc.* and *Ltd.* are set off from the corporate name with commas.

> Brooklyn, New York, was the original home of the Dodgers.

The state is separated from the city by commas.

> Nanette graduated from high school in June, 1980, and began her first job on July 2, 1980.

The year is set off from the month or the day by commas. Although it is acceptable to omit the commas when only the month and year are referred to, be careful *not* to use a single comma. *Never* write:

> Nanette graduated from high school in June, 1980 and began her first job on July 2, 1980.

In such situations, either two commas or no commas are correct, but one comma is ALWAYS wrong.

The punctuation of numbers poses a special problem. As we have seen, the year is set off from the month or day. You probably are also aware that commas are used to separate thousands, hundred thousands, billions, etc., in figures of four or more digits: $2,642,921.

However, some numbers DO NOT take commas:

1. Street numbers and ZIP codes

    1129 Maple Street, Smithtown, Ohio 93011

2. Telephone numbers

    (914) 830-9612

3. Decimals

    49.113207

4. Serial or account numbers

    621 Z78 97

5. Weights and measures

    7 pounds 7 ounces

★ **EXERCISE 5**
Supply commas wherever needed in these sentences.

1. World Transport Ltd. is located at 241 West Decatur Street Rockville Maine 31229.
2. The company founded in 1949 is owned and operated by Diana Forman.
3. Ms. Forman a graduate of the Harvard Business School was one of the first women in the field of interstate trucking.
4. In August 1962 she hired her first female driver.
5. This woman one would imagine had to overcome strong resentment from her male peers.
6. Today Ms. Forman employs over 1200 women many of whom are truck drivers.
7. According to Ms. Forman it is the success of the female drivers not her own achievement that has contributed the most to women's progress.
8. Acceptance of women on the road she believes has contributed to the growth of women's opportunities in the rest of society.
9. World Transport of course employs many men too.
10. But it is the women not the men who are currently making the headlines.

The distinction between RESTRICTIVE and NONRESTRICTIVE expressions is confusing to many writers. A *restrictive* expression is essential to the meaning of the sentence; think of restrictive as meaning "making specific":

Students *who can type 80 words a minute* should have no trouble finding a job.

Here the italicized words are crucial; not all students, but only those "who can type 80 words a minute" should have no trouble finding a job.

On the other hand, a *nonrestrictive* expression is NOT essential to the meaning of the sentence; think of nonrestrictive as simply "adding information" rather than "making specific."

> My mother, *who can type 80 words a minute,* should have no trouble finding a job.

Here the italicized words are *not* crucial. Since "I" can have only one mother, knowing that she can type 80 words a minute doesn't help us identify her; it simply tells us more about her.

Consider these additional examples:

> Mr. Brown's brother John works for the government; his brother Arthur is in private industry.

Since Mr. Brown has more than one brother, their names are *restrictive;* they tell us which brother is which, and so we use *no* commas.

> Mr. Brown's wife, Susan, is an attorney.

Mr. Brown, of course, can have only one wife, so her name is *nonrestrictive.* Therefore, we set *Susan* off with commas.

★ EXERCISE 6
Some of these sentences require commas to set off nonrestrictive expressions. Insert any missing comma and mark those sentences that need no comma with a check in the space provided.

1. People who strive for professional success occasionally entertain business contacts. ____
2. Mr. Chu who strives for professional success must occasionally entertain business contacts. ____
3. Business discussions that begin over lunch may frequently result in a signed contract. ____
4. In his discussion with Mr. Alvarez which began over lunch Mr. Chu settled a major deal. ____
5. Mr. Chu's client Ms. Murphy was delighted with his success. ____
6. Mr. Chu confident of his social manner enjoys taking clients to dinner. ____
7. Businesspersons confident of their social manner enjoy taking clients to dinner. ____
8. Even breakfast which is usually overlooked can be a fruitful occasion for a business chat. ____
9. Mr. Chu has an appointment for breakfast tomorrow. ____
10. Another contract which he anticipates signing will be an enormous boost to his career. ____

THE APOSTROPHE

The apostrophe is used in three ways.

First of all, it is used to indicate the possessive form of nouns and indefinite pronouns.

> The briefcase owned by Martin—Martin's briefcase
> The fault of nobody—nobody's fault
> The property owned by the company—the company's property

In each of the preceding examples, the noun being made possessive is singular and does not end in S. So the possessive form takes *'s* at the end.

If a singular noun already ends in S, however, there are two possibilities. If the noun has only one syllable, add *'s:*

> The telephone number of Bess—Bess's telephone number
> The job of my boss—my boss's job

If the singular noun has more than one syllable, add only an apostrophe:

> The disciples of Jesus—Jesus' disciples

But, if the pronunciation of the possessive gives the word an extra syllable, add *'s:*

> The fatigue of the waitress—the waitress's fatigue
> The car owned by Louis—Louis's car

Plural nouns may also be made possessive. If a plural noun already ends in S, form the possessive by adding only an apostrophe:

> The benefits of the workers—the workers' benefits
> *But*
> The rights of women—women's rights

A confusing point of possession arises with hyphenated nouns:

> the editor-in-chief's office
> my father-in-law's business

Note that possession is indicated by the last word only. This is also the case for nouns in joint possession:

> Ray and Sally's friend
> Tom and Rita's store

(If *separate* possession is intended, both nouns must get an *'s* ending: Al's and Lucy's answers.)

Remember: Possessive pronouns (see Chapter 6) DO NOT take apostrophes!

★ EXERCISE 7
Using a possessive noun, rewrite each of these.

Example:
the orders from my boss
my boss's orders

1. the guess of anybody

_____

2. the responsibility of Rosemary

_____

3. the weapons of the policemen

_____

4. the roles of the actresses

_____

5. the dog owned by Gus

_____

6. the cat owned by Iris

_____

7. the transmission of the cars

_____

8. the tires of the bus

_____

9. the partnership between Alex and Sid

_____

10 the reaction of the passer-by

_____

The second use of apostrophes is in contractions, which are shortened forms of words. The apostrophe goes where the omitted letters or numbers would be.

I would	I'd
can not	can't
they are	they're
1929	'29
because	'cause

Finally, the apostrophe is used to form special plurals.

1. Lowercase letters

The w's on this typewriter come out looking like u's.

2. Abbreviations ending with periods

All the M.D.'s in the theater offered their help.

However, though acceptable, no apostrophe is needed to form these plurals:

1. Capital letters

I recognized your briefcase by the two Rs in the monogram.

2. Abbreviations that are capitalized and unpunctuated

Many MIAs from the Vietnam era are still unaccounted for.

Of course, an apostrophe should be used in the two above cases when it is needed to avoid misreading:

The A's in the letterhead should all be capitalized.

Also, numbers referred to as numbers and words referred to as words similarly take an apostrophe in their plural only when needed for clarity:

During the first round at poker, I had two 10s and two 9s but couldn't draw a third of either.
I tend to abbreviate all my *ands*.

But

In the new shipment of towels, the *his*'s are all blue, but the *hers*'s are turquoise.

★ EXERCISE 8
By inserting apostrophes
where needed, correct
these sentences. If a sentence is correct, put a
check in the space pro-
vided.

1. This companys collection rate is rather high. ____
2. Many of our bills are c.o.d.s. ____
3. Some of our charge accounts havent been paid, however. ____
4. The M.D.s tend to be especially slow. ____
5. Dr. Adlers account, for instance, is now 90 days past due. ____
6. Weve sent him several statements. ____
7. Dr. Moses payments are also behind. ____
8. But she has been our customer since the early 1970s. ____
9. Sometimes I get tired of typing all those *please remits.* ____
10. But its worth it when the checks come in. ____

QUOTATION MARKS

Quotation marks are always used in pairs. They enclose exactly quoted statements from either someone's writing or someone's speech.

> In an article on credit, financial advisor Jane Freund wrote: "Establishing credit before you need it is an intelligent precaution."

A quote within a quote is enclosed in single *quotation* marks:

> Freund noted: "We all have at least one friend who brags, 'I never buy anything on credit.' But that person is establishing no credit history, a hedge against the day he may need credit."

Notice that the speaker and the verb of saying (Jane Freund wrote, for example) are always *outside* the quotation marks.

> DO NOT FORGET TO CLOSE A QUOTATION WITH THE SECOND QUOTATION MARK.

Quotation marks are also used to enclose certain titles: short stories, essays, articles, poems, and chapters. Titles of full-length works (such as books, magazines, newspapers, plays, movies, and television shows) are usually underlined (to indicate italics).

> I found the article "How to Ask for a Raise," in the August issue of Secretary's World, very interesting.

Note that italics (or underlining) are also used for names of ships, aircraft, spacecraft, and trains; titles of works of art; and foreign words.

> The launching of *Apollo VII* was spectacular.
> The *Mona Lisa* has captured men's imaginations for centuries.
> As we parted, he waved and bid me *adieu.*

A third, but often misused, use of quotation marks is to enclose words used in a special sense:

> "Insolvent" means "unable to pay debts."
> The accountant suggested that we "amortize" our expenditures, that is, write them off by prorating them over a fixed period.

* EXERCISE 9
In these sentences, insert quotation marks wherever needed.

1. Julia Lantigua, who has written many articles on personal computers, is the author of The Affordable PC: Power to the People in the August issue of PC Monthly.
2. In the article, Lantigua maintains, computers enable ordinary people to do big projects that they otherwise wouldn't have the resources to do.
3. Lantigua points out, computers provide access to vast amounts of information and simple ways to store it.
4. Lap-top computers, she explains further, enable people to take information wherever they go.
5. In The Affordable PC, Lantigua interviews several professionals who have become dependent on their computers.
6. One, Alan Novak, a short story writer, said, because my computer simplifies revising, I am much more prolific now than I was in my pre-computer days.
7. Similarly, Lois Bagdikian, an advertising executive, said, by storing bits of ideas for new ads on my lap-top, I can work on new campaigns while travelling, with my inspiration right there on my knees.
8. Finally, Robert Ragin, a high school teacher, observed, many of my students are hooked on electronic mail and belong to bulletin-board type clubs.
9. Lantigua elaborates, without the performance pressure of school, the fear of making mistakes, electronic mail encourages people to communicate with words.
10. Reassuringly, she adds, with spelling and grammar software, they may even learn to write with accuracy and precision.

THE HYPHEN

The hyphen is used to join two or more words into a compound:

> do-it-yourself instruction booklets
> a wait-and-see attitude

The hyphen is also used with compound numbers from 21 to 99 and with fractions:

> thirty-eight
> eighty-two
> one-quarter
> four-fifths

And the hyphen is used with such prefixes as *ex-*, *all-*, *self-*, and *pro-*:

> ex-convict
> all-star
> self-help
> pro-tennis

Note: DO NOT leave a single-letter syllable at the beginning or end of a line *(e-liminate, dictionar-y)*. Similarly, DO NOT begin a line with a two-letter word ending *(want-ed)*.

A hyphen may also be used to divide a word at the end of a line. This should only be done between syllables. (Therefore, one-syllable words may NOT be hyphenated.)

> At the end of every semester, you must take an ex-
> amination.

★ **EXERCISE 10**
Revise these phrases, using hyphenated compounds.

Example:

a vacation for three weeks
a three-week vacation

1. a movie that has been rated X

_____

2. a restaurant that is ranked at four stars

_____

3. a garment sewn by hand

_____

4. a question that boggles the mind

_____

5. vegetables that were grown at home

_____

6. negotiations that took all night

_____

7. a tablecloth stained with tea

_____

8. a graduate who is seventeen years old

_____

9. a student who is oriented toward a career

_____

10. a dress covered with polka dots

_____

★ **EXERCISE 11**
In the space provided, write out each word with spaces between syllables, inserting a hyphen at a suitable end-of-line break. If a word should NOT be divided, place an X in the space. Refer to the dictionary if necessary.

1. bankruptcy _____

2. corporation _____

3. price _____

4. depreciation _____

5. liability _____

6. fiscal _____

7. selling _____

8. franchise _____

9. mortgage _____

10. monopoly _____

THE DASH

The dash is used to indicate abruptness, especially a sudden change of thought or tone. To type a dash, use two unspaced hyphens; to write a dash by hand, use an unbroken line about the length of two hyphens.

> I plan to study for the exam all night--if my eyes hold out.
>
> Mr. Rodriguez—do you remember him from last year's conven-
> tion?—will be joining our staff in May.

A dash should be used to break off an unfinished statement:

> Mrs. Olsen mumbled, "I can't seem to remember where—"

A dash should also be used between an introductory list and the explanatory sentence that follows:

> Calmness, confidence, and a copy of your resume—bring all of
> these with you to a job interview.

Remember: The dash should be used discreetly. It is NOT a substitute for
commas or terminal punctuation.

PARENTHESES

Parentheses are used to enclose statements that are completely separate
from the main thought of the sentence. Such statements may serve as
supplement or as reference:

> In some professions (physical therapy, for example), a dress code
> may be strictly enforced.
>
> Margaret Grange (1883–1966) was the author of several books
> on corporate finance.
>
> According to the union contract, all employees are required to
> have a college transcript on file (see section 6, paragraph 1).

Parentheses should also be used for enumeration within a sentence:

> You will need the following: (1) your resume, (2) letters of refer-
> ence, (3) a college transcript, and (4) a pad and pencil.

Note that sentence punctuation comes AFTER the closing parenthesis:

> I have investigated various models of calculators for the office
> (see the attached list), but none has been purchased as yet.

However, if the parentheses enclose a whole sentence, the terminal punctuation is placed inside the closing parenthesis:

> Please submit your time cards by Wednesday evening. (Blank
> time cards are available in the personnel office.)

BRACKETS

Brackets have three uses:

1. Parentheses within parentheses

> The role of business in American life has often been the subject
> of our fiction (see, for example, the novels of William Dean
> Howells [1837–1920]).

2. Interpolations within a quotation

> In *Death of a Salesman* by Arthur Miller, Charlie pays tribute to
> Willy Loman: "[A salesman's] a man way out there in the

blue, riding on a smile and a shoe shine. . . . A salesman is got to dream, boy. It comes with the territory."

3. Editorial corrections and comments

The professor ended his lecture with this remark: "All of you will hopefully [*sic*] read at least some of these books." (*Sic* signifies here that the word *hopefully,* although used incorrectly, is being reproduced from the original quotation.)

★ **EXERCISE 12**
Punctuate each of these sentences by inserting the necessary dashes, parentheses, and brackets.

1. Bernard M. Baruch 1870–1965 was born in Camden, South Carolina.
2. Because he was a renowned financier he made a fortune in the stock market before he was thirty he was often engaged by the government as a special adviser.
3. He contributed to the Allied effort during both World War I national defense adviser and World War II special adviser to James F. Byrne.
4. Later he was a member of FDR's "Brain Trust" a group of unofficial advisers that also included college professors and labor leaders.
5. He even participated in efforts toward international control of atomic energy U.S. representative to the U.N. Atomic Energy Commission.
6. In 1953, a branch of the City University of New York formerly the School of Business Administration of the City College was renamed in his honor the Bernard M. Baruch School of Business and Public Administration.
7. The details of Baruch's life and times may be found in his autobiography see *Baruch* 2 volumes, 1957–60.

Capitalization

There is logic to be found in the rules for capitalization if we think of these rules as falling into three categories:

I. The first word of a sentence should be capitalized.

The man sees the tree.
My mother talks while I listen.

This rule includes complete sentences *within* sentences such as:

QUOTATIONS—My adviser says, "It is never too early to plan your career."
CERTAIN QUESTIONS—The real issue was, What were we to do about the problem?
STATEMENTS AFTER COLONS (when emphasis is desired)—We found a solution: We would do the job ourselves.

★ **EXERCISE 13**
Proofread this paragraph for words that should be capitalized but aren't. Then underline the letters that should be changed to capitals.

"flexible work hours" (or flextime for short) is one of the biggest innovations in employment policy in the past few decades. under flextime, employees choose the times at which they arrive at and depart from work within the limits set by management. usually core hours are established: during this midday period all employees must be present. they may choose, however to come in early or stay late. under flextime, absenteeism has dropped significantly, and productivity has risen. as a result, the Public and World Affairs Committee predicts, "flextime is going to be with us in the coming years."

II. The first and last words of *titles* and *headings* should be capitalized. So should all the other words EXCEPT:

ARTICLES *(a, an, the)*
COORDINATORS (*and, or, but, for, nor; so* and *yet* are flexible)
SHORT PREPOSITIONS (such as *in, on, of*)

Consider these examples:

Advertising Strategy for the Small Business
"Tax Shelters: Are They for You?"
Middle Management Stress
"Latest News in Money Market Funds"
Introduction to Computer Programming
"The Ups and Downs of the Adjustable Mortgage"

★ EXERCISE 14
In the space provided, rewrite these titles, using appropriate capitalization.

1. *secretarial and office procedures for college*

2. *principles of data processing*

3. *how to marry a millionaire*

4. "so you want to be a legal secretary?"

5. "how to ask for a raise"

6. "one hundred ways to supplement your income"

7. *how to find the job you've always wanted*

8. "avoiding three o'clock fatigue"

9. "how to work around a candy machine without gaining weight"

10. *take the money and run*

III. The *names* of specific persons, places, and things should be capitalized.

Michael Jordan, like many other successful athletes, also successfully maneuvered a career in advertising.
A motor trip to Rome from Sicily would be an unforgettable vacation.
The World Trade Center is the tallest structure in New York City.

The names of organizations and institutions are covered by this rule:

> The convention of the American Psychological Association will be held during the week of May 24.
> Warren earned his bachelor's degree at Yale University.

Similarly, historical periods, events, and documents are capitalized:

> Literature of the Renaissance is marked by an awareness of classical culture.
> The Revolutionary War began in 1775 and ended in 1883.
> The Declaration of Independence was adopted on July 4, 1776.

Members of national, political, religious, racial, social and athletic groups are capitalized:

> The Republican candidate for mayor spent the morning shaking hands at the train station.
> Babe Ruth was one of the most famous outfielders to ever play with the Yankees.

Days of the week, months of the year, and names of holidays are capitalized, but seasons of the year are NOT.

> I will have your order ready by Tuesday.
> Winston entered law school in September.
> I always overeat on Thanksgiving.
> Every summer, the Feins rent a cottage on Cape Cod.

Note that compass directions work two ways: When used to refer to a region or place, they are capitalized.

> Voters in the Northeast are often stereotyped as liberals.

But compass points used as *directions* are NOT capitalized.

> Los Angeles is west of Las Vegas.

Finally, words referring to a deity or to religious documents are capitalized.

> In Greek mythology, Zeus was the father of Castor and Pollux.
> The Lord gives and the Lord takes away.
> The Koran is the collection of Moslem scriptural writings.

★ EXERCISE 15
Proofread these paragraphs for words that should be capitalized but aren't. Then underline the letters that should be changed to capitals.

1. On june 28, 1778, the battle of monmouth was fought. The last major battle in the north during the revolutionary war, it took place north of monmouth court house in new jersey. There, george washington led an army of 13,500 troops to victory against the British troops, who were led by henry clinton.

2. Born on february 11, 1847, in milan, ohio, thomas alva edison became one of america's greatest inventors. Although he produced over 1,300 inventions, the most famous remain the light bulb and the phonograph. Edison also built the first central electric power station, erected on pearl street in new york city. Known as the "wizard of menlo park," he considered his genius to be "one percent inspiration and ninety-nine percent perspiration."

A number of special considerations arise with regard to capitalization:

1. Regular nouns are capitalized when they are *part of a name,* for example:

> During lunch hour, the street was teeming with people.

But

> I work at the corner of Twelfth Street and Arthur Avenue.

> Cheryl graduated from high school in 1976.

But

> Her *alma mater* is Madison High School.

> Our office building is thirty stories high.

But

> The Empire State Building is a major New York tourist attraction.

This rule holds true for commercial brand names:

> Kellogg's Corn Flakes

But

> Ivory soap

2. Adjectives that are formed from names are capitalized.

> The American flag is a symbol of democracy.
> *Hamlet* is a frequently produced Shakespearean play.

3. Abbreviations of capitalized words should also be capitalized.

> U.P.S. (United Parcel Service)

But

> c.o.d. (cash on delivery)

4. A person's title should be capitalized when used *before* the name. Titles used *after* names are not capitalized.

> Dean Douglas addressed the student body at the first assembly
>   of the year.

But

> Mr. Paul Douglas, dean of students, attended the first assembly
>   of the year.

Titles of particularly high rank MAY be capitalized when used without a name:

> The President of the United States held a press conference.

But

> The president of U.S. Steel held a press conference.

Similarly, terms of kinship MAY be capitalized when used as the person's name:

> Before I went out, I told Dad that I'd be home by ten.

5. As we have seen frequently, the pronoun *I* is always capitalized.

> I am quite proud of myself.

6. The *first* word of a complimentary closing is capitalized.

> Sincerely yours
> Yours truly

★ **EXERCISE 16**
Proofread this letter for uncapitalized words that should be capitalized. Then underline the letters that should be changed to capitals.

Dear mr. jackson:

i would like to offer my hearty congratulations on your promotion to president of the empire stove company. All of us at seymour's service centers, inc., are pleased that your years of hard work have been rewarded.

Seymour's appreciates the fine quality and serviceability of american-made stoves and appliances. That is why we have always confidently offered empire stoves to our customers.

In closing, president jackson, let me say that we look forward to a long and mutually rewarding business relationship with e.s.c.

sincerely yours,

Abbreviations

As a general rule, you should avoid abbreviations in your writing, unless the writing is technical or you are preparing lists or tables. The following abbreviations *are* acceptable in formal writing.

TITLES

1. *Mr., Mrs., Ms., Dr.,* and *St.* (meaning *Saint*) are always abbreviated when used before a name.

Mr. James Cooper	Mrs. Jane Bowles
Mr. J. F. Cooper	Mrs. J. Bowles
Mr. Cooper	Mrs. Bowles
Ms. Lillian Lewis	St. Peter
Ms. L. Lewis	St. Cecilia
Ms. Lewis	

2. Such abbreviations as *Prof., Gov., Sen.,* and *Rep.* may be used before a *full* name (a first name or initial PLUS a last name).

> Prof. Fred Farkas
> Gov. T. P. Barnes

When only a last name is used, however, the title must be spelled out.

> Professor Farkas
> Governor Barnes

3. The designations *Honorable* and *Reverend,* because they indicate dignity and respect, should *not* be abbreviated except in addresses and lists. Moreover, they must be used with a first name, initial, or title in addition to the last name.

Reverend Tom Payne	Honorable Bruce Ng
Rev. Tom Payne	Hon. Bruce Ng
Rev. T. Payne	Hon. B. Ng
Rev. Dr. Payne	

Using *the* before such designations indicates additional formality.

The Reverend Tom Payne	The Honorable Bruce Ng
The Rev. Tom Payne	The Hon. Bruce Ng

4. Titles appearing *after* names must be spelled out, except Esq., Jr., and Sr., and academic, professional, and religious designations.

> T. P. Barnes, governor

But

> T. P. Barnes, Esq.
> Frieda Farkas, Ph.D.
> Tom Payne, D.D.
> Wayne Reed, C.P.A.

COMPANY NAMES

Abbreviate firm names only when the company prefers it. Their letterhead will provide you with this information; for example, *Con Edison* is acceptable for the *Consolidated Edison Company.* Similarly, using *&* instead of *and* should be limited to the company's official use:

> A & P
> Lord & Taylor

Organizations and governmental agencies that are known by their initials may be abbreviated in writing:

> The OPEC nations have agreed to raise the price of oil by another $2 per barrel.
> The CIA has recalled its agents from the Middle East.

TERMS USED WITH FIGURES AND DATES

1. The designation *A.D.* (*anno Domini* meaning "year of our Lord") and *B.C.* ("before Christ") should always be abbreviated.

> Claudius I was born in the year 10 B.C. and died in the year A.D. 54.

Note that *A.D.* precedes the year while *B.C.* follows it.

2. The abbreviations *A.M.* ("before noon") and *P.M.* ("after noon") may always be used.

> My work day begins at 9:00 A.M. and ends at 4:30 P.M.

Note that *A.M.* and *P.M.* must always be used with figures; do not use them with words or the term *o'clock.*

> My work day begins at nine o'clock in the morning and ends at four-thirty in the afternoon.

3. *Number* and *numbers* may be abbreviated as *no.* (or *No.*) and *nos.* (or *Nos.*) respectively when used before figures.

> The model I am most interested in is no. 131.
> The following checks have not yet cleared: nos. 451, 454, and 458.

However, spell out *number* or *numbers* at the beginning of a sentence:

> Number 62159 is the missing invoice.

4. The dollar sign ($) is permissible in writing. Instead of the cumbersome

> Sue owes Roger nineteen dollars and fifty-five cents.

it is proper to write:

> Sue owes Roger $19.55.

LATIN EXPRESSIONS

The abbreviations of certain Latin expressions are acceptable though in formal writing the English version should be spelled out.

cf.	compare
e.g.	for example
et al	and others
etc.	and so forth
i.e.	that is
viz.	namely
vs.	versus

For example:

> The major oil companies (Gulf, Exxon, *et al*) are passing on the price increase to consumers.

Certain words should NOT be abbreviated in writing. (In addresses, lists, tables, invoices, and the like, abbreviations are acceptable.)

1. Names of cities, states, and countries

> Although Arnold was born in Philadelphia, Pennsylvania, he has lived in West Germany most of his life.

2. Months of the year, days of the week

> The shipment of electric yo-yos arrived Wednesday, October 1.

3. Parts of place names, such as *Street, Avenue, Road, Park, Port, Fort, Mount, River,* as well as compass directions

> The Adirondack Mountains are northeast of the Mississippi River.
> The hardware store is on the west side of Bruckner Boulevard.

4. Units of measure, courses of study, and the words *page, chapter,* and *volume*

> On page 14 of the physics textbook, the speed of light is listed as 186,000 miles per second.

1. The meeting to explore ways of increasing tourism in Greenwood, North Dakota, was called to order at seven-fifteen in the evening.

2. Mister Ashley introduced the guest speaker, the Honorable J. R. Buckley, mayor of Greenwood.

3. The members of the Greenwood Chamber of Commerce, who were present at the meeting, greeted Mayor Buckley with warm applause.

4. Buckley began his speech with an anecdote about ancient Rome in the year 129 before Christ.

5. But he quickly moved to the number one concern of everyone present, namely, how to attract more tourists to Greenwood.

6. The mayor surprised the audience by announcing plans to spend two million five hundred fifty thousand dollars on restoring the town's landmarks and historical sites.

7. He also announced the intentions of International Telephone and Telegraph to erect a Sheraton Hotel on Broad Street in the center of town.

8. After Buckley's address, Lana Stephens, Certified Social Worker, asked a question.

9. Miss Stephens wanted to know if local residents would be employed on the planned construction projects.

10. The mayor assured her that they would, and the meeting adjourned at ten o'clock.

_____

_____

★ **EXERCISE 18**
Proofread this letter for incorrect abbreviations and then rewrite the letter on another sheet of paper, making all necessary corrections.

Dear Mr. Poe:

On Tues., Mar. 17, which happened to be Saint Patrick's Day, I purchased four lbs. of Meunster cheese from your supermarket on Grand St. in Grahamsville, N.J.

I intended to serve the cheese to guests that night. However, when I unwrapped the cheese after getting it home, I discovered that it was green with mold!

The manager of the Grand St. store refused to refund my money. I paid $12.44 for the cheese. I would like you to know that if my claim is not satisfied, I intend to take the matter to the Dept. of Cons. Affairs.

Yours truly,

Numbers

Knowing whether or not to spell out a number or use figures is tricky. But there are some guidelines. A safe rule of thumb is to *spell out numbers that can be expressed in one or two words;* use figures for other numbers.

six million soldiers	6,490,000 soldiers
one-fourth	82¼
fifty dollars	$49.95

Certain numbers should always be spelled out:

1. Numbers that begin a sentence

   One hundred fifty yards of wire are needed to complete the project.
   We will need 150 yards of wire to complete the project.

2. Large round numbers

   Six billion dollars (or) $6 billion
   (Using figures would imply emphasis: $6,000,000,000.)

3. Time expressed as a number alone or with the word *o'clock*

   four in the afternoon
   four o'clock

   Use figures with *A.M.* and *P.M.*

   4 A.M. (or) 4:00 P.M.
   2:30 A.M.

Other numbers should be indicated with figures:

1. Addresses: house, street, and ZIP code numbers

> 252 Ash Street, Greenville, Wyoming 71226
> 11 East 49 Street (or) 11 East 49th Street
> P.O. Box 72
> RFD 2

2. Decimals

> 6.293
> 0.00329

Note that commas are NOT used with decimals.

3. Dates

> January 31, 1951 (or) 31 January 1951
> May twenty-fourth (or) the twenty-fourth of May (or) May 24 (or)
>   May 24th

Note that figures are used when the year is mentioned along with the day. Note, too, that an ordinal ending (1st, 2nd, 4th) is NOT used when the year is mentioned.

4. Expressions requiring two numbers

> 10 fifteen-cent stamps
> 2 five-dollar bills

Note that the first number is indicated in figures and the second is spelled out.

Keep in mind that *consistency* in using numbers is important. In a series, use either all words or all figures:

> On the desk were two pens, one pad, and six manila envelopes.
> I would like to order 10 reams of paper, 4 dozen pencils, and 2
>   boxes of erasers.

Finally, certain words and symbols often used with numbers must be considered:

1. The word *percent* should be spelled out, except on invoices and lists (in which case you may use %).

> nine percent
> 11½ percent

2. The symbol ¢ should only be used in quoting prices. Otherwise, use words or units of a dollar.

> 6¢
> six cents
> $.06

3. The symbol # should only be used in tables, invoices, etc. Instead, use *number* or the abbreviation *no.* or *No.* The symbol should NEVER be used with house numbers or RFD numbers.

★ **EXERCISE 19**
These numbers are all written as words. Some should be written as figures; others should remain words if intended for use in formal writing. In the space provided, convert those numbers that would be acceptable as figures; label CORRECT those numbers that should be left alone.

1. eight dollars and twelve cents

_____

2. three-fifths

_____

3. forty-nine west eleventh street

_____

4. August tenth, 1980

_____

5. seven billion

_____

6. ten men, 8 women, and sixteen children

_____

7. two sixty-cent fares

_____

8. nine-thirty A.M.

_____

9. ten cents

_____

10. Post Office Box Twenty-one

_____

★ **REVIEW EXERCISES**
Proofread these letters for errors in punctuation, capitalization, abbreviation, and use of numbers. Then rewrite each letter on another sheet of paper, making all necessary corrections.

A.

TO: All Sales Representatives

FROM: Fay Sorrell

DATE: November 4, 1981

SUBJECT: Departmental Meeting

There will be a meeting of the sales department on friday November 8, in rm. 110. Mister Arthur Parker will address the meeting on the topic, "Improving Your Sales Through Self-Hypnosis."

Mr. Parker a certified psychoanalyst who has studied at the Alfred Adler institute, is the author of several books including the best-seller It's a Snap (New York, 1991).

Following the lecture, there will be a question and answer period.

Your attendance is required.

B.

Dear Tenant—

Please be advised, that pursuant to the 1992–93 Rent Guidelines Board, the percentages covering Lease Renewals effective July 1st, 1992, have been changed. The renewal percentages are:

Five percent for one-year renewal
9% for two-year renewal
13% for 3-year renewal

Enclosed is your lease renewal. Please sign, and return both copies; along with the additional security of $20.41.

Thank you for your cooperation.

Yours truly,

C.

TO: Michael Moody

FROM: Fred Dobbs, Personnel Insurance Coordinator

DATE: May 15, 1993

SUBJECT: Medical Leave of Absence

On the basis of information provided by your Physician and at your request, you have been placed on medical leave of absence as of May 30, '93.

To maintain your leave, Company policy requires additional written statements from your physician at thirty-day-intervals. These statements, should be sent directly to the Personnel insurance Coordinator at the downtown office.

Failure to return to work on the date indicated by your physician, will be considered a Resignation.

Feel free to contact me, for further information regarding this policy.

D.

Policy Number: 43 681 345
Date: 9/5/91

Dear Mr. & Mrs. Chou:

We are sorry that we cannot provide the additional protection that you requested.

Because you made 5 claims in the past four years, we cannot provide $500.00 Deductible Comprehensive Coverage on the '90 Ford Probe that replaced your old car. Nevertheless—Bodily Injury and Property Damage on the old car have been transferred to your new car.

Although we were temporarily providing the protection while considering your request, we will be unable to continue providing it. You will be covered by the protection only until 12:01 o'clock (A.M.) on September 26, 1991. You will, therefore have a 3-week period in which to apply for the protection elsewhere.

Please understand, Mister and Mrs. Chou, that our decision was made after thorough consideration of your case and based upon the underwriting rules and regulations of our company.

All of your other coverage, remains in full force as it was before your request.

Sincerely,

E.

Dear Doctor Christopher,

Not long ago I spoke with you on the telephone, about a possible teaching position with you next semester. You suggested, I mention this in my letter.

The man who referred me to your school was Prof. Helmsley of the accounting dept.

My most recent job was in the secretarial skills department at Bronxville Comm. College. I was a part-time instructor there, for 4 consecutive semesters.

I have enclosed my resume for your consideration.

Thank you

Sincerely Yours,

Part Two
CORRESPONDENCE

9.
BUSINESS STYLE

Tone

Second to grammatical correctness, achieving an appropriate business style may be the biggest problem for the writer of business letters. A sure sign of an inexperienced writer, in fact, is the obvious attempt to sound too "businesslike."

> As per your request, please find enclosed herewith a check in the amount of $16.49.

Such expressions as "herewith" and "as per" contribute nothing to the message while making the letter sound stilted and stiff.

The first step, then, to writing successful business correspondence is to relax. While business letters will vary in tone from familiar to formal, they should all sound natural. Within the limits of standard English, of course, you should try to say things in a "regular" way:

> As you requested, I am enclosing a check for $16.49.

If you resist the temptation to sound businesslike, you will end up being more business-minded. The second version of our sample sentence is not only more personal and friendly; it is also more efficient. It uses fewer words, taking less time to write and type as well as to read and comprehend.

With this initial piece of advice in mind, review the following list of words and expressions. Then plan to eliminate these terms from your business writing vocabulary.

EXPRESSIONS TO AVOID IN BUSINESS LETTERS

according to our records
acknowledge receipt of
as to, with reference to, with
   regard to, with respect to
at hand, on hand
attached please find, attached
   hereto, enclosed herewith,
   enclosed please find
beg to inform, beg to tell
duly
for your information
hereby, heretofore, herewith

I have your letter
I wish to thank, may I ask
in due time, in due course of time
in receipt of
in the near future
in view of
our Mrs. Campbell
permit me to say
pursuant to
thank you again
thank you in advance
thereon

Instead of . . .	*Use . . .*
advise, inform	say, tell, let us know
along these lines, on the order of	like, similar to
as per	as, according to
at an early date, at your earliest convenience	soon, today, next week, *a specific date*
at this time, at the present time, at this writing	now, at present
check to cover	check for
deem	believe, consider
due to the fact that, because of the fact that	because
favor, communication	letter, memo, *et al.*
for the purpose of	for
forward	send
free of charge	free
in accordance with	according to
in advance of, prior to	before
in compliance with	as you requested
in re, re	regarding, concerning
in the amount of	for
in the event that	if, in case
kindly	please
of recent date	recent
party	person, *a specific name*
said	*not to be used as an adjective*
same	*not to be used as a noun*
subsequent to	after, since
the writer, the undersigned	I/me
up to this writing	until now

Consider the difference between these two versions of the same letter:

Dear Mr. Singh:

With reference to your order for a Nashito camcorder, we are in receipt of your check and are returning same.

I beg to inform you that, as a manufacturer, our company sells camcorders to dealers only. In compliance with our wholesale agreement, we deem it best to refrain from direct business with private consumers.

For your information, there are many retailers in your vicinity who carry Nashito camcorders. Attached please find a list of said dealers.

Hoping you understand.

Yours truly,

Dear Mr. Singh:

We have received your order for a Nashito camcorder but, unfortunately, must return your check.

As a manufacturer, we sell only to dealers, with whom we have very explicit wholesale agreements.

Nevertheless, we sincerely appreciate your interest in Nashito products. We are therefore enclosing a list of retailers in your community who carry a full line of our camcorders. Any one of them will be happy to serve you.

Sincerely yours,

Outlook

While striving for a natural tone, you should also aim for a positive outlook. Even when the subject of your letter is unpleasant, it is important to remain courteous and tactful. Building and sustaining the goodwill of your reader should be an underlying goal of nearly any letter you write. Even a delinquent account may someday become a paying customer.

A simple "please" or "thank you" is often enough to make a mundane letter more courteous. Instead of:

> We have received your order.

you might try:

> Thank you for your recent order.

Or, in place of the impersonal:

> Checking our records, we have verified the error in your November bill.

you could help retain a customer by writing:

> Please accept our sincere apologies for the error in your November bill.

Saying "We are sorry" or "I appreciate" can do much to build rewarding business relations.

On the other hand, you must be tactful when delivering unpleasant messages. NEVER accuse your reader with expressions like "your error" or "your failure." An antagonistic letter would say:

> Because you have refused to pay your long overdue bill, your credit rating is in jeopardy.

A more diplomatic letter (and therefore one more apt to get results) might say:

> Because the $520 balance on your account is now over ninety days past due, your credit rating is in jeopardy.

Because the second sentence refrains from attacking the reader personally (and also includes important details), it will be read more receptively.

A word of caution is necessary here. Some writers, in an effort to be pleasant, end their letters with sentence fragments:

> Looking forward to your early reply.
> Hoping to hear from you soon.
> Thanking you for your interest.

These participial phrases (note the -ING form in each) should NOT be used to conclude a letter. There is never an excuse for grammatical flaws, especially when complete sentences will serve the purpose well:

> We look forward to your early reply.
> I hope to hear from you soon.
> Thank you for your interest.

Consider the difference between these two versions of the same memo:

```
TO: Department Supervisors

FROM: Assistant Director

Inform your subordinates:

1  Because so many have taken advantage of past leniency,
   lateness will no longer be overlooked. Paychecks will
   be docked as of Monday, March 6.

2  As a result of abuses of employee privileges, which have
   resulted in exorbitant long distance telephone bills,
   any employee caught making a personal call will be sub-
   ject to disciplinary action.

As supervisors, you will be required to enforce these new
regulations.
```

```
TO: _____
FROM: Wanda Hatch, Assistant Director
```

Unfortunately, a few people have taken advantage of le-
nient company policies regarding lateness and personal
phone calls. As a result, we must all now conform to
tougher regulations.

Please inform the members of your department that:

1 Beginning Monday, March 6, the paychecks of employees
  who are late will be docked.

2 Personal phone calls are no longer permitted.

It is a shame that the abuses of a few must cost the rest
of us. But we are asking all department supervisors to
help us enforce these new rules.

The "You Approach"

Courtesy and tact are sometimes achieved by what is called a *"you approach."* In other words, your letter should be reader oriented and sound
as if you share your reader's point of view. For example:

> Please accept our apologies for the delay.

is perfectly polite. But:

> We hope you have not been seriously inconvenienced by the delay.

lets your reader know that you care.

This, of course, does NOT mean you should avoid "I" and "we" when
necessary. When you do use these pronouns, though, keep a few pointers
in mind:

1. Use "I" when you are referring to yourself (or to the person who will
   actually sign the letter.)
2. Use "we" when you are referring to the company itself.
3. DO NOT use the company name or "our company," both of which,
   like the terms listed earlier in this chapter, sound stilted. This practice
   is rather like referring to oneself by one's name, rather than "I" or
   "me."

Also, you should be careful to use your reader's name sparingly in the
body of your letter. Although this practice seems, at first glance, to per-
sonalize a letter, it can sound condescending.

Now, compare the two letters that follow, and see if you recognize the
features that make the second letter more *"you*-oriented."

Dear Ms. Biggs:

Having conducted our standard credit investigation, we have concluded that it would be unwise for us to grant you credit at this time.

We believe that the extent of your current obligations makes you a bad credit risk. As you can understand, it is in our best interest to grant charge accounts only to those customers with proven ability to pay.

Please accept our sincere regrets and feel free to continue to shop at Allen's on a cash basis.

Sincerely yours,

Dear Miss Biggs:

I am sorry to inform you that your application for an Allen's charge account has been turned down.

Our credit department believes that, because of your current obligations, additional credit might be difficult for you to handle at this time. Your credit reputation is too valuable to be placed in jeopardy. We will be delighted, of course, to reconsider your application in the future should your financial responsibilities be reduced. Until then, we hope you will continue to shop at Allen's where EVERY customer is our prime concern.

Sincerely yours,

Organization

One further word about style: a good business letter must be well organized. You must *plan in advance* everything you want to say; you must *say everything necessary* to your message; and then you must stop. In short, a letter must be logical, complete, and concise.

When planning a letter and before you start to write, jot down the main point you want to make. Then, list all the details necessary to make that point; these may be facts, reasons, explanations, and so on. Finally, rearrange your list; in the letter you will want to mention things in a logical order so that your message will come across as clearly as possible.

Making a letter complete takes place during the planning stage, too. Check your list to make sure you have included all the relevant details; the reader of your finished letter must have all the information he or she will need. In addition to facts, reasons, and explanations, necessary information could also entail an appeal to your reader's emotions or understanding. In other words, SAY EVERYTHING YOU CAN TO ELICIT FROM YOUR READER THE RESPONSE YOU'D LIKE.

On the other hand, you must be careful not to say too much. You must know when a letter is finished. If a message is brief, resist the temptation to "pad" it; if you've said what you have to say in just a few lines, don't try to fill the letter out. One mistake is to reiterate an idea. If you've already offered your thanks, you will upset the logical order and, therefore, the impact of your letter if you end with:

> Thank you once again.

Tacking on a separate additional message will similarly weaken the effect of your main point. Imagine receiving a collection letter for a long overdue bill that concludes:

> Let us take this opportunity to remind you that our January White Sale begins next week, with three preview days for our special charge customers.

Don't, moreover, give your reader more information than is needed:

> Because my husband's birthday is October 12, I would like to order the three-piece luggage ensemble in your fall catalog.

Certainly, an order clerk would much prefer to know the style number of the luggage than the date of your husband's birth.

In a similar vein, you should strive to eliminate redundant words and phrases from your letters. For example:

> I have received your invitation *inviting me* to participate in your annual Career Conference.

Since all invitations invite, the words *inviting me* are superfluous. Another common mistake is to say:

> the green-colored carpet

or:

> the carpet that is green in color

Green *is* a color, so to use the word *color* is wordy.

Adverbs are often the cause of redundancy:

> If we cooperate together, the project will be finished quickly.

Cooperate already means work together, so using the word *together* is unnecessary.

Also, when one word will accurately replace several, use the one word. Instead of:

> Mr. Kramer handled the job *in an efficient manner.*

say:

> Mr. Kramer handled the job *efficiently.*

The following list of common redundancies should help you eliminate the problem from your writing:

REDUNDANT EXPRESSIONS

Don't Use . . .	*Use . . .*
and et cetera	et cetera
as a result of	because
as otherwise	otherwise
at about	about
attached hereto	attached
at this point in time	at this time; now
avail oneself of	use
be of the opinion	believe
both alike	alike
both together	together
check into	check
connect up	connect
continue on	continue
cooperate together	cooperate
customary practice	practice
during the time that	while
each and every	each *or* every
enclosed herewith	enclosed
enter into	enter
forward by post	mail
free gift	gift
have a tendency to	tend to
in many instances	often
in spite of the fact that	although
in the amount of	for
in the event that	if
in the matter of	about
in the process of being	being
in this day and age	nowadays
inform of the reason	tell why
is of the opinion	believes
letter under date of	letter of
letter with regard to	letter about
new beginner	beginner
on account of the fact that	because
owing to the fact that	because, since
past experience	experience
place emphasis on	emphasize
place an order for	order
repeat again	repeat
same identical	identical

send an answer	reply
up above	above
whether or not	whether
write your name	sign

Now consider the following two sample letters. Notice the redundancies in the first that are eliminated in the second.

Dear Ms. Rodriguez:

I am very pleased with the invitation that I received from you inviting me to make a speech for the National Association of Secretaries on June 11. Unfortunately, I regret that I cannot attend the meeting on June 11. I feel that I do not have sufficient time to prepare myself because I received your invitation on June 3 and it is not enough time to prepare myself completely for the speech.

Yours truly,

Dear Ms. Rodriguez:

I am pleased with the invitation to speak to the National Association of Secretaries. Unfortunately, I cannot attend the meeting on June 11.

I feel that I will not have sufficient time to prepare myself because I received your invitation on June 3.

I will be happy to address your organization on another occasion if you would give me a bit more notice. Best of luck with your meeting.

Sincerely yours,

Note: Composing on a word processor can streamline your efforts toward a business style. No equipment will compose your message, but you will find it easier to make changes and corrections when you "write" at the screen rather than on paper. On the other hand, because they simplify the act of revision, word processors leave you no excuse for careless turns of phrase or grammatical errors.

Of course, as you exclude irrelevant details and redundancies, you should be careful NOT to cut corners by leaving out necessary words. For example, some writers, in a misguided attempt at efficiency, omit articles (*the, a,* and *an*) and prepositions:

Please send order special delivery.

The only effect of omitting "the" and "by" here is to make the request curt and impersonal. The correct sentence is:

Please send the order by special delivery.

Electronic Mail

When you use a computer terminal to communicate either inside or outside your organization, you should not abandon the basic principles of business writing. You should still strive for CLARITY, COMPLETENESS, CORRECTNESS, and COURTESY as you would in more traditional forms of correspondence. But when using electronic mail, there are a few additional provisions:

1. Keep your message short: You want your message to fit on one screen, whenever possible, thus keeping all important information visible at once.
   DO use short phrases, abbreviations, industry jargon known to your correspondent.
   DON'T be so brief that your meaning is lost or your approach seems unprofessional.
2. Be sure your message is easy to answer: Let your reader know at the start what your subject is *and* what you want done.
   DO ask questions that can be given a one-word response.
   DON'T give lengthy instructions that require your reader to leave the terminal or possibly clear the screen for information.
3. Beware of electronic eavesdroppers: Not only can your message be forwarded by the receiver or printed for others to read; it will also be stored in the computer's memory (even if you delete the message!).
   DO take advantage of the speed and efficiency of electronic mail.
   DON'T send any message that could cast doubt on your character or capabilities.

★ PRACTICE 1
In the space provided, rewrite each sentence to eliminate the stilted tone.

Example:
We are in receipt of your letter dated December 13, 19--.
We have received your letter of December 13, 19--.

1. Please advise us as to your decision.

   _____

   _____

2. In the event that your bill has already been paid, kindly disregard this reminder.

   _____

   _____

3. Due to the fact that your subscription has not been renewed, the next issue of *Run!* will be your last.

   _____

   _____

4. Feel free to contact the undersigned if you have any questions.

   _____

   _____

5. Pursuant to our telephone conversation of Friday last, I would like to verify our agreement.

_____

_____

6. Subsequent to last month's meeting, several new policies have gone into effect.

_____

_____

7. Please forward your order at your earliest convenience.

_____

_____

8. Our deluxe model copier is on the order of a Rolls Royce in terms of quality and precision.

_____

_____

9. Enclosed please find a self-addressed reply card for the purpose of your convience.

_____

_____

10. I beg to inform you that, despite your impressive background, we feel that your skills do not quite match our needs.

_____

_____

★ PRACTICE 2
In the space provided, replace each expression with one or two words that convey the same meaning.

1. type out from shorthand notes

_____

2. a shopkeeper with a good reputation

_____

3. performed the work with great effect

_____

4. a sharp rise in prices accompanied by a fall in the value of currency

_____

5. some time in the near future

_____

6. ran off several copies of the original on a duplicating machine

_____

7. people with the responsibility of managing an office

_____

8. suffering from fatigue

_____

9. in a decisive way

_____

10. handwriting that is nearly impossible to read

_____

★ PRACTICE 3
On another sheet of
paper, rewrite these letters
to make them more
courteous, concise, and
"you-oriented."

A.

Dear Ms. Lawson:

I regret to inform you that we are completely booked up for the week of August 22. We have no rooms available because the National Word Processors Association will be holding their convention at our hotel during the week of August 22. As you will surely understand, we have to reserve as many rooms as possible for members of the association.

If you can't change the date of your trip, maybe you could find the double room with bath that you want at another hotel here in Little Rock.

Cordially,

B.

Dear Mr. Ross:

With reference to your letter of Thursday last, I can't answer it because my boss, Ms. Leonard, is out of town. If I gave you any information about the new contract with Hastings Development Corporation, she might not like it.

If Ms. Leonard wants you to have that information, I'll have her write to you when she returns in two weeks.

Yours truly,

C.

Dear Ms. Graham:

The information you want having to do with filing for an absentee ballot for the upcoming Presidential election, is not available from our office.

Why don't you write your local Board of Elections?

Sorry.

Sincerely yours,

10.
LETTER FORMAT

Before we begin to discuss letter *content*, we must examine letter appearance, for it is the physical condition of a letter that makes the first impression on your reader. Before reading even one word you have written, the reader has formed an opinion based on the way your letter looks—the arrangement, the typing quality, and so on.

When you have composed the body of your letter and are ready to print, keep in mind three things:

Typing Letters should be single-spaced with double-spacing between paragraphs. Typing should be neat and dark. Errors should not be erased.

Paragraphing Paragraph breaks should come at logical points in your message and should also result in an EVEN appearance. A one-line paragraph followed by an eight-line paragraph will look bottom heavy. Paragraphs of *approximately* the same length will please the eye.

White space In addition to the space created by paragraphing, leave space by centering your letter on the page. An ample margin of white space should surround the message, top and bottom as well as both sides. If a letter is brief, avoid beginning to type too high on the page; if a letter is long, do not hesitate to use an additional sheet of paper. (See Figure 10-1 for recommended spacing between letter parts.)

Note: Although preparing your letter on a word processor will facilitate the job of formatting, *you* still control the organization of your message and remain ultimately responsible for the final appearance of your letter.

Parts of a Business Letter

While the horizontal placement of letter parts may vary (see the next section, "Arrangement Styles"), the vertical order of these parts is standard. Refer to the model letter (Figure 10-1) as you study the following list of letter parts.

1. LETTERHEAD: This, of course, is printed and supplied by your employer. It is used only for the first page of a letter.
2. DATELINE: The date on which the letter is being prepared is typed a few lines below the letterhead.
3. INSIDE ADDRESS: The address of your reader is typed as it will appear on the envelope.
4. ATTENTION LINE: This is not always required. It should be used when the letter is addressed to a company or organization as a whole, but you want it to be handled by a specific individual at the company or within the organization. It should be underlined or typed in capitals.

5. SALUTATION: While "Dear Sir," "Dear Madam," "Dear Madam or Sir," "Gentlemen," "Gentlemen and Ladies" are acceptable in cases of extreme formality, you should otherwise use an individual's name whenever it is known. When the reader's name is *not* known, the person's title is the next best term in a salutation.

6. SUBJECT LINE: Like the attention line, this is often omitted, but its inclusion is a courtesy to your reader. By alerting him to the content of your message, you enable him to decide whether the letter requires immediate attention. It should be underlined or typed in capitals.

7. BODY: This is the actual message of your letter.

8. COMPLIMENTARY CLOSING: This is a polite, formal way to end a letter; standard forms are "Yours truly" or "Truly yours," "Sincerely yours," "Respectfully yours," and so on. Excessively familiar closings should be avoided, except in special situations. "Best wishes," for example, could be used when the reader is well known to you. Expressions such as "Fondly" or "Love" should, obviously, be reserved for private correspondence.

9. COMPANY SIGNATURE: Another item often omitted from less formal correspondence, it should be used when the signer of the letter is writing as a spokesperson for the company, not as an individual. Since this information appears in the letterhead, some companies omit it altogether.

10. SIGNER'S IDENTIFICATION: Typed four lines below the previous item to allow space for the signature, this includes the signer's name and any relevant titles.

11. REFERENCE INITIALS: Consisting of the signer's initials in capitals followed by a slash or colon followed by the typist's lowercase initials, this item serves as a reminder of who prepared the letter.

12. ENCLOSURE REMINDER: Consisting of the word "enclosure," or the word "enclosure" followed by a list of the enclosed items, this is a practical courtesy to prevent your reader from discarding important matter with the envelope.

13. "CC" NOTATION: Also a courtesy, this tells the reader who has been sent a carbon copy of the letter.

Arrangement Styles

As previously noted, the horizontal placement of letter parts is flexible—within the limits of five basic styles. Often, however, a company will have a preferred arrangement style which employees are required to use.

FULL-BLOCKED (Figure 10-2): All letter parts begin at the left margin. It is therefore the fastest traditional arrangement style to type.

(1) **Flanagan's** Department Store
12207 Sunset Strip
Los Angeles, California 91417

(2)   June 7, 19--

(3) Ketchum Collection Agency
1267 Hollywood Boulevard
Los Angeles, California 91401

(4) ATTENTION: MS. TERRY ROBERTS

(5) Gentlemen and Ladies:

(6) Subject: Mr. Gary Daniels, Account #69 112 003

We would like to turn over to your services the account of
Mr. Gary Daniels, 4441 Natick Avenue, Sherman Oaks, California
91418. The balance on Mr. Daniels' account, $829.95, is now
120 days past due; and, although we have sent him four statements and five letters, we have been unable to collect his debt.

(7) Mr. Daniels is employed by West Coast Furniture Showrooms, Inc.
He banks at the Natick Avenue branch of Third National City
Bank and has been a customer of ours for four years. We have
enclosed his file for your reference.

We are confident that we can rely on Ketchum as we have in the
past. Please let us know if there is any further information
with which we can furnish you.

(8)   Sincerely yours,

(9)   FLANAGAN'S DEPARTMENT
STORE

(10)   Martha Fayman
Credit Manager

(11) MF/wg
(12) Enclosure
(13) cc Mr. Norman Hyman

Figure 10-1

THE PARTS OF A BUSINESS LETTER

BLOCKED (Figure 10-3): Like full-blocked, all letter parts begin at the left margin, *except* the dateline, complimentary closing, company signature, and writer's identification, which start at the horizontal center of the page. (Options—the dateline may end at the right margin; attention and subject lines may be centered or indented five or ten spaces.)

SEMI-BLOCKED *or* MODIFIED BLOCKED (Figure 10-4): This is the same as a blocked letter with one change: the beginning of each paragraph is indented five or ten spaces.

SQUARE-BLOCKED (Figure 10-5): This is the same as a full-blocked letter with two changes: the date is typed on the same line as the start of the inside address and ends at the right margin; reference initials and enclosure reminder are typed on the same lines as the signature and signer's iden- tification. As a result, corners are squared off. This arrangement saves space, allowing longer letters to be fit onto a single page. (Be sure to use a line at least 50 spaces long so that the inside address won't run into the dateline.)

SIMPLIFIED *or* AMS (Figure 10-6): Designed by the Administrative Man- agement Society, this style uses open punctuation and is the same as full- blocked, except: (1) no salutation or complimentary closing is used; (2) an entirely capitalized subject line (without the word "subject") *must* be used; (3) the signer's identification is typed in all capitals; and (4) lists are indented five spaces unless numbered or lettered (in which case they are blocked with no periods after the numbers or letters). This style is extremely efficient, requiring much less time to type than other styles. However, it is also impersonal. For this reason, the reader's name should be mentioned at least once in the body.

Punctuation Styles

Regardless of punctuation style, the *only* letter parts (outside of the body) to be followed by punctuation marks are the salutation and complimentary closing. Within the body, the general rules of punctuation apply.

OPEN: No punctuation is used, except in the body. (See Figure 10-2.)

STANDARD: The salutation is followed by a colon; the complimentary closing is followed by a comma. (See Figure 10-3.)

Note: The salutation and closing should be punctuated consistently: either *both* are followed by punctuation or *neither* is followed by punctua- tion. Note, too, that a comma is NOT used after the saluta- tion. (This practice is reserved for private correspondence.)

NORP
NATIONAL ORGANIZATION OF RETIRED PERSONS
Freeport High School, Freeport, Vermont 66622

October 14, 19--

Ms. Iva Stravinsky
Attorney-at-Law
200 Center Street
Freeport, Vermont 66622

Dear Ms. Stravinsky

Subject: Guest Lecture

The members of the Freeport chapter of the National Organization
of Retired Persons would indeed be interested in a lecture on
"Proposed Changes in The Financing of Medicare." Therefore, with
much appreciation, I accept your offer to address our club.

The NORP meets every Tuesday at 8 P.M. in the auditorium of
Freeport High School. The programs for our meetings through November 20 have already been established. However, I will call
you in a few days to schedule a date for your lecture for the first
Tuesday after the 20th that meets your convenience.

The membership and I look forward to your lecture on a topic so
important to us all.

Sincerely yours

NATIONAL ORGANIZATION OF RETIRED PERSONS

Henry Purcell
President

HP/bm

Figure 10-2

FULL-BLOCKED LETTER STYLE

NORP
NATIONAL ORGANIZATION OF RETIRED PERSONS
Freeport High School, Freeport, Vermont 66622

October 14, 19--

Ms. Iva Stravinsky
Attorney-at-Law
200 Center Street
Freeport, Vermont 66621

Dear Ms. Stravinsky:

Subject: Guest Lecture

The members of the Freeport chapter of the National Organization
of Retired Persons would indeed be interested in a lecture on
"Proposed Changes in the Financing of Medicare." Therefore, with
much appreciation, I accept your offer to address our club.

The NORP meets every Tuesday at 8 P.M. in the auditorium of
Freeport High School. The programs for our meetings through
November 20 have already been established. However, I will call
you in a few days to schedule a date for your lecture for the first
Tuesday after the 20th that meets your convenience.

The membership and I look forward to your lecture on a topic so
important to us all.

Sincerely yours,

Henry Purcell
President

HP/bm

Figure 10-3

BLOCKED LETTER STYLE

NORP
NATIONAL ORGANIZATION OF RETIRED PERSONS
Freeport High School, Freeport, Vermont 66622

October 14, 19--

Ms. Iva Stravinsky
Attorney-at-Law
200 Center Street
Freeport, Vermont 66621

Dear Ms. Stravinsky:

Subject: Guest Lecture

The members of the Freeport chapter of the National Organization of Retired Persons would indeed be interested in a lecture on "Proposed Changes in the Financing of Medicare." Therefore, with much appreciation, I accept your offer to address our club.

The NORP meets every Tuesday at 8 P.M. in the auditorium of Freeport High School. The programs for our meetings through November 20 have already been established. However, I will call you in a few days to schedule a date for your lecture for the first Tuesday after the 20th that meets your convenience.

The membership and I look forward to your lecture on a topic so important to us all.

Sincerely yours,

Henry Purcell
President

HP/bm

Figure 10-4

SEMI-BLOCKED LETTER STYLE

NORP

NATIONAL ORGANIZATION OF RETIRED PERSONS
Freeport High School, Freeport, Vermont 66622

Ms. Iva Stravinsky   October 14, 19--
Attorney-at-Law
200 Center Street
Freeport, Vermont 66621

Dear Ms. Stravinsky:

        SUBJECT: GUEST LECTURE

The members of the Freeport chapter of the National Organization of
Retired Persons would indeed be interested in a lecture on "Proposed
Changes in the Financing of Medicare." Therefore, with much
appreciation, I accept your offer to address our club.

The NORP meets every Tuesday at 8 P.M. in the auditorium of
Freeport High School. The programs for our meetings through November 20 have already been established. However, I will call you
in a few days to schedule a date for your lecture for the first Tuesday
after the 20th that meets your convenience.

The membership and I look forward to your lecture on a topic so
important to us all.

Sincerely yours,

NATIONAL ORGANIZATION OF RETIRED PERSONS

Henry Purcell
President   HP/bm

Figure 10-5

SQUARE-BLOCKED LETTER STYLE

NORP

NATIONAL ORGANIZATION OF RETIRED PERSONS
Freeport High School, Freeport, Vermont 66622

October 14, 19--

Ms. Iva Stravinsky
Attorney-at-Law
200 Center Street
Freeport, Vermont 66621

GUEST LECTURE

The members of the Freeport chapter of the National Organization
of Retired Persons would indeed be interested in a lecture on
"Proposed Changes in the Financing of Medicare." Therefore, with
much appreciation, I accept your offer to address our club.

The NORP meets every Tuesday at 8 P.M. in the auditorium of
Freeport High School. The programs for our meetings through
November 20 have already been established. However, I will call
you in a few days to schedule a date for your lecture for the
first Tuesday after the 20th that meets your convenience.

The membership and I look forward, Ms. Stravinsky, to your
lecture on a topic so important to us all.

HENRY PURCELL, PRESIDENT

HP/bm

Figure 10-6

SIMPLIFIED LETTER STYLE

Postscripts

It is advisable to avoid postscripts; when a letter is well planned, all pertinent information will be included in the body. However, when a postscript is required, it is arranged as the other paragraphs in the letter have been, preceded by "P.S." or "PS":

P.S. Let me remind you of our special discount on orders for a dozen or more of the same model appliance.

Special Paragraphing

When a message contains quotations of prices or notations of special data, this information is set in a special paragraph (see Figure 10-7), indented five spaces on the left and right, preceded and followed by a blank line.

The Envelope

An envelope should be addressed to correspond with the inside address. On an envelope, though, the state name may be abbreviated in accordance with the United States Postal Service ZIP-code style. On a standard business-size envelope, the address should begin four inches from the left edge, fourteen lines from the top (see Figure 10-8).

In accordance with Postal Service guidelines, the address should be blocked and single-spaced; and it should include the ZIP code one space after the state. Because NO information should appear below the ZIP code, special instructions (such as *ATT: Mr. Smith* or *Please Forward*) should be placed four lines below the return address. Similarly, mailing services, such as *Airmail* or *Certified Mail,* should be placed below the stamp.

The return address, matching the letterhead, is usually printed on business envelopes.

FRANKLIN AND GORDON OFFICE SUPPLIES, INC.
72-01 Lefferts Boulevard, Rego Park, New York 11206

September 15, 19--

Robert Nathan, CPA
222 Bergen Street
New Orleans, Louisiana 77221

Dear Mr. Nathan:

We appreciate your interest in Franklin and Gordon office supplies
and are delighted to send you the information you requested:

    Ruled ledger paper, by the ream only, costs $45; with the
    purchase of six or more reams, the price is reduced to $42
    per ream, a savings of at least $18.

    Black, reinforced ledger binders are $25 each; with the
    purchase of six or more binders, the price is only $23 each,
    a savings of at least $12.

Because we are the manufacturers of many other fine office supplies,
ranging from ball-point pens to promotional novelties, we have enclosed for your consideration a copy of our current catalog. Should
you decide to place an order, you may use the convenient order form
in the center of the catalog or call our 24-hour toll free number
(1-800-999-9000).

Please let us know if we may be of further assistance.

Sincerely yours,

FRANKLIN AND GORDON OFFICE SUPPLIES, INC.

George Gillian
Customer Service Manager

GG:jc
Enclosure

Figure 10-7

SPECIAL PARAGRAPHING

Flanagan's Department Store
12207 Sunset Strip
Los Angeles, California 91417

Attention Ms. Terry Roberts   Registered Mail

                    Ketchum Collection Agency
                    1267 Hollywood Boulevard
                    Los Angeles, CA 91401

Figure 10-8

THE ENVELOPE

⋆ PRACTICE
**Type this letter in each of
the five arrangement styles:
(A) Full-blocked, (B)
Blocked, (C) Semi-blocked,
(D) Square-blocked, and (E)
Simplified.**

Dateline: July 9, 19—
Inside Address: The Middle Atlantic Institute of Technology, 149 Danbury
                  Road, Danbury, Connecticut 50202
Attention Line: Attention Dean Claude Monet
Salutation: Gentlemen and Ladies
Subject Line: Educational Exchange
Body:
   The Commission for Educational Exchange between the United States
and Belgium has advised me to contact you in order to obtain employment
assistance.
   I received my Doctor's Degree with a "grande distinction" from the University of Brussels and would like to teach French (my mother tongue),
English, Dutch, or German.
   My special field is English literature; I wrote my dissertation on James
Joyce, but I am also qualified to teach languages to business students. I
have been active in the field of applied linguistics for the past two years
at the University of Brussels.
   I look forward to hearing from you.
Complimentary Closing: Respectfully yours
Signer's Identification: Jacqueline Brauer
Reference initials: JB:db

11.
REQUEST LETTERS

As a businessperson, you will inevitably have to write many request letters. The need for information or special favors, services, or products arises daily in almost every type of business. The reasons for writing a request letter are diverse:

1. to obtain information (such as prices or technical data);
2. to receive printed matter (such as booklets, catalogs, price lists, and reports);
3. to receive sample products;
4. to order merchandise;
5. to engage services (including repair or maintenance services);
6. to make reservations (at hotels, restaurants, theaters,);
7. to seek special favors (such as permission, assistance, or advice).

While certain requests, such as ordering merchandise, are routine matters, the general guidelines for business letter writing are especially important when writing any request. Tact and courtesy are essential when you want your reader to *act*. And if you want him to act *promptly*, your letter must encourage him to do so. Therefore, all requests should:

1. be specific and brief;
2. be reasonable;
3. provide complete, accurate information.

Inquiries

Usually, an inquiry offers the recipient no immediate reward or advantage beyond the prospect of a future customer or the maintenance of goodwill. Therefore, your inquiry must be worded in such a way that the recipient will respond despite a hectic schedule. To do this, you must make your inquiry *easy to answer*.

First of all, you should decide exactly what you want *before* you write. This should include the specific information that you need as well as the course of action you would like your reader to take. Consider this request:

```
Dear Sir or Madam:

Please send us information about your office copiers so
that we will know whether one would be suited to our type
of business.

Yours truly,
```

The recipient of this letter would be at a total loss to respond. Other than simply sending a brochure or catalog, she could not possibly explain the advantages of her company's machines without knowing your company's needs. You have *not* made it easy for her to act.

Such an inquiry should include specific questions worded to elicit specific facts. Since the manufacturer of copiers may make dozens of models, the inquiry should narrow down the type your company would consider.

Mahoney and Millman, Inc.
1951 Benson Street
Bronx, New York 10465

May 2, 19--

RBM Manufacturing Company, Inc.
4022 Ninth Avenue
New York, New York 10055

Dear Sir or Madam:

We intend to purchase a new office copier before the end of the fiscal year. We would like to consider an RBM copier and wonder if you have a model that would suit our needs.

Our office is small, and a copier would generally be used by only three secretaries. We run approximately 3,000 copies a month and prefer a machine that uses regular paper. We would like a collator, but rarely need to run off more than 25 copies at any one time.

We would also like to know about your warranty and repair service.

Since our fiscal year ends June 30, 19--, we hope to hear from you soon.

Sincerely yours,

William Wilson
Office Manager

WW/sw

Figure 11-1

INQUIRY

Note how the revised letter (Figure 11-1) makes it easier for your reader to respond. You have given a clear picture of what you're looking for, so she can determine which of the company's products might interest you. Moreover, by mentioning the REASON for your inquiry, you motivate her response. (Your intended purchase is a real potential sale for RBM.) Finally, by letting her know WHEN you intend to buy, you've encouraged her to reply promptly.

When a request does *not* hold the prospect for a potential sale, you should make your letter even more convenient for your reader:

1. Itemize and list the specific facts you want.
2. Enclose a self-addressed, stamped envelope.
3. Suggest a way in which you can reciprocate.

Dear Mr. Greenbaum:

I am taking a course in Principles of Advertising at Smithville Community College in Smithville, Ohio, and am doing my term project on the ways in which American automobile manufacturers have been competing in the small-car market.

I would therefore greatly appreciate your sending me the following specifications on the new RX—7:

1 Fuel economy statistics

2 Technological advances (such as steering system, brake system, and engine capacity)

3 Available options

I would also find it very helpful if you told me in which magazine (or other mass media) you began your advertising campaign.

I am certain my classmates will find this information extremely interesting. I will be sure to send you a copy of my report as soon as it is complete.

Respectfully yours,

Orders

Many companies use special forms for ordering merchandise or service. They may use their own, called a *purchase order,* or one provided by the seller, called an *order form.* These forms have blank spaces to insure the inclusion of all necessary information. Their advantage is that they enable a company to number and so carefully file all expenditures.

Nevertheless, there will be times when an order must be put into letter format. At such times, you must be sure to include COMPLETE, ACCURATE INFORMATION because incomplete orders result in delayed deliveries, and inaccurate facts result in receipt of the wrong merchandise.

Every order should include:

1. the name of the item being ordered;
2. the item's number (catalog number, style number, model number, etc.);
3. quantity desired (often in large units such as dozens, cases, reams, etc.);
4. description (such as size, weight, color, material, finish, extra features);
5. unit price;
6. applicable discounts;
7. applicable sales tax;
8. total price;
9. method of payment (such as charge account, including the account number; c.o.d.; check; etc.);
10. desired delivery date;
11. method of shipment (such as parcel post or air express);
12. delivery address (which may vary from the billing address);
13. authorized signature.

In addition, if your order is in response to an advertisement, you should mention the source (such as the title and issue date of a magazine or newspaper).

The following letter would run into trouble:

Dear Sirs:

Please send me one of your weather vanes which I saw advertised for $34.95. We have recently repainted our garage, and a weather vane would be a wonderful finishing touch.

My check is enclosed.

Sincerely,

First of all, an order clerk would not know what to send this customer unless the company manufactured only one style of weather vane for $34.95. Moreover, instead of providing NECESSARY FACTS, the writer included unnecessary details. Generally, it is <u>NOT</u> NECESSARY TO MENTION A REASON FOR AN ORDER. Orders are routine and handled in quantity; as long as you are a paying customer, your motive for buying does not interest the seller.

While the preceding letter would require interim correspondence before the order could be shipped, the letter in Figure 3-2 would elicit prompt delivery.

```
                                        250 Commonwealth Avenue
                                        Boston, Massachusetts 02118
                                        February 14, 19--


Cape Cod Ornaments, Inc.
94 State Road
West Yarmouth, Massachusetts 02757

Dear Madam or Sir:

I have seen your ad in the Boston Globe of Sunday, February 12,
and would like to order the following weather vane:

    Model EPC-18" eagle with arrow, copper, $34.95.

I would like the weather vane sent to the above address by parcel
post and charged, with any applicable sales tax and handling costs,
to my VISA account (number 003 0971 A109; expiration date, 3/93).

                            Yours truly,
```

Figure 11-2

ORDER

★ PRACTICE
For each of the following activities, prepare a request letter using appropriate arrangement and punctuation styles.

A. You are the program chairperson of the Harrisburg Civic Association. Write a letter to Margaret Belmont, mayor of Harrisburg, asking if she would be willing to attend a future meeting of the association and address the members on a topic of general interest. Meetings are held the second Wednesday of every month at 7:30 P.M. in the basement meeting room of the community center. Previous speakers have included Hiroko Kamata, president of Grand Northern Motels, Inc., who spoke on the topic "Increasing Tourism in Harrisburg," and Gregory Lardas, CPA, who spoke on the topic "Local Property Tax: Boost or Burden?" You may explain that meetings are attended by approximately 75 community-minded people and that the lecture segment of the meeting usually lasts about one hour.

B. As assistant buyer for Fenway's Toy Store, 1704 North Broadway, Richmond, Virginia 23261, write a letter to the Marco Toy Company, Inc., 223 Sunrise Highway, Glen Cove, New York 11566, to order two dozen Baby Jenny dolls (at $10 each), one dozen Baby Jenny layette sets (at $15 each), and three dozen 18-inch Tootsie-Wootsie teddy bears (at $7 each). You would like to have these items in stock in time for the pre-Christmas selling season. You want to make this purchase on account and have it shipped air express. If Marco has available any special Christmas displays for their merchandise, you would like to receive these, too.

C. As assistant finance manager of your company, it is your responsibility to report to your supervisors about year-end tax saving measures that can be taken within the organization. Write a letter to Wilda Stewart (Stewart and Stewart CPA's, 466 Main Street, Eugene, Oregon 84403), an accountant you met recently at a seminar on the new federal tax laws. Ask her for information for your report, including pointers on deferring income and accelerating deductions as well as year-end expenditures.

D. Answer the following advertisement in the current issue of *Office Workers' Weekly:*

COPY KWIK COPYSTAND

America's widest used copystand: Functional, good-looking . . . saves precious desk space . . . relieves neck and eye strain . . . attaches easily to any computer monitor . . . comes with copy clip and magnetic line guide. One-year warranty. $24 plus $2.95 postage and handling (NJ residents please add appropriate sales tax). CKC, Inc., 2019 Logan Street, Paramus, NJ 70622.

E. You are the supervisor of the secretarial pool of the Am-Lux Company, Inc., 51 West 42 Street, New York, New York 10031. You recently read an article by Loretta Lawrence entitled "Ten Pitman Pitfalls to Watch Out For" in *Sten* magazine. You believe the twenty-five secretaries in your department would benefit from reading the article. Write a letter to Ms. Lawrence, in care of *Sten,* 705 Tenth Avenue, New York, New York 10048, requesting her permission to make twenty-five copies of her article for circulation only within your company.

12.
REPLIES

A large part of handling a company's correspondence involves ANSWER-ING the mail. The ability to phrase an appropriate response is, therefore, a valuable and marketable skill.

Letters of response fall into a number of categories, including:

1. acknowledgments
2. follow-ups
3. confirmations
4. remittances
5. order acknowledgments
6. stopgap letters
7. inquiry replies
8. referrals
9. refusals

Many companies use form letters for certain types of replies, such as order acknowledgments. Nevertheless, a reply is often a fertile sales opportunity, and a personal, carefully worded letter can reap both profits and goodwill.

Like a request, a reply should be *specific* and *complete*. However, a reply need not be brief. Indeed, because a reply must be both *helpful* and *sales oriented,* brevity is often impossible to achieve.

On the other hand, it is essential that a reply be *prompt*. In striving for a *"you* approach," this promptness may even be pointed out to the reader:

```
Dear Mr. Mechanic:

I received your letter this morning and wanted to be sure
you would have our current price list before the end of
the week. . . .
```

Without patting yourself on the back, such an opening lets your reader know you are *interested* and want to be *helpful*. In fact, whenever possible, a response should go a little further than the original request. An extra bit of information or unasked-for help can turn an inquirer into a steady customer.

Acknowledgments   An acknowledgment (Figure 12-1) should be written as a courtesy when you receive merchandise, material, money, or information to let your reader know that you have received it. When the matter received was not an order, an acknowledgment can also serve as a thank-you note.

Markham's Cards and Gifts
400 Paseo de Peralta, Santa Fe, New Mexico 87501

October 23, 19--

Mr. Herbert Benjamin
Sales Representative
Newmart Cards, Inc.
399 North Canon Drive
Beverly Hills, California 90210

Dear Mr. Benjamin:

Thank you for arranging for us to receive our Christmas card displays
a bit early this year. We installed them as soon as they arrived on
Monday, and we've already sold out two lines!

The two months between now and Christmas seem destined to be busy
ones, and I suspect you'll be hearing from us again soon.

Best wishes,

Hedy Rosen
Assistant Buyer

Figure 12-1

ACKNOWLEDGMENT

Follow-Ups   After a decision or agreement has been made, either at a meeting or in conversation, it is wise to send a follow-up letter (Figure 12-2) to establish a written record of the transaction.

THE COMMITTEE TO KEEP MINNESOTA GREEN
24 NORTH MAIN STREET, BLACKDUCK, MINNESOTA 56630

June 3, 19--

Ms. Christine Solars
Solars, Solars, and Wright
62 Onigum Road
Walker, Minnesota 56484

Dear Ms. Solars:

We are pleased that you will be participating in the Ecology
Colloquium sponsored by the Committee to Keep Minnesota Green.
As we discussed in our telephone conversation this morning, the
Colloquium will take place on June 29 in the convention room at
the Blackduck Inn.

The Colloquium will begin with the keynote address at 10:30 A.M.
At 11:00, you will join our other guests of honor in a debate on
the topic, "The Cost of Conservation: Public or Private Responsibilities?" Following the debate, luncheon will be served in the
main dining room, where you will, of course, be a guest of the
Committee.

Along with the other members of the Committee, I am looking forward to our meeting on the 29th.

Sincerely yours,

Figure 12-2
FOLLOW-UP

Confirmations   While confirmations are routine for such businesses as hotels and travel agencies, other businesses may also require them. Doctors, for example, and repair services can avoid wasted time by contacting patients and customers a day or so in advance of scheduled appointments. Such confirmations are frequently made by telephone, but a form letter or postcard will also effectively transmit *clear, correct,* and *complete* information, particularly when the type of business requires large numbers of confirmations. As is often the case, however, an individually written letter, such as Figure 12-3, can turn a customer into a *regular* customer by adding a personal touch.

The Barclay

5500 South 96th Street, Omaha, Nebraska 68127

August 10, 19--

Mr. Yegor Volsky
2233 Connecticut Avenue, N.W.
Washington, D.C. 20008

Dear Mr. Volsky:

This letter will confirm your reservation for a single room with bath for August 24-27. Your room will be available after 2 P.M. on the 24th.

Since you will be arriving in Omaha by plane, you may want to take advantage of The Barclay's Shuttle. Our limousine departs from the domestic terminal every hour on the half hour, and the service is free for guests of the hotel.

Cordially yours,

Figure 12-3
CONFIRMATION

Remittances Companies often request that their bill, or a portion of their bill, accompany a remittance. When this is not the case, a cover letter is necessary to explain what your enclosed check is for. This letter should contain any information regarding your order that will be needed for the proper crediting of your account: include your account number, the invoice number, and the amount of the check. DO NOT include superfluous information that could confuse an accounts receivable clerk. Remarks not directly related to the remittance should be reserved for a separate letter.

    Dear Gentlemen and Ladies:

    The enclosed check for $312.68 is in payment of invoice
    no. 10463. Please credit my account (no. 663-711-M).

    Yours truly,

Order
Acknowledgments Many companies today have abandoned the practice of acknowledging orders, particularly when the order will be filled promptly. Some companies respond to orders by immediately sending an invoice, and some employ the halfway measure of using printed acknowledgment forms. But however handled, confirming an order helps to establish goodwill by reassuring the customer that the order has been received.

First orders SHOULD be acknowledged in order to welcome the new customer and encourage further business (Figure 12-4). Similarly, an unusually large order by a regular customer deserves a note of appreciation.

Any order acknowledgment, whatever the circumstances, should contain specific information. It should let the customer know exactly what is being done about the order by

1. mentioning the date of the order;
2. including the order or invoice number;
3. explaining the date and method of shipment;
4. acknowledging the method of payment.

Of course, all order acknowledgments should also express appreciation for the order and assure the customer that it will be filled.

An acknowledgment is often an opportunity for a salespitch. First of all, if a salesperson was involved in the order, his or her name should appear somewhere in the letter. But beyond this, a letter may also include a description of the merchandise to reaffirm the wisdom of the customer's purchase. Other related products may also be mentioned to spark the customer's interest and future orders.

Because orders cannot always be filled promptly and smoothly, situations arise in which a wise businessperson will send more than a mere acknowledgment.

Customers, for example, cannot always be relied on to submit complete orders. When an essential piece of information has been omitted, the order must be delayed and a tactful letter sent. Although the customer in such a case is at fault, the letter must neither place any blame nor express impatience. Indeed, the customer's own impatience must be allayed with a positive, friendly tone. A bit of reselling—reminding the customer of the order's desirability—is often in order in a letter of this kind.

Dear Mr. Hassan:

Thank you for your order of October 22 for 6 rolls of black nylon webbing. We are eager to deliver Order 129 to your store as soon as possible.

But first, please let us know whether you'd like the webbing in 1-, 1⅓-, or 2½-inch widths. If you note your preference on the bottom of this letter and mail it back to us today, we can have your order ready by the beginning of next week.

Olsen's Upholstery products are among the finest made, and we're sure you'd like to receive your purchase without further delay.

Sincerely yours,

PAYTON'S PLASTICS, INC.
1313 Spruce Street
Philadelphia, PA 17512

September 16, 19--

Ms. Cybel Megan
FRAMES-BY-YOU
126 Walnut Street
Philadelphia, PA 17503

Dear Ms. Megan:

We are pleased to have received your order of September 15 and
would like to welcome you as a new customer of Payton's Plastics.

Your order (No. 62997) for one dozen 4' X 5' sheets of 1/8" Lucite
is being processed and will be ready for shipment on September 21.
It will be delivered to your workshop by our own van, and payment
will be c.o.d. (our policy for all orders under $100).

We are sure you will appreciate the clear finish and tensile strength
of our entire line of plastics. Ms. Julie Methel, your sales representative, will call on you soon with a catalog and samples.

Cordially,

PAYTON'S PLASTICS, INC.

Howard Roberts
Customer Relations

Figure 12-4

ORDER ACKNOWLEDGMENT

Sometimes a *delayed delivery* is caused by the seller, not the buyer—a delicate situation that requires a carefully written letter (Figure 12-5). When an order cannot be filled promptly, the customer is entitled to an explanation. Assurance should be given that the delay is unavoidable and that everything is being done to speed delivery.

Such a letter must be especially "*you*-oriented." It should express that you understand the customer's disappointment and regret the inconvenience. At the same time, the letter must avoid a negative tone and not only stress that the merchandise is worth waiting for, but assume that the customer is willing to wait. The form letter in Figure 12-5 could be used in a mass mailing but sounds, nevertheless, as if it has the individual customer in mind.

1066 Third Avenue

American Electric Company, Inc.

New York, New York 10081

Dear

Requests for our pamphlet, "10 Points to Consider When Buying Home
Video Equipment," have been overwhelming. As a result, we are
temporarily out of copies.

Nevertheless, the new printing is presently being prepared, and
I have added your name to the mailing list to receive a copy as
soon as it is available.

In the meantime, you may find an article by Professor Leonard Mack,
of the Pennsylvania Institute of Technology, to be of some help.
The article, entitled "The Latest Crop of Home Video Centers,"
appeared in the September issue of Consumer Digest.

Sincerely,

Figure 12-5

DELAYED DELIVERY

Silver Imports, Ltd.

609 San Anselmo Avenue
San Anselmo, California 94960

March 4, 19--

Ms. Bonnie Corum
Bonnie's Baubles
4091 West Ninth Street
Winston-Salem, North Carolina 27102

Dear Ms. Corum:

Thank you for your recent order, number 622. We are always especially delighted to serve an old friend.

Your six pairs of Chinese Knot earrings (item 15b) and one dozen
Primrose pendants (item 8a) have been shipped by United Parcel
and should arrive at your boutique within the week.

Unfortunately, our stock of cloisonné bangle bracelets (item 9d)
has been depleted because of a delay in shipments from China.
Our craftsmen have been at great pains to keep up with the demand
for these intricate and finely wrought bracelets. We have put
your one dozen bracelets on back order and hope to have them on
their way to you before the end of the month.

Very truly yours,

Chun Lee Ng
Manager

Figure 12-6

PARTIAL DELIVERY

When a *partial shipment* can be made, the customer must be informed
that certain items have been *back ordered*. Again, the letter should assume
the customer's willingness to wait. But it should also make an attempt to
"resell" the merchandise by stressing its finer features without emphasizing
the missing items (see Figure 12-6).

When an order cannot be filled at all, a letter suggesting a *substitute order* (Figure 12-7) is occasionally appropriate. The suggested merchandise must, naturally, be comparable to the original order and should be offered from a perspective, not of salvaging a sale, but of helping the customer. The letter must include a sales pitch for the suggested item, but it should emphasize the customer's needs. Of course, the letter should also explain why the original order cannot be filled.

 Books-By-Mail P.O. Box 799 Dallas, Texas 75220

April 10, 19--

Mrs. Donna Phillips
RFD 2
Crosby, Texas 77532

Dear Mrs. Phillips:

Thank you for ordering Indra Madhur's outstanding book, An Intro-duction to Indian Cooking. As you know, in the fifteen years since its first publication, Mr. Madhur's book has become a classic and a standard for great cooks everywhere.

Sadly, An Introduction is no longer in print, and I am returning your check for $15.95. But to satisfy your interest in Indian cuisine, I would like to suggest an alternative, Purnamattie Jaffre's Indian Gourmet. Ms. Jaffre was a student of Mr. Madhur, and her recently published volume has been widely hailed by both food and cookbook critics.

If you would like a copy of Indian Gourmet, which costs only $13.95, please let me know, and I will immediately send it to you.

Cordially,

David Ewing
Order Department

Figure 12-7

SUBSTITUTE DELIVERY

Stopgap Letters

When a thorough response to an incoming letter must be delayed, receipt of the letter at least should be promptly acknowledged. Such letters of acknowledgment are called STOPGAP LETTERS. They let your customer know that his inquiry has not been ignored and will be attended to as soon as possible.

Like a delayed delivery letter, a stopgap letter informs your customer that time is needed to process his request. Necessary information or materials, for example, may not be immediately available. Or your company may have prescribed channels for reacting to certain inquiries. Credit applications and insurance claims, for instance, take time to be processed and so are often answered promptly with a stopgap acknowledgment.

A stopgap letter will also be called for when your employer is out of town. The correspondent should be assured that his letter will be relayed to your employer as soon as he returns. You should be careful NOT to commit your employer to any action, nor should you explain his absence.

Dear Reverend Hollingsworth:

Your request to meet with Rabbi Tucker to discuss his participating in an interfaith symposium on world peace arrived this morning. However, Rabbi Tucker is out of town and is not expected back before the 15th.

I will be sure to inform Rabbi Tucker of the planned symposium as soon as he returns.

Yours truly,

Inquiry Replies

All inquiries should be answered, even those that cannot for some reason be given a complete response. An inquiry indicates interest in your company and a potential customer. The inquiry reply should be designed not only to increase that interest, but to inspire the inquirer to action.

An inquiry reply should begin by thanking the reader, acknowledging the interest in your company. As in Figure 12-8, it should end by offering further assistance—but ONLY if you actually want additional inquiries from this person.

The substance of an inquiry reply is usually *information*. You should include not just the specific facts your correspondent requested, but any others that may be of help. (This is, of course, assuming that the original inquiry or request was reasonable.) If you cannot provide all the relevant data right away, you should promise it.

A&M Sewing Supplies, Inc. 40-04 Summit Avenue, Fairlawn, NJ 07662

June 2, 19--

Mr. Samuel Long
Maxine Sportswear Manufacturing Co., Inc.
842 Seventh Avenue
New York, New York 10018

Dear Mr. Long:

Thank you for your interest in A & M equipment. We are happy
to supply you with the information you requested.

The following prices are quoted per dozen. Individual units
are slightly higher:

Item	1 Dozen @:
A-1 Garment Turner	$180.00
A-1 Automatic Winder	90.00
Ace Thread Trimmer	120.00
No-Slip Feed Puller	132.00

In case you have any further questions, Mr. Long, please do not
hesitate to call. I can be reached between 8:30 A.M. and 6:00
P.M. at (201) 881-9412.

Sincerely yours,

Figure 12-8

INQUIRY REPLY I

If the information requested cannot be provided at all (as in Figure 12-9),
or if it is confidential, you should explain this in your letter. You must be
careful, however, to word your explanation tactfully and resist the impulse to
accuse your reader of trying to gather information to which she is not entitled.
Assume the inquiry was innocent and try to maintain goodwill.

Maxine Sportswear Manufacturing Co., Inc
842 Seventh Avenue, New York, New York 10018

June 10, 19--

Mrs. Sharon Tong
693 Pelham Parkway
Bronx, New York 10422

Dear Mrs. Tong:

We certainly appreciate your interest in Maxine Sportswear. Nevertheless, I am afraid I cannot supply you with the information you
request.

Because we do not sell our garments directly to the consumer, we try
to keep our wholesale prices between ourselves and our dealers. It is
our way of meriting both the loyalty and good faith of those with
whom we do business. Clearly, divulging our wholesale prices to a
consumer would be a violation of a trust.

However, I have enclosed for your reference a list of our dealers in
the Bronx and Manhattan. A number of these dealers sell Maxine
Sportswear at discount.

Very truly yours,

Figure 12-9

INQUIRY REPLY II

Sometimes a request for information about a company's products or
services may be answered with a brochure or catalog. Such materials,
though, must always be accompanied by a personalized cover letter. You
should not only explain why you've sent the brochure and arouse your
reader's interest in it; you should also call attention to the particulars of the
brochure and attempt to encourage a sale.

A good practice for a manufacturer, moreover, who doesn't sell directly
to the public, is to pass along copies of the inquiry and reply to a dealer,
who may pursue the sale further.

Dear Mr. Godonov:

Thank you for your request for information about the Teaneck Tennis Center. One of New Jersey's newest facilities, we are a full-service tennis club just 15 minutes
from Manhattan.

The enclosed brochure describes our special features,
including championship-size courts and professional in-
struction. You may find the section on our Businessperson's Special of particular interest.

If you drop by Teaneck Tennis anytime between 7 A.M. and 10
P.M., we would be delighted to give you a personal tour of
the Center--at no obligation of course.

Cordially yours,

Referrals

Business people often receive inquiries that can best be answered by
another person. In that case, the correspondent must be informed that the
inquiry is being passed on.

A letter of referral should *acknowledge receipt* of the inquiry and *explain*
why and to whom it is being referred. Alternately, you may find it more
efficient to advise the correspondent of the proper source of information
and tell exactly where to write.

Again, a manufacturer should be especially careful to sustain the reader's
interest even while referring her to a dealer. The address of a local dealer
or a list of dealers in the area should be included in this kind of referral.
Too, the reader should *never* be chastised for bypassing the middleman;
instead, she should be politely referred to the appropriate source.

Dear Mrs. Simpson:

Your request for information regarding marriage counselors in your community can best be answered by the Board
of Community Services.

I am therefore referring your letter to Mr. Orlando Ortiz
at the Whitestone Community Board. He will, I am sure, be
in touch with you soon.

Yours truly,

Refusals

There are many times when a businessperson must say no. When granting
a favor, awarding a contract, hiring an applicant, or for that matter making
any decision, saying yes to one person often means saying no to another.
The key, however, is to say no gracefully. Here, as in most correspondence,
maintaining goodwill is extremely important.

When saying no, you should first of all never actually say *no*. Your letter should be as positive as you can make it. The actual refusal should be stated once and briefly. The rest of the letter should be reader oriented and very friendly.

No matter what the request, your reader deserves an explanation of your refusal. Your reason should be based on facts, not emotions, although an appeal to your reader's sense of fair play or business savvy is often appropriate (see Figure 12-10). NEVER make the reader himself the reason for your refusal.

AGNES CAFIERO, M.D.

California Institute of Psychiatry
629 Seventh Avenue
San Francisco, California 94120

September 1, 19--

The Honorable Nelson McKenzie
The State Capitol Building
Sacramento, California 91400

Dear Mr. McKenzie:

Thank you for your recent request for my endorsement of your campaign for United States Senator. I am honored that you believe my name could be of value to you.

My professional policy, however, is to refrain from public endorsements. In my practice, I treat patients of all political parties, and I strongly believe that it is in their best interest that I maintain a nonpartisan position.

Privately, of course, I allow myself more leeway. I have always been impressed by your stand on the issues, particularly your support for national health insurance. I wish you all the best in your campaign and am enclosing a personal contribution of $100.

Sincerely yours,

Agnes Cafiero, M.D.

Figure 12-10

REFUSAL

Rarely will you want in a refusal to sever all business connections. Therefore, you should be careful to keep your letter "open-ended." Express appreciation for the request though it is being denied, and if possible suggest an alternative course of action. A "not-at-this-time" refusal keeps open the possibility of future business.

* PRACTICE
On another sheet of paper, prepare a letter of response for each of the following situations.

A. You are employed in the shipping department of Kinbote Products, Inc., 200 Southeast Fourth Street, Miami, Florida 33131. Write a letter acknowledging the following order from Ellen Minsky, buyer for Gold's Specialty Shops, 3636 West Grace Street, Tampa, Florida 33607.

Dear Gentlemen and Ladies:

Please send me two dozen exercise suits (Style L-29) in the following assortment of sizes and colors:

    Vanilla—3 petite, 3 small, 4 medium, 2 large
    Chocolate—2 petite, 4 small, 4 medium, 2 large

Charge my account (882GSS) for the wholesale price of $35 per suit.

I would like the order shipped air express and would appreciate your letting me know how soon I may expect delivery.

Yours truly,

B. Cornell Peal, vice president of the General Communications Corporation, 600 North Milwaukee Street, Milwaukee, Wisconsin 53202, is out of town attending a four-day meeting of the regional directors of the company. As his administrative assistant, send a stopgap letter in response to the following request from Professor Anne Boleyn, Department of Media and Communications, University of Wisconsin, Menomonie, Wisconsin 54751.

Dear Mr. Peal:

Last month, I telephoned your office to invite you to give a guest lecture to my graduate seminar in teletronics. You said you would be pleased to give such a lecture but asked that I contact you again, in writing, later in the semester.

If you are still interested in visiting the class, I would very much like to set a date for the lecture. The class meets on Tuesdays from 4:30 to 6:00 P.M. and runs for six more weeks.

I would appreciate your letting me know as soon as possible which Tuesday would be most convenient for you.

Sincerely yours,

C. You have just made a luncheon engagement for your employer Sook Chang, an architect with Fulson Contractors, Inc., 4444 Western Avenue, Boulder, Colorado 80301. The appointment is with a prospective client, Justin Michaels, 622 Garth Street, Boulder, Colorado 80321. Write a letter to Mr. Michaels to confirm the lunch date, which will take place at Trattoria di Marco, at the corner of Tenth Street and Western Avenue, on April 7 at 1 P.M.

D. You are employed by the Lawsen Linen Company, P.O. Box 762, Bloomfield, New Jersey 07003. Write a letter to Mrs. Marianne Rollins, 444 Ross Avenue, Caldwell, New Jersey 07006, to explain a delay in shipping her order for one set of Floral Mist queen-size sheets and pillowcases. Because of a factory strike, all orders have been held up, but assure her that negotiations are progressing and a settlement is expected soon. Convince her to wait and not cancel her order.

E. Arthur Edwards, owner of Edwards Drug Store, 1540 Peachtree Street, N.E., Atlanta, Georgia 30309, has been a customer of the Southern Cosmetics Company, 2109 Lenox Road, N.E., Atlanta, Georgia 30326, for seven years. Because Mr. Edwards has placed an unusually large order, he has requested a special discount. As a representative of Southern Cosmetics, write a letter to Mr. Edwards refusing the discount.

13.
CREDIT AND COLLECTION LETTERS

Credit Letters

Credit involves the purchasing and receiving of goods without immediate payment. Being able to "buy now and pay later" enables a purchaser to acquire desired goods even when cash is not currently available. Allowing individuals and businesses to buy on credit can increase a company's volume of sales. Therefore, buying and selling on credit have become a common and essential business practice.

Of course, before granting credit, a company must be reasonably sure of the customer's financial stability, and her ability and willingness to pay. These are verified by the exchange of credit information. Five types of letters are involved in credit correspondence:

1. applications for credit
2. inquiries about credit worthiness
3. responses about credit worthiness
4. letters granting credit
5. letters refusing credit

APPLICATIONS

Consumer applications for charge accounts, with businesses such as department stores or gasoline companies, are usually made by filling out an application blank. This form typically allows space for home and business addresses, names of banks and account numbers, a list of other charge accounts, and, perhaps, a list of references.

Business account applications are more often made by letter (Figure 13-1). A new business, for example, may wish to place a first order with a supplier or manufacturer and establish a credit line or open account. A letter of this kind should include credit references (such as banks and other businesses that have extended credit).

CREDIT INQUIRIES

Department stores usually turn credit applications over to a *credit bureau.* Such bureaus keep files on people and businesses whose credit references and histories they have investigated. When they determine an applicant's *credit standing* (that is, reputation for financial stability), they give the applicant a *credit rating* (the bureau's evaluation of the credit standing). On the basis of this rating, the store decides whether or not to grant the applicant credit.

When checking a business's credit standing, a company may contact the references. The letter of credit inquiry (see Figure 13-2) should contain all known information about the applicant, and it should assure the reference that all information will remain confidential. The inclusion of a reply envelope is a wise courtesy.

KRETCHMER'S APPLIANCE STORE
1135 STATE STREET, CHICAGO, ILLINOIS 60688

February 3, 19--

Standard Electric Corporation
2120 Oak Terrace
Lake Bluff, Illinois 60044

Dear Madam or Sir:

Enclosed is our purchase order 121 for 6 four-slice toasters, model 18E.

We would like to place this order on open account according to your regular terms. Our store has been open for two months, and you may check our credit rating with Ms. Peggy Sawyer, branch manager of the First Bank of Chicago, 1160 State Street, Chicago, Illinois 60688.

You may also check our credit standing with the following companies:

The Kenso Clock Company, 150 Ottawa, N.W., Grand Rapids, Michigan 49503

National Kitchen Products, Inc., 55 East Main Street, Round Lake Park, Illinois 60733

Eastern Electric Corporation, 750 East 58 Street, Chicago, Illinois 60637

Please let us know your decision regarding our credit as well as an approximate delivery date for our first order.

Sincerely yours,

Bruce Kretchmer

Figure 13-1

CREDIT APPLICATION

CREDIT RESPONSES

Companies that receive large numbers of credit inquiries often use their own form for responding. In this way, they can control the information given out and, especially, limit the information to hard facts: amounts owed and presently due, maximum credit allowed, dates of account's opening and last sale, degree of promptness in payment, and so on.

Standard Electric Corporation
2120 Oak Terrace
Lake Bluff, Illinois 60044

February 7, 19--

Ms. Keisha Sawyer
Branch Manager
The First Bank of Chicago
1160 State Street
Chicago, Illinois 60688

Dear Ms. Sawyer:

Kretchmer's Appliance Store, 1135 State Street, Chicago, has placed an order with us for $120 worth of merchandise and listed you as a credit reference.

We would appreciate your sending us information regarding Kretchmer's credit rating. We would especially like to know how long the owner, Bruce Kretchmer, has had an account with you and whether or not any of his debts are past due. We will, of course, keep any information we receive in the strictest confidence.

A reply envelope is enclosed for your convenience.

Sincerely yours,

STANDARD ELECTRIC CORPORATION

Milton Smedley
Credit Department

Figure 13-2
CREDIT INQUIRY

Because an individual's or business's reputation is at stake, opinions should be expressed discreetly, if at all. Particularly when a credit reference is unfavorable, it is advisable to state only objective facts in order to avoid a possible libel suit. Most companies, moreover, reiterate somewhere in the letter (see Figure 13-3) that they expect the information provided to remain confidential.

The First Bank Of Chicago
1160 State Street
Chicago, Illinois 60688

February 14, 19--

Mr. Milton Smedley
Credit Department
Standard Electric Corporation
2120 Oak Terrace
Lake Bluff, Illinois 60044

Dear Mr. Smedley:

We are happy to send you, in confidence, the credit information you requested concerning Mr. Bruce Kretchmer, owner of Kretchmer's Appliance Store.

Mr. Kretchmer, who was appliance department supervisor at Lillian's Department Store until last fall, has had personal checking and savings accounts with us for the past ten years. His accounts were always in order, with adequate balances to cover all checks drawn.

His appliance store, at 1135 State Street, was opened last December. For this undertaking, he borrowed $8,000 from this bank and has begun making regular payments against the loan. We are unaware of any further outstanding debts he may have.

On the basis of our experience with him, we believe Mr. Kretchmer to be credit worthy.

Yours truly,

THE FIRST BANK OF CHICAGO

Keisha Sawyer
Branch Manager

Figure 13-3

CREDIT REFERENCE

CREDIT-GRANTING LETTERS

When all credit references are favorable, a letter is sent granting credit to the customer (Figure 13-4). Whether for a consumer charge account or a dealer open account, the acceptance letter should:

1. approve the credit;
2. welcome the customer and express appreciation;

Standard Electric Corporation

2120 Oak Terrace
Lake Bluff, Illinois 60044

February 18, 19--

Mr. Bruce Kretchmer
Kretchmer's Appliance Store
1135 State Street
Chicago, Illinois 60688

Dear Mr. Kretchmer:

It is my pleasure to welcome you as an SEC credit customer, for your request for credit has been approved.

Your first order, for 6 Model 18E toasters, will be ready for shipment on Monday, February 22.

On the first of each month, we will prepare a statement of the previous month's purchases. Your payment is due in full on the tenth. With each statement, you will also receive a supply of order forms and return envelopes.

Arlene Ryan, your personal SEC sales representative, will visit you some time next week. In addition to bringing you catalogs and samples, she will explain our special dealer options, such as advertising campaigns and rebate programs.

We are delighted that SEC can be a part of your store's beginnings and look forward to serving you for many years to come.

Sincerely yours,

Milton Smedley
Credit Department

Figure 13-4

CREDIT-GRANTING LETTER

3. explain the credit terms and privileges;
4. establish goodwill and encourage further sales.

CREDIT-REFUSING LETTERS

Sometimes, of course, credit must be denied (Figure 13-5). A letter refusing credit must give the customer a reason, which, however, may be expressed vaguely for purposes of tact and protection of references.

The credit-refusal letter must also try to encourage business on a cash basis; the tone, therefore, must be positive and in some way "*you*-oriented." In addition, it is a good idea to suggest that the customer reapply for credit in the future, thereby letting him know that you nevertheless desire and appreciate his business.

 HANS & MEYER'S ▪ Suppliers to the Plumbing Trade ▪1010 Broadway, New York, NY 10033

August 10, 19--

Mr. Donald Cortland
Cortland Hardware Store
20-67 Kissena Blvd.
Queens, NY 11203

Dear Mr. Cortland:

Thank you for your recent application for Hans & Meyer's
60-day terms of credit. However, we believe it would not be in
your best interest to grant you credit at this time.

An impartial credit investigation indicates that your company's
present financial obligations are substantial. We fear that adding
to those obligations could jeopardize your sound credit standing
in the community.

Of course, Mr. Cortland, you are always welcome to buy from Hans &
Meyer's, on a COD basis. We will try our best to serve you in
all ways possible. And if, in the future, your obligations should
be reduced, feel free to apply again for terms of credit. We
shall be delighted to reconsider.

Cordially yours,

Figure 13-5

CREDIT-REFUSING LETTER

Collection Letters

No matter how carefully a company screens its credit customers, there will be times when a bill goes unpaid and steps to collect must be taken. The problem when writing a collection letter is how to exact payment and simultaneously keep a customer. The writer of a collection letter wants to get the money owed *and* maintain goodwill.

Collection letters, therefore, should be *persuasive* rather than forceful, *firm* rather than demanding. A fair and tactful letter gets better results than a sarcastic or abusive one. In fact, even collection letters should be *"you-oriented"*: courteous, considerate, and concerned about the customer's best interest.

Collection letters are usually sent in a series. The first tends to be mildest and most understanding, with the letters getting gradually more insistent. The final letter in a series, when all else has failed, threatens to turn the matter over to a lawyer or collection agency. Of course, the tone of any letter in the series will vary, from positive and mild to negative and strong, depending upon the past payment record of the particular customer. The intervals between the letters may also vary, from ten days to a month at the start, from one to two weeks later on.

Every letter in a collection series should contain certain information:

1) the amount owed;
2) how long the bill is overdue;
3) a specific action the customer may take.

Some companies also like to include a SALES APPEAL, even late in the series, as an extra incentive for payment.

The majority of bills are paid within ten days of receipt, with nearly all the rest being paid within the month. Therefore, when a bill is a month overdue, action is called for. Still, the collection process must begin gently.

Step 1

The *monthly statement* reminds the customer of outstanding bills. If it is ignored, it should be followed (about a week or ten days later) by a second statement. The second statement should contain a notice (in the form of a rubber stamp or sticker) stating "Past Due" or "Please Remit." An alternative is to include a card or slip with the statement, alerting the customer to the overdue bill. This notice should be phrased in formal, possibly even stilted language; it is an *objective* reminder that does not embarrass the customer with too early a personal appeal.

> Our records indicate that the balance of $ _____ on your account is now past due. Payment is requested.

Step 2

If the objective statement and reminder fail to get results, the collection process must gradually become more emotional and personal. (Form letters may be used, but they should *look* personal, adapted to the specific situation.) The second collection message, however, should still be friendly. It should seek to excuse the unpaid bill as an oversight; the tone should convey the assumption that the customer intends to pay. At this stage, too, a stress on future sales, rather than on payment, may induce action.

COLLECTION LETTER I

Dear _____ :

Snow may still be on the ground, but the first signs of spring are already budding. And we know you will be planning your Spring Sales soon. You may already have your order in mind.

When you send us a check for $ _____ , now _____ past due, you will guarantee that your next order will be promptly filled.

Oversights, of course, do happen, but we know you won't want to miss the opportunity, not only of stocking up for the coming season, but of taking advantage of our seasonal ad campaign as well.

Sincerely yours,

Step 3

The next letter in the series should still be friendly, but it should also now be firm. While expressing confidence in the customer's intention to pay, it should inquire about the *reason* for the delay. The third collection message should also make an appeal to the customer's sense of:

1. fairness;
2. cooperation;
3. obligation;

or desire to:

1. save her credit reputation;
2. maintain her credit line.

This letter should stress the customer's self-interest by pointing out the importance of prompt payment and the dangers of losing credit standing. The letter should convey the urgency and seriousness of the situation.

COLLECTION LETTER II

Dear _____ :

We are truly at a loss. We cannot understand why you still have not cleared your balance of $ _____ , which is now _____ overdue.
Although you have been a reliable customer for _____ years, we are afraid you are placing your credit standing in jeopardy. Only you, by sending us a check today, can secure the continued convenience of buying on credit.

We would hate to lose a valued friend, Mr./Ms. _____ .

Please allow us to keep serving you.

Sincerely,

Step 4

Ultimately, payment must be demanded. The threat of legal action or the intervention of a collection agency is sometimes all that will induce a customer to pay. In some companies, moreover, an executive other than the credit manager signs this last letter as a means of impressing the customer with the finality of the situation. Still, the fourth collection letter should allow the customer one last chance to pay before steps are taken.

Note: Before threatening legal action, it is advisable to have a Final Collection Letter reviewed by an attorney.

FINAL COLLECTION LETTER

Dear _____ :

Our Collection Department has informed me of their intention to file suit as you have failed to answer any of our requests for payment of $ _____ , which is now _____ overdue.

Before taking this action, however, I would like to make a personal appeal to your sound business judgment. I feel certain that, if you telephone me, we can devise some means to settle this matter out of court.

Therefore, I ask that you get in touch with me by the _____ of the month so that I may avoid taking steps which neither of us would like.

Truly yours,

Note: If a customer responds to a collection letter, STOP THE COLLECTION SERIES, even if the response is not full payment.

A customer may, for example, offer an excuse or promise payment; he may make a partial payment or request special arrangements. At this point, the series would be inappropriate.

For instance, if your customer has owed $600 on account for two months and sends you a check for $150, you may send a letter such as the following:

```
Dear Mr. Marsh:

Thank you for your check for $150. The balance remaining
on your account is now $450.

Since you have requested an extension, we offer you the
following payment plan: $150 by the 15th of the month for
the next three months.

If you have another plan in mind, please telephone my of-
fice so that we may discuss it. Otherwise, we will expect
your next check for $150 on September 15.

Sincerely yours,
```

★ **PRACTICE**
For each of the following, prepare a credit or collection letter, as specified in the directions.

A. Mr. Marvin Gold of 1602 Arlington Avenue, Bronx, New York 10477, has had a charge account at Manson's Department Store, 4404 Madison Avenue, New York, New York 10008, for six years. His credit limit is $400. He has always paid his bills on time although he currently has an outstanding balance of $182.54, forty-five days overdue. The National Credit Bureau has contacted Manson's for credit information about Mr. Gold. Write the letter Manson's should send to the National Credit Bureau.

B. The credit references of Ms. Migdalia Ruiz (818 Ocean Parkway, Brooklyn, New York 11202) are all favorable, and so her new charge account with Manson's Department Store has been approved. Write the letter Manson's should send to Ms. Ruiz.

C. Ms. Hiroko Osawa's credit references indicate that, although she has no outstanding debts or record of poor payment, her employment history is unstable. Manson's Department Store, therefore, concludes that she would be a poor credit risk. Write the letter that Manson's should send to Ms. Osawa (6061 Valentine Lane, Yonkers, New York 80301), denying her application for a charge account.

D. Weimar's Furniture Emporium (617 Sherman Road, North Hollywood, California 91605) has owed the Eastgate Furniture Manufacturing Company, Inc., $750 for forty-five days. Eastgate has sent two statements and one letter, which Weimar's has ignored. Write the next letter that Eastgate (305 Bush Street, San Francisco, California 94108) should send to Weimar's.

E. For eight years, Mr. Josef Larsen, of 1 Penny Lane, Summit, Pennsylvania 17214, has been a charge customer of Browne's Department Store (900 Chestnut Street, Philadelphia, Pennsylvania 19107). A "slow pay," he has nevertheless always remitted within sixty days of purchase. However, Mr. Larsen's balance of $269.48 is now ninety days past due. He has not responded to the two statements and two letters Browne's has already sent him. Write the next letter that Browne's should send to Mr. Larsen.

14.
COMPLAINTS, CLAIMS, AND ADJUSTMENTS

Business transactions will from time to time go awry, and the exchange of money, merchandise, or service will not occur as expected. In such situations, the customer must promptly notify the company of the problem by letter; such a letter is logically called a *complaint*. A complaint that calls upon the company to make restitution is called a *claim*. The company, responding to the claim, will write a letter of *adjustment*.

Complaints

When a customer is dissatisfied with goods or services, a complaint letter will inform the company or organization of the problem. Such a letter should both present the facts and express the customer's dissatisfaction.

Because a complaint, unlike a claim, does not necessarily call for action or compensation from the company, it should be answered gracefully. Indeed, the writer of a complaint is offering help to the offending organization, an opportunity to improve its operations. Therefore, the response to a complaint should be concerned and courteous, *not* defensive. It may offer an explanation and suggest remedies that are being followed. It definitely should extend an apology.

Claims

Countless aspects of business dealings can break down, but the most common causes for claims are:

1. an incorrect bill, invoice, or statement (Figure 14-3);
2. a bill for merchandise ordered but never received;
3. delivery of unordered merchandise;
4. delivery of incorrect merchandise;
5. delivery of damaged or defective merchandise (Figure 14-4);
6. an unusually delayed delivery.

Two other more specialized types of claims are:

1. a request for an adjustment under a guarantee or warranty;
2. a request for restitution under an insurance policy.

21 West Main Street
Cochecton, NY 11222
October 9, 19--

Dr. Linda Peters, Director
County General Hospital
Route 97
Callicoon, NY 11203

Dear Dr. Peters:

On the afternoon of October 8, my neighbor's son, Kevin Sawyer,
was raking leaves in his family's yard when he tripped and fell.
From the degree of pain he was obviously experiencing, I suspected he might have broken his ankle. Thus, as the only adult
around at the time, I drove him to your hospital.

When we arrived at the emergency room, no one was available to
help Kevin from the car, and I had to help him hobble in as best
I could. The effort increased his pain, yet when we were inside,
the receptionist, without looking up, told us to take a number and
wait our turn. We waited for more than two hours before Kevin was
seen by a doctor.

As a member of the community your hospital serves, I am outraged by
the treatment my young neighbor received. The lack of concern was
upsetting; the lack of attention could have been life threatening.
All of us in Wayne County deserve better treatment, and I hope you
will look into the situation to see that the suffering caused Kevin
Sawyer is never again inflicted by an employee of your institution.

Yours truly,

Michelle Sussman

Figure 14-1

COMPLAINT

County General Hospital
Route 97
Callicoon, NY 11203

October 12, 19--

Ms. Michelle Sussman
21 West Main Street
Cochecton, NY   11222

Dear Ms. Sussman:

Thank you for bringing to my attention the inexcusable wait you and Kevin Sawyer endured in the emergency room on October 8. I am extremely sorry for any additional pain Kevin may have experienced and any emotional stress you may have felt under the circumstances.

Allow me, however, to offer an explanation. Shortly before you arrived, an automobile accident just outside Callicoon resulted in four seriously injured people being rushed to County General. Since we are, as you know, a small rural hospital, our emergency staff was stretched to its limits to assist these people simultaneously.

Nevertheless, you and Kevin should not have been ignored for two hours. I have spoken to the receptionist with whom you dealt, and I can assure you that in the future arrivals to our emergency room will be treated with concern and prompt attention.

Again, I apologize for the events of October 8 and greatly appreciate your letting me know about them.

Yours truly,

Linda Peters, M.D.

Figure 14-2

COMPLAINT RESPONSE

A claim is written to *inform* the company of the problem and *suggest* a fair compensation. No matter how infuriating the nature of the problem nor how great the inconvenience, the purpose of a claim is NOT to express anger, but to get results.

Therefore, it is important to avoid a hostile or demanding tone. A claim must be calm and polite though, of course, also firm.

A claim should begin with the facts, first explaining the problem (such as the condition of the merchandise or the specific error made). Then all the necessary details should be recounted in a logical order. These details may include the order and delivery dates, the order or invoice number, the account number, the method of shipment, and so on. A copy of proof of purchase, such as a sales slip or an invoice, should be included whenever possible. (Always, of course, retain the original.)

Remember: You are more likely to receive a favorable response from an adjuster who understands your problem thoroughly.

---

811 Regent Street
Phoenix, Arizona 99087
December 3, 19--

Gleason's Department Store
2297 Front Street
Phoenix, Arizona 99065

Dear Sir or Madam:

I have just received the November statement on my charge account (No. 059-3676). The statement lists a purchase for $83.95, including tax, which I am sure I did not make.

This purchase was supposedly made in Department 08 on November 12. But because I was out of town the week of the tenth and no one else is authorized to use my account, I am sure the charge is in error.

I have checked all the other items on the statement against my sales receipts, and they all seem to be correct. I am therefore deducting the $83.95 from the balance on the statement and sending you a check for $155.75.

I would appreciate your looking into this matter so that my account may be cleared.

Sincerely yours,

Figure 14-3

CLAIM I

Jack's Hardware Store
72 Elm Street
Kennebunk, Maine 06606

April 12, 19--

Eterna-Tools, Inc.
Route 9
Saddlebrook, New Jersey 07666

Dear Gentlemen and Ladies:

On March 1, we ordered and subsequently received one case of
handsaws, model 88b. We paid for the order with our check no. 7293,
a photocopy of which is enclosed.

When we decided to order these saws instead of model 78b, it was at
the urging of your sales representative, Harold Saunders. He assured
us that the new saws were more durable and efficient than the older
model.

However, we have now had the saws on our selling floor for three
weeks, and already six have been returned with broken teeth by extremely dissatisfied customers.

We are therefore returning the entire order of 88b saws and would
like to be refunded for their full purchase price plus shipping expenses.

Yours truly,

Figure 14-4

CLAIM II

The second part of the claim should emphasize the loss or inconvenience
that has been suffered. Again, the account should be factual and une-
motional, and naturally you should NOT exaggerate.

Finally, you should state a *reasonable* adjustment. This should be worded
positively and convey your confidence that the company will be fair.

As you read the sample claims, notice especially how they state
all the *facts calmly. The writer never loses his or her temper, never makes
a threat, and never attempts to place blame.* At all times, the letter is
directed toward the solution.

Adjustments

Claims should be answered *promptly* with a letter that will restore the customer's goodwill and confidence in the company. Like a claim, a letter of *adjustment* should emphasize the solution rather than the error and convince the customer that you understand and want to be fair.

An adjustment letter should begin with a positive statement, expressing sympathy and understanding. Near the start, it should let the reader know what is being done, and this news, good or bad, should be followed by an explanation. The letter should end with another positive statement, reaffirming the company's good intentions and the value of its products, but NEVER referring to the original problem.

Whether or not your company is at fault, even the most belligerent claim should be answered politely. An adjustment letter should NOT be negative or suspicious; it must NEVER accuse the customer or grant any adjustment

leason's
DEPARTMENT STORE

2297 Front Street
Phoenix, Arizona 99065

December 8, 19--

Ms. Rosetta Falco
811 Regent Street
Phoenix, Arizona 99087

Dear Ms. Falco:

As you mentioned in your letter of December 3, you were indeed billed for a purchase you had not made.

According to our records, you should not have been charged the $83.95, and the sum has been stricken from your account.

Thank you for bringing this matter to our attention. We hope you have not been inconvenienced and will visit Gleason's soon so that we may again have the pleasure of serving you.

Sincerely yours,

Figure 14-5

LETTER OF ADJUSTMENT I

Eterna-Tools, Inc. Route 9, Saddlebrook, N.J. 07666

April 19, 19--

Mr. Jack Patterson
Jack's Hardware Store
72 Elm Street
Kennebunk, Maine 06606

Dear Mr. Patterson:

We are sorry that the model 88b handsaws you purchased have not
lived up to your expectations. Frankly, we are surprised they have
proved so fragile and appreciate your returning them to us. Our lab
people are already at work trying to discover the source of the
problem.

We are glad to assume the shipping costs you incurred, Mr. Patterson.
But may we suggest that, instead of a refund, you apply the price of
these saws to the cost of an order of model 78b saws. Your own experience will bear out their reliability, and we are sure your customers will be pleased with an Eterna-Tool Product.

If you will drop us a line okaying the shipment, your 78b handsaws
will be on their way within the week.

Sincerely yours,

Figure 14-6

LETTER OF ADJUSTMENT II

grudgingly. Remember, your company's image and goodwill are at stake when you respond even to unjustified claims.

When the facts of a claim have been confirmed, one of three fair solutions is possible:

1. The requested adjustment is granted.
2. A compromise adjustment is proposed.
3. Any adjustment is denied.

Responsibility for the problem, reliability of the customer, and the nature of the business relationship are all considered in determining a fair adjustment. But the ultimate settlement must always be within the bounds of *company policy*.

GRANTING AN ADJUSTMENT

This letter should be cheerful, freely admitting errors and willingly offering the adjustment. It should express appreciation for the information provided

ATLAS PHOTOCOPIERS, INC.
81 WARREN STREET
NEW YORK, NEW YORK 10003

August 28, 19--

Mr. Thomas Shandy
Finance Director
Handleman & Burns, Ltd.
41 Maiden Lane
New York, New York 10002

Dear Mr. Shandy:

We are sorry that you are not completely satisfied with your
Atlas photocopier. You are entirely justified in expecting
more than eighteen months of reliable performance from an
Atlas office machine, and we are always eager to service any
product that does not for some reason live up to standards.

We appreciate your giving us the opportunity to inspect the
malfunctioning copier. According to our service representative, two problems contributed to the unit's breakdown. It
is apparently being used for a significantly higher volume
of copying than it was built for (as is clearly indicated in
both the sales material and user's manual with which you were
provided). Furthermore, there are indications that a number
of people in your department are not properly closing the
cover before copying documents. The resultant "sky-shots"
can lead to the burn-out of a number of mechanical parts.

Although we are not prepared to offer you a replacement copier
as you suggested (indeed the one-year warrantee has been ex-
pired for six months), we would be happy to take the damaged
copier as a trade-in on another, larger-capacity Atlas copier.
We believe this arrangement would better meet your department's
needs and be more economically advisable than additional
repairs on the old unit. Please let us know if you would like
to speak to a sales representative about the terms of a
trade-in.

Yours truly,

Figure 14-7

LETTER OF ADJUSTMENT III

in the claim. The letter *may* include an explanation of what went wrong; it *should* include an indication that similar errors will be unlikely in the future. Finally, it should *resell* the company, perhaps by suggesting future business (see Figure 14-5).

OFFERING A COMPROMISE ADJUSTMENT

This letter will be written when neither the company nor the customer is entirely at fault. It must express an attitude of pleasant cooperation. It should be based on facts and offer a reason for refusing the requested adjustment. As in Figure 14-6, it should immediately make a counteroffer that meets the customer halfway. Of course, it should leave the decision to accept the adjustment to the customer and suggest a course of action.

REFUSING AN ADJUSTMENT

Like all refusals, this adjustment letter is most difficult to write, for you must try nevertheless to rebuild your customer's goodwill. It must say no graciously but firmly while convincing the customer of the company's fairness and responsibility.

A letter refusing an adjustment should begin by expressing the customer's point of view (see Figure 14-7). It should demonstrate your sympathy and desire to be fair. It should emphasize the careful consideration the claim received.

When saying no, it is often tactful, moreover, to present the explanation *before* the decision and to include an appeal to the customer's sense of fair play. Also, an effective conclusion might suggest an alternative course of action the customer could take.

★ PRACTICE
The situations described in these problems call for either a claim or an adjustment letter. Prepare the appropriate letter as instructed.

A. In order to entertain and impress an important out-of-town business associate, you made dinner reservations at Club Bruce, a prestigious restaurant known to cater to a business clientele. Your reservations were for 7:00 P.M. on June 8, and you and your guest arrived promptly. Your table, however, was not ready, and you were kept waiting for one hour and fifteen minutes. Intermittent inquiries were received by the maitre d' with rude indifference. Consequently, your guest became extremely annoyed with the restaurant as well as with you. Write an appropriate complaint letter to the restaurant's owner (Bruce Bedford, Club Bruce, 2 Merrimac Road, Merrimac, NH 03113).

B. Refer to Exercise A and write the response that Bruce Bedford should send to placate his dissatisfied customer and preserve his reputation in the Merrimac business community.

C. On September 5, Arnold Hayes received a monthly statement from Nayak & Nolan (10 French Market Place, New Orleans, Louisiana 70153), where he has had a charge account for eight years. The statement included a "previous balance" from the August statement. However, Mr. Hayes had promptly paid that balance (of $81.23) on August 7 and has a canceled check to prove it. Write the claim from Mr. Hayes, 80 Arch Drive, New Orleans, Louisiana 70155, asking that his account be cleared up. Mention his enclosure of a check to cover the remaining balance on his account ($107.80).

D. Refer to Exercise C and write the letter of adjustment from Nayak and Nolan, acknowledging the error.

E. On October 7, the Kitchen Korner, 47-03 Parkway Drive, St. Paul, Minnesota 55104, placed an order for two dozen poultry shears from the Northridge Cutlery Company, 2066 Yellow Circle, Minnetonka, Minnesota 55343. By November 30, the shears have still not arrived, and there has been no letter from Northridge Cutlery explaining the delay. Write the claim from Kitchen Korner inquiring about the order. Emphasize these concerns: Did the order arrive? Why was neither an acknowledgment nor a stopgap letter sent? Will the shears arrive in time for pre-Christmas shopping?

F. Refer to Exercise E and write the letter from Northridge Cutlery answering Kitchen Korner's claim. Explain the delay as caused by a strike of local truckers. Apologize for failing to notify the customer.

15.
SALES AND PUBLIC RELATIONS LETTERS

All business letters are in a sense sales letters, as we have already observed. And all business letters are also public relations letters in that one must always seek to establish and maintain goodwill. But some letters are written for the express purpose of selling, and others are written for no other reason than to earn the reader's goodwill.

These letters—*sales* letters and *public relations* letters—require a highly specialized style of writing. Both demand a writer with *flair* and the ability to win the reader with words. For this reason, most large companies employ professional writers—advertising and public relations specialists—who handle all the sales and publicity writing.

Not only do advertising or public relations writers know how to appeal to people's buying motives; they know how to *find* potential buyers. They must know how to acquire mailing lists (such sources as a company's own files, telephone books, and directories are good starts) and how to select the right audience from those lists.

Nevertheless, and especially in smaller companies, there are times when almost any businessperson will have to compose either a sales letter or a public relations letter. While the nuances of style may be beyond the scope of this chapter, certain basic guidelines can help you win a desired sale or earn an associate's goodwill.

Sales Letters

Sales letters may be broken down into three categories: Direct Mail, Retail, and Sales Promotion. While the manner of the sale is different for each, all share a common purpose—to sell a product or service.

DIRECT MAIL SALES LETTERS

Direct mail, or mail order, attempts to sell directly to the customer *through the mail* (Figure 15-1). The direct mail sales letter, therefore, does the entire selling job. A salesperson never calls on the customer; the product is never even seen in person. Solely on the basis of the description and inducements in the letter, the customer is urged to buy—to mail a check and wait for his purchase to arrive.

A direct mail letter must, consequently, include a "hard sell." It must grab the reader's attention with its physical appearance; the use of flashy envelopes and the inclusion of brochures or samples often help. It must

AP All-Pro Sporting Supplies, Inc.
Box 8118, Phoenix, Arizona 85029

March 3, 19--

Dear

What do Miss Universe and Mr. America have in common? They both
lift weights to keep in shape--with very different results, of
course. And many women across the country are discovering--just
like Miss Universe--that weight lifting is an effective and fun
way to a better-looking body and better health in the bargain.

All-Pro has put together a special package to help women get started.
We will send you a pair of three-pound dumbbells and a fully illustrated body-building regime. In just 45 minutes a day, three days
a week, these easy-to-follow exercises will firm up every muscle of
your body from your deltoids to your calves.

Despite the myths that have grown up around body-building, lifting
weights will <u>not</u> make a woman look like a man. Does Cher look like
Arnold Schwarzenegger? And weight lifting is completely safe. According to Dr. Leonard Paddington of the Phoenix Sports Medicine
Institute, "Weight lifting, which strengthens the cardiovascular
system, is safe for people of all ages. If you start a weight-
lifting program now, you will be able to continue to whatever age
you want."

Weight lifting shows results faster than any other form of exercise.
Get started now and you'll be all set for your bathing suit and the
beach this summer.

Our Women'n'Weights package, with the two dumbbells and complete
exercise regime, at the low low price of $21.95, is available only
through the mail. You can't buy it in any store. And for a limited
time only, we will send you, along with your purchase, an exercise mat
FREE. This 100% cotton, quilted mat is machine washable, a $6.96
value.

To order your Women'n'Weights package, and your free exercise mat,
SEND NO MONEY NOW. Just fill in the enclosed postage-paid reply
card, and your better body will be on its way to you.

Yours truly

Figure 15-1

DIRECT MAIL SALES LETTER

develop the reader's interest with appealing headlines and thorough physical description of the product; several pictures, from different angles, are a good idea.

Moreover, a direct mail letter must convince the reader of the product's quality and value; such evidence as details and statistics, testimonies, and guarantees are essential when a customer cannot see or test a product for herself. And finally, to clinch the deal, a direct mail letter must facilitate action: clear directions for ordering plus a reply card and postage-paid envelope make buying easy; a "send-no-money-now" appeal or the offer of a premium provides additional inducement.

RETAIL SALES LETTERS

Retail sales letters (Figure 15-2) are commonly used by retail businesses to announce sales or stimulate patronage. Their advantage over other forms of advertising (such as television, radio, or newspaper ads) is that letters can be aimed selectively—at the specific audience most likely to buy. An electronics store, for example, holding a sale on electronic phone

Justin's

Winston Salem, NC 27106

January 24, 19--

Dear Customer:

Now that the scaffolds are down and the hammering has stopped, you are probably aware that Justin's has opened a new store in the Bethabara Shopping Center. We are extremely proud of this gleaming new addition to the Justin family.

To celebrate the occasion, we are having a Grand Opening Sale, and every Justin store will be in on it.

EVERYTHING in ALL our stores will be marked down 10-30%. Designer jeans that were $60-$90 are now $40-$60. An assortment of 100% silk blouses, originally $60-$95, are on sale for $40-$65. The savings are incredible.

The sale is for one day only, January 31. But the doors will open at 9 A.M., so you can shop early for the best selection. And, of course, your Justin's and VISA cards are always welcome.

Sincerely yours,

Figure 15-2

RETAIL SALES LETTER

books and digital diaries, could target letters specifically to business people and professionals as opposed to, say, homemakers or educators, thus reaching customers with the clearest need for the product.

A letter announcing a sale must contain certain information:

1. the reason for the sale (a seasonal clearance, holiday, special purchase);
2. the dates on which the sale will take place;
3. an honest description of the sale merchandise (including a statement of what is and is not marked down);
4. comparative prices (original price versus sale price or approximate markdown percentages);
5. a statement encouraging the customer to act fast.

SALES PROMOTION LETTERS

A sales promotion letter (Figure 15-3) solicits interest rather than an immediate sale. It is written to encourage inquiries rather than orders. A product that requires demonstration or elaborate explanation, for example, could be introduced in a promotional letter; interested customers will inquire further. Similarly, products requiring elaborate and expensive descriptive material (for example, a large brochure or sample) could be introduced in a promotional letter; uninterested names on a mailing list would then be screened out, leaving only serious potential customers and thereby cutting costs.

Like other sales letters, a promotional letter must stimulate the reader's interest and describe the product. But it need not be as detailed: customers desiring further information are invited to send in a reply card, contact a sales representative, or visit a local dealer. Of course, such inquiries MUST be answered promptly by either a salesperson or a letter. And the follow-up letter (which could include a leaflet or sample) should provide complete information, including specific answers to questions the customer may have asked. The follow-up must also attempt to convince the reader to buy and tell how to make the purchase.

All of the sales letters described in this chapter have certain features in common: they convey *enthusiasm* for the product and employ *evocative language.* They demonstrate the writer's knowledge of both product and customer. And they illustrate the advertising principles known as AIDA:

1. **A**ttention: The letter opens with a gimmick to grab the reader's attention and create the desire to know more.
2. **I**nterest: The letter provides information and plays up certain features of the product to build the reader's interest.
3. **D**esire: The sales pitch appeals to one or more personal needs (such as prestige, status, comfort, safety, or money) to stimulate the reader's desire.
4. **A**ction: The letter makes it easy for the reader to buy and encourages immediate action.

Smith & Marcus

Financial Consultants

732 Commonwealth Avenue

Boston, Massachusetts 62633

February 10, 19--

Dear

In times of economic uncertainty, personal financial planning can
pose more challenges than running your own business. Determining
the investment vehicles that will protect your own and your family's
future requires financial insight and information.

That is why many successful business owners like yourself have engaged the services of the personal financial consultants at Smith &
Marcus. We have both the expertise and objectivity to help you sort
out your long and short term financial goals and then select the investment strategies that will meet those goals. Whether your immediate concerns are tax planning or estate planning, we believe we
have the answers to your financial questions.

To introduce you to the sort of answers we have, you are cordially
invited to a seminar, "What a Personal Financial Planner Can Do for
You." The seminar will take place on Wednesday, March 1, 19--, at
7 P.M. in the Essex Room of the Essex-Marlboro Hotel. Because seats
are limited, we would appreciate your letting us know if you plan to
attend by telephoning Dorothy Phillips at 771-3102, extension 222.

Yours truly,

Figure 15-3

SALES PROMOTION LETTER

*Public Relations
Letters*

Public relations concerns the efforts a company makes to influence public
opinion, to create a favorable company image. Its purpose is NOT to make
a sale or stimulate immediate business, but rather to convey to the public
such positive qualities as the company's fair-mindedness, reliability, or
efficiency.

Public relations is big business, and large corporations spend millions
of dollars a year on their public relations campaigns. When a major oil
company sponsors a program on public television, that is public relations;
when a large chemical company establishes a college scholarship fund,
that is public relations, too.

The public relations specialist knows how to use all the mass media (television, radio, magazines, newspapers, and films); she knows how to compose press releases and set up press conferences, prepare broadcast announcements, and arrange public receptions.

But public relations exists on a smaller scale as well. It is the local butcher's remembering a shopper's name, and it is the local hardware store buying T-shirts for the Little League. For, basically, public relations is the attempt to establish and maintain GOODWILL.

Public relations letters, therefore, are those letters written for the purpose of strengthening goodwill. Some of these can be considered *social business letters* (see Chapter 16), such as invitations, thank-you notes, and letters of congratulations. Others are akin to advertising, such as announcements of openings or changes in store facilities or policies. Still others are simply

---

Pine & White

100 Massachusetts Avenue
Boston, Massachusetts 02116

June 12, 19--

Ms. Beverly May
100 Gould Street
Needham, Massachusetts 02194

Dear Ms. May:

Now that you've used your Pine & White credit card for the very first time, we are sure you have seen for yourself the convenience and ease a charge account provides. So we won't try to "resell" you on all the benefits you can take advantage of as a new charge customer.

We'd simply like to take this time to thank you for making your first charge purchase and assure you that everyone at Pine & White is always ready to serve you. We are looking forward to a long and mutually rewarding association.

Welcome to the "family."

Sincerely yours,

Ms. Christine Popoulos
Customer Relations

Figure 15-4

PUBLIC RELATIONS LETTER I

friendly gestures, such as a note welcoming a new charge customer or thanking a new customer for her first purchase (Figure 15-4).

A specific kind of public relations letter is designed to demonstrate a company's interest in its customers. This letter (Figure 15-5) is written *inviting* complaints; its purpose is to discover causes of customer dissatisfaction before they get out of hand. (Responses to such letters must always get a prompt follow-up assuring the customer that the reported problem will be looked into.)

Pine & White   100 Massachusetts Avenue
Boston, Massachusetts 02116

May 26, 19--

Mrs. Addison Tanghal
14 East Elm Street
Brookline, Massachusetts 02144

Dear Mrs. Tanghal:

It's been more than six months since you charged a purchase at Pine & White, and we can't help worrying that we've done something to offend you. We are sure you are aware of the convenience and ease your charge account provides, but we would like to assure you once again that everyone at Pine & White is always ready to serve you.

If you have encountered a problem with our service or merchandise, we want to know. It is our sincere desire to give you the personal attention and satisfaction you have come over the years to expect from Pine & White. And we welcome the advice of our customers and friends to keep us on our toes.

Please fill out the enclosed reply card if something has been troubling you. We will give your comments immediate attention, as we look forward to seeing you once again at our Brookline store and all our other branches.

Sincerely,

Ms. Christine Popoulos
Customer Relations

Figure 15-5

PUBLIC RELATIONS LETTER II

Similarly, to forestall complaints (and of course encourage business), large companies frequently send *informative* letters that *educate* the public (Figure 15-6). A supplier of gas and electricity, for example, may include with the monthly bill an explanation of new higher rates. Or a telephone company will enclose a fact sheet on ways to save money on long distance calls.

Whatever the ostensible reason for a public relations letter—to establish, maintain, or even revive business—remember that *all* public relations letters must be *friendly,* for their overriding purpose is to create a friend for the company.

Murgano's Office Equipment, Inc.•Montgomery, Alabama•36044

October 19, 19--

Dear Office Manager:

Few business folks these days would deny that the fax machine has become an indispensable tool. Instead of waiting days for a letter to cross the country by mail, you can push a button and fax it in seconds. Instead of paying the high price for an overnight courier to deliver your document, you can fax the same document anywhere in the world for the price of a phone call.

Short for <u>facsimile</u>, a fax machine consists of three parts. A <u>scanner</u> reads your original document and converts the images on the page into a digital code. A <u>modem</u> translates this code into a transmittable analog signal. Finally, a <u>telephone</u> calls the receiving fax machine and sends the message. When you receive a document, the process reverses. The telephone answers the call and receives the message. The modem translates the message back to a digital code, and then this code is converted to images on a page and printed. Thus, the received document is a <u>facsimile</u> of the original, transmitted document.

Fax machines are available with a wide range of useful features, from conveniences such as autodialer and on-hook dialing to qualities such as fine mode and half-tone (for sending finely detailed documents). Our on-staff experts can help you determine which features will best meet your business's needs.

Indeed, everyone at Murgano's is eager to make your fax purchase as uncomplicated as possible. Just give us a call or drop by our showroom. We'll put a fax in your future fast.

Sincerely yours,

Figure 15-6

PUBLIC RELATIONS LETTER III

★ PRACTICE
On another sheet of paper, prepare either a sales or public relations letter as called for in each of the following situations.

A. Select a product (such as kitchen gadgets, magazines, or cosmetics) that you have considered purchasing (or have actually purchased) by mail. Write a letter that could be used to stimulate direct mail sales for the product.

B. Geoffrey's, a fine men's clothing store located at 10 Arlington Street, Boston, Massachusetts 02116, is having its annual fall clearance sale. All summer and selected fall merchandise will be on sale with discounts up to 60% on some items. The sale will begin on September 10. Write a letter to be sent to all charge customers, inviting them to attend three presale days, September 7–9, during which they will find a full selection of sale merchandise before it is advertised to the public.

C. You work for the ABC Corporation, Fort Madison, Iowa 52622, manufacturer of electric typewriters. Write a letter to be sent to the heads of all business schools in the area, inviting them to inquire about your latest model. Describe some of the typewriter's special features and tell the reader how to receive additional information.

D. You are employed by the First National Bank of Dayton, 1742 Broad Street, Dayton, OH 45463. You recently opened both a savings and a checking account for Claire Paulsen, a new resident of Dayton. Write a letter to Ms. Paulsen (222 Elm Street, Dayton, Ohio 45466) to welcome her to the city and to the bank.

E. Imagine that you work in the customer relations department of a large furniture store. Write a letter that could be sent to customers who have bought furniture for one room of their home, encouraging them to buy furniture for another room. Remind them of the quality and service they received when they did business with you in the past. Urge them to shop with you again.

16.
SOCIAL BUSINESS LETTERS

Like public relations letters, social business correspondence does not promote immediate business. Yet an astute businessperson will recognize the writing of a letter of congratulations or appreciation as a fertile chance to build goodwill.

The occasions that call for social business letters are many; such letters may express congratulations, sympathy, or thanks, or may convey an invitation or announcement. These messages may be extended to friends and personal acquaintances, to co-workers and employees, and to business associates. They may even be sent to persons who are unknown to the writer but who represent potential customers.

While the *tone* of a social business letter will vary with the relationship between the correspondents, all such letters must sound SINCERE. And, with the possible exception of an announcement, they should avoid any hint of a sales pitch.

Social business letters are often written on smaller stationery than letterhead. Some may be handwritten or formally engraved, rather than typed. Moreover, as an additional personalized touch, the salutation in a social business letter may be followed by a comma instead of a colon.

Because the language of a social business letter must strike a delicate balance between the personal and professional, the friendly and formal, it is a good idea to refer to a current book of etiquette for proper wording. Such a reference work will serve as a reliable guide, especially when composing formal invitations and letters of condolence.

Letters of Congratulations

A letter of congratulations builds goodwill by stroking the reader's ego: everyone likes to have accomplishments acknowledged.

The occasions for congratulatory messages are numerous: promotions (Figure 16-1), appointments, and elections; achievements, awards, and honors; marriages and births (Figure 16-2); anniversaries and retirements.

Whether written to a close friend or a distant business associate, any letter of congratulations must be SINCERE and ENTHUSIASTIC. It may be short, but it should contain PERSONAL remarks or references.

A letter of congratulations should contain three essential ingredients; it should:

1. begin with the expression of congratulations;
2. mention the reason for the congratulations with a personal or informal twist;

Dear Alan,

Congratulations on your promotion to senior accounts executive. You have worked hard for Rembow Consultants, and I am delighted that your efforts have been rewarded.

As you move into your new office and assume the weight of responsibilities that go along with your new position, please let me know if I can be of any assistance.

Sincerely,

Figure 16-1

LETTER OF CONGRATULATIONS I

Ruth T. Travis
1156 Clearview Avenue
Cold Spring Harbor, New York 11798

Dear Monica,
Congratulations on the birth of your grandchild, David Gary. You and Jim must be thrilled by the experience of becoming grandparents.
Please extend my warmest wishes to your daughter Jane and her husband. May this new addition to your family bring you all joy.
Sincerely,
Ruth

Figure 16-2

LETTER OF CONGRATULATIONS II

3. end with an expression of goodwill (such as praise or confidence—NEVER say "Good luck," which implies chance rather than achievement).

Letters of Sympathy

When an acquaintance experiences the death of a loved one, it is proper, although difficult, to send a message of condolence (see Figures 16-3 and 16-4). To avoid awkwardness, many people opt for commercially printed sympathy cards, but a specially written note is more PERSONAL and GENUINE.

A message of condolence lets your reader know that you are aware of his personal grief and wish to lend sympathy and support. The message, therefore, should be SIMPLE, HONEST, and DIRECT, and it should express SORROW with DIGNITY and RESPECT. (The expression "I am sorry," however, should be avoided, for as a cliché it sounds flat and insincere.)

The message of condolence should begin by referring to the situation and the people involved. This should be a bland statement that avoids unpleasant reminders. The note may use the word *death* but should NOT describe the death.

The rest of the note should be brief: an encouraging reference to the future (which should be uplifting but realistic) or, if appropriate, a gesture of goodwill (such as an offer of help).

Note: A letter of sympathy is also sent to someone who is ill or who has suffered an accident or other misfortune.

Dear Mr. Summers,

    I would like to extend the deep sympathy of all of us at Jason Associates.

    We had the privilege of knowing and working with Edith for many years, and her friendly presence will be sadly missed.

    Please consider us your friends and telephone us if we can be of any help.

               Sincerely,

Figure 16-3

LETTER OF CONDOLENCE I

Michael Barrett
2368-83 Street, Brooklyn, New York 11214

Dear Hal,

Roseann and I were deeply saddened to learn of your great loss. We hope the love you and Edith shared will help comfort you in the days ahead.

If there is anything we can do for you now or in the future, please let us know.

With much sympathy,
Michael

Figure 16-4

LETTER OF CONDOLENCE II

Letters of Appreciation

In business, as in the rest of life, it is important to say "thank you."

We have already seen (in Chapter 15) that letters of appreciation should be sent to new customers upon the opening of an account or the making of a first purchase. But many other occasions call for a "thank you" as well; a note of appreciation should always be sent after receiving:

1. gifts
2. favors
3. courtesies
4. hospitality
5. donations

A note of thanks should also be sent in response to a letter of congratulations.

A thank-you note may be BRIEF, but it must be PROMPT, for it must, like all social business letters, sound SINCERE.

A proper letter of appreciation (see Figures 16-5 and 16-6) will contain three key elements; it will:

1. begin by saying "thank you";
2. make a sincere personal comment;
3. end with a positive and genuine statement (NEVER say "Thank you again.")

Dear Mr. Yoshimura,

    Thank you very much for referring Natalie Slate to us. We are, of course, pleased to take on a new client. But even more, we appreciate your confidence in our legal ser- vices and your willingness to communicate this confidence to others.

    Be assured that we will continue to make every effort to live up to your expectations.

                    Cordially,

Figure 16-5

LETTER OF APPRECIATION I

Lisa Longo
9 Nutmeg Lane
Framingham, Massachusetts 01708

Dear Lucy,
    Thank you for the wonderful set of cookbooks. This thoughtful gift helped to make my birthday a very special occasion
          Sincerely,
          Lisa

Figure 16-6

LETTER OF APPRECIATION II

Invitations

While such events as openings, previews, and demonstrations may be advertised in newspapers or on handbills, guests may be more carefully selected if invitations are sent by letter.

Formal events, such as a reception, open house, or formal social gathering, *require* formal invitations. These invitations can be engraved or printed, or they can be handwritten on note-size stationery.

A general invitation (Figure 16-8) should be cordial and sincere; a formal invitation (Figure 16-7) should be less personal, written in the third person. Either kind of invitation, however, must do three things:

1. Invite the reader to the gathering.
2. Give the date, time, and place of the gathering.
3. Offer a reason for the gathering.

A formal invitation should, in addition, include the R.S.V.P. notation. This abbreviation stands for *répondez s'il vous plaît;* it asks the reader to please respond, that is, "Please let us know if you plan to attend."

The Brookdale Chamber of Commerce
requests the pleasure of your company
at a dinner honoring
the Honorable Stacy Coughey
Wednesday, the third of June
at seven o'clock
The Stardust Room of the Excelsior Hotel
R.S.V.P.

Figure 16-7

INVITATION I

Jaco Films, Inc.
1120 Avenue of the Americas, New York, New York 10036

January 3, 19--

Dear

In a few weeks, JACO will proudly release its new feature-
length film, <u>The Purchase</u>, starring Amanda Theriot in her
first appearance in seventeen years.

A special preview showing of <u>The Purchase</u>, for friends of
Ms. Theriot and of JACO Films, will be held on January 19, at
8 P.M., at the Regent Theater on Broadway and 52nd Street.

You are cordially invited to attend this preview. Admission
will be by ticket only, which you will find enclosed. Following
the film, refreshments will be served.

Sincerely yours,

Figure 16-8

INVITATION II

Announcements

Announcements may rightly be considered closer to public relations than social business letters. They may take the form of news releases, advertisements, or promotional letters. But *formal announcements* resemble invitations in both tone and format. Indeed, the combination of formal announcement/invitation (Figure 16-10) is not an uncommon form of correspondence.

Business events such as openings (see Figure 16-9), mergers, and promotions (see Figure 16-11) may be the subject of both formal and informal announcements.

Dr. Richard Levine
announces the opening of his office
for the practice of pediatric medicine
1420 North Grand Street
Suite 1B
Miami, Florida
(402) 889-7626

Figure 16-9

FORMAL ANNOUNCEMENT

The ALDO Corporation
is pleased to announce the appointment of
Ms. Firuz Darkhosh
as its new executive vice-president
and requests the pleasure of your company
at a reception in her honor
Friday, the twelfth of April
at four o'clock
The President's Suite   Room 510

Figure 16-10

COMBINATION ANNOUNCEMENT/INVITATION

```
TO:  All Personnel

FROM:  George Hart, President

DATE:  April 3, 19--

SUBJECT:  The New Executive Vice President

We are pleased to announce the appointment of Ms. Firuz
Darkhosh to the position of executive vice president.

Ms. Darkhosh has been with ALDO for eight years, first as
assistant manager of marketing and then, for the past five
years, as manager of marketing.  She attended Baruch College
and Pace University, where she earned a master's degree in
business administration.

I'm sure you will all join me in extending hearty congratu-
lations to Ms. Darkhosh and best wishes for her future here
at ALDO

                       GH
```

Figure 16-11

INFORMAL ANNOUNCEMENT

* **PRACTICE**
For each of the social situations described, prepare a correspondence that is appropriate to business relationships.

A. You are administrative assistant to the president of Burton and Doyle, Inc., 355 Bond Street, Oshkosh, Wisconsin 549091. Your boss, Mr. Arthur J. Burton, asks you to write a letter of congratulations, which he will sign, to Theodore Manning, 72 North Eden, La Crosse, Wisconsin 54601, a junior executive who has just been named "Father of the Year" by the La Crosse Boy Scouts Council.

B. You are employed by American Associates, Inc., 2870 North Howard Street, Philadelphia, Pennsylvania 19122. Your boss, Jacqueline Austin, 450 Poplar Street, Hanover, Pennsylvania 17331, has not been in the office for several days, and it has just been announced that her mother died. Since Ms. Austin will not be returning to work for a week or two, write a letter to express your condolence.

C. You have worked for the law firm of Lederer, Lederer and Hall, 407 East 23 Street, New York, New York 10013, for many years. On the occasion of your tenth aniversary with the company, an office party is held in your honor, and Mr. Gerald Hall presents you with a wristwatch as a token of the company's appreciation. Write a letter to Mr. Hall thanking him and the entire company for the party and the gift.

D. The Merchants Insurance Company of Tucson is holding its annual executive banquet on September 8, 19--, at 7 P.M. It will be held in the Gold Room of the Barclay Country Club, 700 Country Club Road, Tucson, Arizona 85726. Design a *formal* invitation which the company can send to all its executives. Include a request for response by August 24th.

E. A baby, Angela May, has been born to Mr. and Mrs. Andrew Lopato. She was born at Community General Hospital on February 9th at 7 A.M. and weighed seven pounds seven ounces. Prepare a *formal* announcement which the Lopatos could use to inform friends and associates of Angela's birth.

17.
EMPLOYMENT CORRESPONDENCE

Of all the different kinds of letters this book discusses, perhaps none are more important for your personal career than those letters you write to apply for a job. Your letter of application and accompanying resume, if well planned and written, can do much to help you secure the job of your choice.

Before you can write your resume or prepare a cover letter, you must do some thinking about yourself, for your employment correspondence must present a prospective employer with a favorable—and desirable— picture of your personality, background, and experiences.

A good way to start is to make a list. In any order, as you think of them, jot down such facts as:

> Jobs you have held
> Schools you have gone to
> Areas you have majored in
> Special courses you have taken
> Extracurricular activities you have joined in
> Memberships you have held
> Awards or honors you have received
> Athletics you enjoy
> Languages you speak
> Special interests you have
> Special skills you have

Try to include on your list any FACT that could help an employer see your *value* as an employee.

After you are satisifed with your list, rewrite it, arranging the facts into categories. This will serve as your worksheet when you are ready to write your resume and letter of application.

The Resume

The resume, which is sometimes called a *data sheet* or *vita*, is an OUTLINE of all you have to offer a prospective employer (see Figures 17-1 and 17-2). It is a presentation of your qualifications, your background, and your experiences, arranged in such a way as to convince a businessperson to grant you an interview.

Your resume, with its cover letter, is the first impression you make on an employer. For that reason, it must look PROFESSIONAL and exemplify those traits you want the employer to believe you possess.

Olga Godunov
2500 North Fruitridge Road
Terre Haute, Indiana 47811
(519) 772-1248

CAREER OBJECTIVE:
To obtain a position as an executive secretary with a large
corporation.

WORK EXPERIENCE:

March 1989   Secretary, the Benlow Corporation. 620 West
 to Present   Second Street, Terre Haute, Indiana.
                      Responsible for general running of the office
                      of a small private firm; duties included typing,
                      filing, billing, answering telephones,
                      scheduling appointments, etc.

October 1987   Receptionist, Dr. Mark Roan, 702 South Fulton
 to March 1989   Street, Berne, Indiana.

January 1987   File Clerk, Ajax Insurance Company, 277
 to October 1987   Westgate Avenue, Berne, Indiana.

EDUCATION:

Judson Secretarial School, Berne, Indiana. September 1986–
January 1987. Courses in typing, filing, Gregg shorthand, and
business machines operation.

Central High School, Berne, Indiana. Diploma, June 1986.

SPECIAL SKILLS:

Typing--70 w.p.m.
Shorthand--120 w.p.m.
Languages--French

REFERENCES:

Ms. Alba Cruz, Owner   Dr. Mark Roan
The Benlow Corporation   702 South Fulton Street
620 West Second Street   Berne, Indiana 46711
Terre Haute, Indiana 47814   (777) 803-9171
(519) 793-8686

Ms. Sarah Cohen, Instructor
Judson Secretarial School
141 River Road
Berne, Indiana 46781

Figure 17-1

RESUME I

Arnold Stevens • 25-92 Queens Boulevard, Bayside, NY 11202 • (212) 884-7788

Career Objective

An entry-level position in the travel industry

Education

The Bowker Business Institute, 600 Fifth Avenue, New York, New York 10011
        Associate degree, June 1990
        Major: Travel and Tourism
        Courses included: The World of Travel
                           Reservations and Ticketing
                           World Geography
                           Salesmanship
                           Business Management
                           Accounting 1
                           Travel Sales and Services
                           Travel Industry Organization

Bayside High School, Bayside, New York
        Diploma, June 1988
        Technical courses included: Typing
                                      Bookkeeping

Work Experience

Sales Assistant M & M Shoe Store, 70-19 Lefferts Boulevard,
                 Bayside, New York 11202
                 September 1988 to present

Stock Clerk   Same as above
                 September 1987 to September 1988

Skills

Typing: 50 w.p.m.
Language: Spanish

References

References will be furnished on request.

Figure 17-2

RESUME II

First of all, a resume *must* be PRINTED on business-size bond. It is acceptable to send photocopies, but these must be PERFECT and look like originals. This can be accomplished by engaging the services of a quick print shop where your resume can be professionally copied on bond paper. When your resume is updated and you add new experiences, you must REPRINT the whole thing. *Never* send a resume with handwritten, or even typed, additions squeezed in. This looks careless, unorganized, and lazy.

The resume must have an overall NEAT appearance: margins should be wide and balanced. Headings should stand out (for example, be underlined, capitalized, or printed in bold face type) and should be PARALLEL.

The information contained on your resume must be ACCURATE and COMPLETE. It should consist of FACTS. (You will be able to *interpret* the facts in your application letter.) Because you are presenting these facts in *outline form,* the information should be expressed in short phrases rather than whole sentences.

Nowadays, it is preferable to keep a resume to *one page.* This means that you must be efficient in selecting the facts to include and clever in arranging them.

Working from your casual list, decide which facts you would like an employer to know. (Eliminate those you would rather he not know.) Consider as well what the employer would like to know about you. (Eliminate those facts that he would probably consider irrelevant.)

In making these decisions, keep in mind the specific job for which you are applying. What facts on your list best qualify you for the job? *These* are the facts to emphasize on your resume.

Having narrowed down your list, recopy it—again arranging the facts into logical order.

Now you are ready to set up your resume. At the top, put your name, address, and telephone number (including your area code). This information can be centered or blocked along the left margin. In either case, it provides a sufficient heading. (The word *resume* is unnecessary.)

The rest of the resume consists of the facts from your list, categorized and printed under headings. Some recommended headings are:

> Employment (or Career) Objective
> Education and/or Training
> Awards and Honors
> Work Experience
> Related or Extracurricular Activities
> Special Skills
> Personal Data
> References

You need not use all of these categories; use, of course, only those that relate to facts on your list. Also, the order in which you list the categories is flexible. You may list your strongest sections first, or you may list first the section that is most relevant to the job in question.

For example, if you have had little business experience but are thoroughly trained, list EDUCATION first. On the other hand, if your college education was in an unrelated field but you have had relevant part-time jobs, list WORK EXPERIENCE first.

Let's look at some of these headings in greater detail.

EMPLOYMENT OBJECTIVE

Many career counselors recommend that this be included and listed first, immediately after your name and address. Mentioning a clearly defined job goal creates the favorable impression that you are a well-directed, motivated individual. On the other hand, many business people now prefer applicants with flexible objectives. Thus, you might consider under this heading a general statement such as, "Acceptance in a management training program" or "Entry-level position in an accounting environment."

EDUCATION

List, in reverse chronological order, the schools you have attended, with names, dates of attendance, and degrees or diplomas awarded. (If you have gone to college, you may omit high school unless your high school experiences are relevant to the job being applied for.) You should list, as well, any job-related courses you have taken. (If you attended a school but did not graduate, include it but be sure to list special courses taken there.)

WORK EXPERIENCE

Between WORK EXPERIENCE and EDUCATION, you must account for *all* your time since high school. (Yes, being a wife and mother for eight years counts as WORK—you've planned and kept a budget, run a household, cared for children—think of the specific responsibilities you have had.) Part-time and summer jobs count here, too, as does volunteer work. (You needn't have gotten paid to have developed a valuable and marketable skill.)

Each job experience should be listed (again, with the most recent job first) with your position or title, employer's name and address (and preferably telephone number), dates of employment, and a brief description of your responsibilities.

Note: If you have been in the armed services, this may be included under WORK EXPERIENCE or a separate heading. Be sure to list the branch of the military, dates, special duties, and highest rank held.

EXTRACURRICULAR ACTIVITIES AND SPECIAL SKILLS

Under these headings you may list any facts that don't fit under EDUCATION or WORK EXPERIENCE but which demonstrate an important aspect of your value to an employer. For example, if you can type and take dictation but have never held a secretarial position, here is where to list your speeds. If you can operate specialized machinery or speak a foreign language, note these facts as well.

Similarly, if you were treasurer of an after-school club, your experience handling money and specific duties that you performed are all important to mention. Indeed, all such memberships and activities are worth noting, for they help draw a picture of a vital, well-rounded individual.

Note: Nowadays, it has become trendy to arrange your entire resume around employment skills. The FUNCTIONAL RESUME lists your employment skills in order of relevance to the job at hand, filling out in a brief paragraph what you've done to acquire or demonstrate that skill. BE AWARE that many employers are suspicious of such resumes for they do not present your career chronologically and may thus conceal an erratic or sporadic work history.

PERSONAL DATA

It is not necessary to list such facts as age, height, weight, health, and marital status. Indeed, FEDERAL and many STATE LAWS prohibit employers from asking about race, religion, or sex. Therefore, some career counselors advise omitting this category altogether.

However, if a personal fact is particularly relevant to the job you are seeking, it may be worth mentioning (though using a heading such as MISCELLANEOUS may be better than PERSONAL DATA). For example, having a family member employed in the field could indicate that you have a thorough understanding of the responsibilities, as well as advantages and disadvantages, of the job; or being in perfect health could be important on a job that requires a great deal of physical activity or even long or irregular hours.

REFERENCES

The *last* section of your resume is a list of those people willing to vouch for your ability and experience. Former employers and teachers (especially teachers of job-related courses) are the best references. Friends or members of the clergy may be used as character references, but their word regarding your skills will have little weight.

Each reference should be listed by name, position or title, business address, and telephone number. A minimum of three names is recommended. Alternatively, under this heading, you may simply state, "References furnished on request," if you prefer to give a prospective employer photostated copies of previously prepared letters of reference.

Note: Be sure to ask permission of each individual before you list anyone as a reference. Also, while some employers prefer to contact your references directly, it is a good idea to get a general letter of reference from each to keep for your own files. (Businesses move or go bankrupt; people move, retire, or die; and, after many years, you may simply have been forgotten!)

Letters of Application

A *letter of application* is a *sales letter* in which you are both salesperson and product, for the purpose of an application is to *attract* an employer's attention and *persuade* her to grant you an interview. To do this, the letter presents what you can offer the employer, rather than what you want from the job.

Like a resume, the letter of application is a *sample of your work;* and it is, as well, an opportunity to *demonstrate,* not just talk about, your skills and personality. If it is written with flair and understanding and prepared with professional care, it is likely to hit its mark.

There are two types of application letters. A SOLICITED letter is sent in response to a help-wanted ad (see, for example, Figure 17-3). Because such a letter will be in competition with many, perhaps several hundred, others, it must be composed with distinction. At the same time, it must refer to the ad and the specific job advertised.

An UNSOLICITED letter (Figure 17-4) is sent to a company for which you would like to work though you know of no particular opening. The advantage of this type of application, however, is that there will be little competition and you can define yourself the position you would like to apply for. Too, you can send out as many of these letters as you wish, to as many companies as you are aware of; it is a good idea, though, to find out the name of a specific person to whom you can send the letter—a more effective approach than simply addressing a letter to "Personnel."

Your letter of application should *look* as good as your resume and be prepared with the same care on plain business-size bond. Here, again, the services of a quick-print shop can be useful.

2500 North Fruitridge Road
Terre Haute, Indiana 47811
March 1, 19--

Mr. Ikuo Saito, Vice President
Indiana Gas and Electric Company
1114 Broad Street
Terre Haute, Indiana 47815

Dear Mr. Saito:

Having served for the past several years as the sole secretary of a private business, I would like to apply for the position of executive secretary which you advertised in the Terre Haute <u>Gazette</u> of Sunday, February 28, 19--.

As secretary to the Benlow Corporation here in Terre Haute, I was directly responsible to Ms. Alba Cruz, the company's owner. My services were generally those of a "gal Friday." In addition to the usual typing, filing, and taking dictation, I was responsible for scheduling all of Ms. Cruz's appointments, screening her telephone calls and visitors, and organizing her paperwork and cor-respondence.

Essentially, I did everything I could to make Ms. Cruz's heavy responsibilities easier. Thus, I am familiar with the duties of an executive secretary and believe I am prepared to anticipate and meet all your expectations. I am confident, too, that, with enthusiasm and sincere effort, I can make the transition from a small business to a large corporation smoothly.

I would appreciate your giving me the opportunity to discuss my qual-ifications in person. I would be happy to come for an interview at your convenience, and I can be reached after 5 P.M. at 772-1248.

Sincerely yours,

Figure 17-3

LETTER OF APPLICATION I

Because a letter of application must sell your qualifications, it must do more than simply restate your resume in paragraph form. While the resume must be factual, objective, and brief, the letter is your chance to interpret and expand. It should state explicitly how your background relates to the specific job, and it should emphasize your strongest and most pertinent characteristics. The letter should demonstrate that you know both yourself and the company.

A letter of application must communicate your ambition and enthusiasm. Yet it must, at the same time, be *modest*. It should be neither aggressive nor meek: neither pat yourself on the back nor ask for sympathy. It should *never* express dissatisfaction with a present or former job or employer. And

---

25-92 Queens Boulevard
Bayside, New York 11202
June 15, 19--

Ms. Loretta Vasquez
The Vasquez Travel Agency
1402 Broadway
New York, New York 10032

Dear Ms. Vasquez:

This month I completed a two-year course of study in Travel and Tourism at the Bowker Business Institute, and my placement counselor, Mr. Robert Feiner, suggested I apply to you for a position as assistant travel agent.

As you will see from my enclosed resume, I have taken courses in nearly every aspect of the travel industry. I have participated in workshops simulating computer and telephone operations, and I have had extensive practice in ticketing and reservations.

My work experience, moreover, has helped me develop an ability to deal with the public, a valuable asset for a travel agency. Not only as a sales assistant, but even as a stock clerk, I have learned to be customer oriented; I have found that courtesy and a smile keep business flowing smoothly.

I would like very much, Ms. Vasquez, to put my skills to work for your travel agency. I am available for an interview Monday through Friday during business hours. You can reach me at 884-7788.

Yours truly,

Figure 17-4

LETTER OF APPLICATION II

you should avoid discussing your reasons for leaving your last job. (If asked this question at an interview, your answer, though honest, should be positive and as favorable to yourself as you can make it.)

When you begin to write your letter of application, keep in mind the principles of writing sales letters:

1. *Start by attracting attention.* You must say, of course, that you are applying and mention both the specific job and how you heard about it (or, in an unsolicited letter, why you are interested in the particular company). But try to avoid a mundane opening. Instead of:

   > I would like to apply for the position of legal secretary which you advertised in the *Los Angeles Times* of Sunday, August 10, 19--.

try something a *bit* more original:

   > I believe you will find that my experiences in the Alameda District Attorney's office have prepared me well for the position of legal secretary which you advertised in the *Los Angeles Times* of Sunday, August 10, 19--.

2. *Continue by describing your qualifications.* Highlight your strengths and achievements and *say* how they suit you for the job at hand. Provide details and explanations (even brief anecdotes) not found on your resume, and refer the reader to the resume for the remaining, less pertinent facts.
3. *Assure the employer that you are the person for the job.* List verifiable facts that prove you are not exaggerating or lying. Mention the names of any familiar or prominent references you may have. In some way distinguish yourself from the mass of other qualified applicants.
4. *Conclude by requesting an interview.* Without being coercive, urge the employer to action by making it easy to contact you. Mention your telephone number (even though it is on your resume) and the best hours to reach you, or state that you will call him within a few days. (Keep in mind that, while some employers will consider a follow-up call admirably ambitious, others will consider it pushy and annoying. Use your judgment.)

A complete application should contain both a letter of application and a resume. While it is possible to write a letter so complete in detail that a resume seems redundant, it is always most professional to include both.

It is best NOT to include copies of your letters of reference or of your school transcripts. These can be provided later if you are granted an interview. In a similar vein, do not include a photograph of yourself. The briefer the original application, the better.

A final word about salary: basically, unless instructed by the want ad, it is best that you not broach the subject. Indeed, even if an ad requires that you mention your salary requirements, it is advisable simply to call them "negotiable." However, when you go on an interview, you should be prepared to mention a salary range (e.g., $20,000–$25,000). For this reason, you should investigate both your field and, if possible, the particular company. You don't want to ask for less than you deserve or more than is reasonable.

Follow-up Letters

Few people nowadays send a *follow-up letter* (Figure 17-5) after an interview. For this reason alone, it can be highly effective.

A follow-up letter should be *courteous* and *brief*. It should merely thank the employer for the interview and restate your interest in the job. A reference to a successful moment at the interview is a good, personalizing touch.

25-92 Queens Boulevard
Bayside, New York 11202
June 25, 19--

Ms. Loretta Vasquez
The Vasquez Travel Agency
1402 Broadway
New York, New York 10032

Dear Ms. Vasquez:

Thank you for allowing me to discuss my travel qualifications in person.

Having met you and Mrs. DeLoia, and seen your agency in operation, I sincerely hope I will have the chance to put my training to work for you.

Enclosed is a copy of my transcript from the Bowker Business Institute, along with the letters of reference you requested. I can be reached at 884-7788 during regular business hours.

Sincerely yours,

Figure 17-5

FOLLOW-UP LETTER

Letters of Reference and Recommendation   The difference between letters of reference and recommendation is slim. A *recommendation* (Figure 17-7) is an endorsement while a *reference* (Figure 17-6) is simply a report. A recommendation is persuasive while a reference verifies facts.

Both types of letters start out the same. Each should include:

1. a statement of the letter's purpose;
2. an account of the duties performed by the applicant or of the applicant's general qualifications.

A letter of recommendation would add a third item—a concluding statement specifically *recommending* the applicant for the particular position.

---

m&m shoe store
70-19 Lefferts Boulevard
Bayside, New York 11202

June 17, 19--

Ms. Loretta Vasquez
The Vasquez Travel Agency
1402 Broadway
New York, New York 10032

Dear Ms. Vasquez:

I am happy to provide the information you requested regarding
Arnold Stevens, with the understanding that this information will
be kept confidential.

Mr. Stevens has been a stock clerk and then a sales assistant in
my store since September 19--. He has always been willing to work
odd hours, including weekends and holidays, and has proven to be a
hardworking and trustworthy employee.

Sincerely yours,

Otto Munson
Proprietor

Figure 17-6

LETTER OF REFERENCE

BBI The Bowker Business Institute, 600 Fifth Avenue New York, N Y 10011

June 17, 19--

Ms. Loretta Vasquez
The Vasquez Travel Agency
1402 Broadway
New York, New York 10032

Dear Ms. Vasquez:

Arnold Stevens was a student in three of my travel courses since
the Fall 19-- semester. He was always an outstanding student.

Mr. Stevens demonstrated his thorough grasp of the subject matter
in his class performance as well as written work. His assignments
were always executed with conscientiousness and punctuality.
Moreover, he was an enthusiastic participant in class discussions
and helped to make the courses rewarding experiences for everyone
else involved.

Therefore, I can recommend Mr. Stevens, without hesitation, for
the position of assistant in your travel agency.

Yours truly,

Jack Adler
Instructor

Figure 17-7

LETTER OF RECOMMENDATION

Note: Before you write a
reference or recommenda-
tion, be sure your company
has no policy forbidding them
(to avoid possible lawsuits or
complaints). If you do write
such a letter, it is advisable to
mark both the envelope and
letter "Confidential" to protect
both yourself and the
applicant.

Letters Declining a Job Offer

A fortunate job applicant may find himself or herself in the position of choosing from several job offers. Or a job may be offered that does not meet the applicant's needs or expectations. In such situations, a courteous, discreet letter declining the job will preserve a potentially valuable business contact and leave open the possibility of future employment.

25-92 Queens Boulevard
Bayside, New York 11202
July 1, 19--

Mr. Paul Nguyen
Nguyen Travel Associates
1133 Third Avenue
Flushing, New York 11217

Dear Mr. Nguyen:

Thank you for taking time to discuss with me both my career goals and the needs of your organization. I appreciate your offering me a position as receptionist.

Unfortunately, I must decline your offer at this time. As I mentioned when we met, I am eager to put my newly acquired travel agent skills to work and would like to begin as an assistant travel agent.

I am, nevertheless, disappointed that we will not be working together. I hope you will understand my decision.

Yours truly,

Figure 17-8

LETTER DECLINING A JOB OFFER

Letters Rejecting
a Job Applicant

Every employer must face the unpleasant task of rejecting job applicants. When the search for a new employee has been properly conducted, the successful candidate will be greatly outnumbered by the unsuccessful candidates. While a personal letter explaining specific reasons for an applicant's rejection is professional and preferable, a form letter is more often used as a way to reject in general terms all the unsuccessful candidates.

Ahmed Abudan Travel, Inc.
312 Lexington Avenue
New York, NY 10021

July 2, 19--

Dear

    I am sorry to inform you that we have filled the position of assistant travel agent for which you recently applied.

    Please be assured that your qualifications were thoroughly reviewed, and it was only after careful consideration that we offered the position to the candidate whose experience and career goals were most compatible with the direction of our organization.

    Thank you for your interest in Abudan Travel. We wish you success in your career.

Yours truly,

Figure 17-9
APPLICANT REJECTION LETTER

Letters of
Introduction

Rather different from but not entirely unrelated to employment letters are *letters of introduction* (Figure 17-10). These are written to a business associate on behalf of a third person (such as an employee, customer, or client). Such a letter is written when one person you know would like to establish a business relationship with another person whom you also know but whom he himself does not.

The letter of introduction you would write in such a situation should include three points:

1. the relationship between you and the person being "introduced";
2. your reason for introducing him to your reader;
3. what you (or he) would like the reader to do for him.

The Vasquez Travel Agency

1402 Broadway

New York, New York 10032

May 20, 19--

Mr. Jonathan Vecchio
Alpine Leisure Village
Aurora, Colorado 80707

Dear Jonathan:

Arnold Stevens has been my assistant for the past year, and he is currently touring the Denver-Aurora area.

So that he may knowledgeably inform our clients of the many delights of Alpine Leisure Village, I would greatly appreciate your giving him a tour of your facilities when he visits.

With much appreciation,

Loretta Vasquez

Figure 17-10

LETTER OF INTRODUCTION

The letter of introduction is sort of a cross between a request and a reference. It should be worded with *courtesy*.

Generally, the letter of introduction is given to the individual being introduced, who in turn delivers it in person. However, it is customary to forward a copy of the letter, along with an explanatory (and less formal) cover letter, so that your reader will anticipate the visit.

★ PRACTICE
Prepare your own employment correspondence according to the following instructions.

A. List all the facts you can think of about your personality, background, and experiences. Then arrange the list in a logical order and decide on categories under which to group the facts. From this worksheet, prepare your resume.

B. Imagine the ideal job for which you would like to apply. With this job in mind, write an unsolicited letter of application to a prospective employer and ask for an interview.

C. Prepare a letter of application answering the following classified advertisement.

> **OFFICE ASST**
>
> Textile distributor has highly diversified position for person who enjoys detailed work & has good typing. Business background helpful. $400/wk. Box 7705

18.
IN-HOUSE CORRESPONDENCE

The letters discussed so far were, for the most part, intended to be sent to people outside one's own company. Messages to customers, clients, and other business associates, they placed heavy emphasis on business promotion and goodwill. But business people frequently must communicate in writing with employees of their own company. The primary purpose of *in-house correspondence* is to share information.

The Interoffice Memorandum

While the ever-growing use of personal computers has reduced the need, within an organization, to communicate on paper, the need does still exist. *Memorandums,* more usually called *memos,* are the form commonly used for *short,* relatively *informal* messages between members of the same organization (see Figure 18-1). The memo provides a simplified, standardized format for communicating information *concisely.* The many uses of memos include announcements and instructions, statements of policy, and informal reports.

Because memos are usually used between people who have a regular working relationship, the *tone* of memos tends to be more informal than the tone of other business letters. Company jargon, for example, is permissible in a memo. Similarly, the writer can usually assume that the reader knows the basic facts and so can get to the heart of the message with little buildup. Note, however, that the level of formality should reflect the relationship between the writer and the reader.

At the same time, a memo, like any piece of written communication, must be prepared with care. It must be TYPED neatly and contain COMPLETE, ACCURATE information. It should adhere to the principles of standard English and maintain a COURTEOUS tone no matter how familiar the correspondents may be.

Unlike other types of business letters, the memo is NOT prepared on company letterhead. Nor does it include an inside address, salutation, or complimentary closing. A memo is a streamlined form and, indeed, many companies provide printed forms to speed up memo preparation even further.

Whether or not a printed form is available, most memos use a standard heading: the company name about one inch from the top followed by the term "Interoffice Memo." Beneath this, four basic subheadings are used:

TO:
FROM:
DATE:
SUBJECT:

C.P. Dalloway & Sons
Interoffice Memo

TO: Charles Dalloway, Jr.

FROM: Clarissa Woolf

DATE: August 18, 19--

SUBJECT: Search for a New Secretary for the Legal Department

Here is the progress report you requested about our search for a
new secretary.

We have now interviewed eight individuals and have narrowed our
choices to three:

1 Margaret O'Connell--types 65 w.p.m., takes dictation at 120
   w.p.m., has had five years' experience in a law office.

2 Daisy Robinson--types 70 w.p.m., takes dictation at 120 w.p.m.,
   has just graduated from Providence Community College (majoring
   in Secretarial Studies).

3 Donald Trumbo--types 65 w.p.m., takes dictation at 100 w.p.m.,
   has worked as a legal assistant for three years and taken
   paralegal courses at Providence Community College.

Members of the Legal Department will meet tomorrow, August 19, at
9:30 A.M., to discuss the candidates and make a decision. Your
presence at the meeting (in Ms. Gray's office) is, of course,
welcome.

                                CW

Figure 18-1

INTEROFFICE MEMORANDUM

(Some companies also include space for such details as office numbers
or telephone extensions.)

The TO: line indicates the name of the person to whom the memo is sent.
Courtesy titles (such as *Mr.* or *Ms.*) are generally used only to show respect
to a superior; job titles, departments, and room numbers may be included
to avoid confusion. When several people will be receiving copies, a CC
notation may be added or an inclusive term used (such as "TO: All Personnel").

The FROM: line indicates the name of the person sending the memo. No courtesy title should be used, but a job title, department, or extension number may be included for clarity or convenience.

The DATE: line indicates in standard form the date on which the memo is sent.

The SUBJECT: line serves as a title and so should briefly but thoroughly describe the content of the memo.

The body of the memo begins three to four lines below the subject line. Like any piece of writing, it should be logically organized. But it should also be CONCISE: the information should be immediately accessible to the reader. For this reason, data are often itemized in memos and paragraphs are numbered. Too, statistics should be presented in tables.

The body of most memos can be divided into three general sections:

An introduction states the main idea or purpose.
A detailed discussion presents the actual information being conveyed.
A conclusion may make recommendations or call for further actions.

Note: Memos are not usually signed. The writer's initials are typed below the message, and if she chooses she may sign her initials over the typed ones or at the FROM line. Reference initials and enclosure notation are typed below the writer's initials along the left margin.

MINUTES

Within most organizations, meetings among members of departments or committees are a regular occurrence. Some meetings are held at fixed intervals (such as weekly or monthly) and others are called for special reasons. *Minutes* (Figure 18-2) are a written record of everything that transpires at a meeting. They are prepared for the company files, for the reference of those in attendance, and for the information of absentees.

Minutes are prepared by a secretary who takes thorough notes during the proceedings. Afterwards, he prepares a *draft* and includes all the pertinent information. (It is usually the secretary's responsibility to decide which statements or actions at a meeting are insignificant and so should be omitted from the minutes.)

In preparing the minutes, the secretary may include complete versions of statements and papers read at the meeting. (Copies are provided by the member involved.) The minutes of *formal* meetings (of, for example, large corporations or government agencies), where legal considerations are involved, are made *verbatim,* that is, they include, word for word, everything that is said or done.

The format used for minutes varies from one organization to another. But the minutes of any meeting should contain certain basic facts:

1. the name of the organization;
2. the place, date, and time of the meeting;
3. whether the meeting is regular (monthly, special, and so on);
4. the name of the person presiding;
5. a record of attendance (for small meetings, a list of those present or absent; for large meetings, the number of members in attendance);
6. a reference to the minutes of the previous meeting (a statement that they were read and either accepted or revised, or that the reading was dispensed with);
7. an account of all reports, motions, or resolutions made (including all necessary details and the results of votes taken);
8. the date, time, and place of the next meeting;
9. the time of adjournment.

Formal minutes would include, in addition to greater detail, the names of all those who make and second motions and resolutions, and the voting record of each person present.

```
                    Minutes of the Meeting of the
                    CAPITOL IMPROVEMENTS COMMITTEE
                    The Foster Lash Company, Inc.
                         October 8, 19--

Presiding:  Patricia Stuart

Present:    Mike Negron
            Sheila Gluck
            Ellen Franklin
            Samuel Browne
            Lisa Woo

Absent:     Fred Hoffman
            Gina Marino
```

The weekly meeting of the Capitol Improvements Committee of the
Foster Lash Company was called to order at 11 A.M. in the conference
room by Ms. Stuart. The minutes of the meeting of October 1 were
read by Mr. Negron and approved.

The main discussion of the meeting concerned major equipment that
should be purchased by the end of the year. Among the proposals
were these:

Ms. Woo presented information regarding three varieties of office
copying machines. On the basis of her cost analysis and relative
performance statistics, it was decided, by majority vote, to recommend
the purchase of a CBM X-12 copier.

Mr. Browne presented a request from the secretarial staff for new
typewriters. Several secretaries have complained of major and
frequent breakdowns of their old machines. Ms. Franklin and Mr.
Browne are to further investigate the need for new typewriters and
prepare a cost comparison of new equipment versus repairs.

The committee will discuss the advisability of providing account executives with laptop computers. The report will be presented by Sheila
Gluck at the next meeting, to be held on October 15, 19--, at 11 A.M.
in the conference room.

The meeting adjourned at 11:45 A.M.

                              Respectfully submitted,

                              Ellen Franklin, Secretary

Figure 18-2

MINUTES

★ PRACTICE
Prepare the in-house
correspondence called for
in each of the following
situations.

A. Your employer, Penelope Louden, requested a schedule of the data processors' planned vacations so that she may decide whether or not to arrange for temporary help during the summer months. The schedule is as follows: Josie Thompkins, July 1–15; Calvin Bell, July 15–29; Stephen James, July 22–August 5; Jennifer Coles, August 12–26. Prepare a memo to Ms. Louden informing her of the schedule and observing that at least three processors will always be present—except during the week of July 22, when both Mr. Bell and Mr. James will be on vacation. Ask if she'd like you to arrange for a temporary processor for that week.

B. As administrative assistant to the president of Conway Products, Inc., it is your responsibility to make reservations at a local restaurant for the annual Christmas party. Because of the high cost per person, you would like to have as accurate a guest list as possible. Therefore, write a memo to all the employees requesting that they let you know by December 1 whether they plan to attend.

C. As secretary to the Labor Grievances Committee of the Slate and Johnson Luggage Company, you must prepare the minutes of the monthly meeting held on September 23. At the meeting, you took the following notes:

1. Called to order 4 P.M., employees' cafeteria, by Mr. Falk.
2. Presiding: Mr. Falk; Present: Mr. Baum, Ms. Dulugatz, Mr. Fenster, Ms. Garcia, Ms. Penn; Absent: Mr. Sun.
3. Correction made in minutes of previous meeting (August 21): Ms. Dulugatz, not Ms. Penn, to conduct study of employee washroom in the warehouse. Approved as corrected.
4. Mr. Fenster presented results of survey of office employees. Most frequent complaints agreed on. Fenster to arrange to present these complaints to Board of Directors.
5. Report on condition of warehouse employee washrooms presented by Ms. Dulugatz. Accepted with editorial revision.
6. Adjourned 5:15 P.M. Next meeting at same time and place on October 22.

D. As secretary to the Highridge Tenants Association, prepare minutes from the following notes taken at the emergency meeting on May 4, 19--.

1. Called to order 7:30 P.M., lobby, by Ms. Gingold.
2. 102 members present, 13 absent, all officers present.
3. Reading of minutes of last meeting dispensed with.
4. Officers' Reports—
   Vice-President read through the "red herring" sent by landlord to tenants. Explained more difficult clauses. Explained lengthy court procedure before actual cooperative offering can be made.
   Treasurer reported balance of $87.10. Observed need for minimum

of $1000 to retain an attorney to negotiate with landlord. Requested members with unpaid dues to see him after meeting.

5. Motions—

The President called for a committee to search for a lawyer to represent tenants. Motion made and carried that floor captains will constitute the committee headed by the President.

Motion to meet again to vote on search committee's selection made and carried.

6. Adjourned 9:30 P.M.

19.
NEWS RELEASES

A *news release* is a form of publicity writing. It is usually an announcement of an event or development within a company. Such occurrences as meetings, appointments, promotions, and expansions, as well as the introduction of new products or services and the dissemination of financial information, are all potential subjects for news releases.

News releases are sent to company publications and the mass media (specifically newspapers, radio, and television) in the hope that the editor will approve the release for publication or broadcast. In order to be accepted by an editor, therefore, a release must do more than promote a company's image and goodwill; it must be NEWSWORTHY and TIMELY; that is, it must interest the audience.

Like memos and minutes, news releases do not use standard business letter format. Nor do they use the "*you*-oriented" tone of voice referred to so often in this book. Both the layout and language of a news release are aimed at making it "copy ready." The less rewriting a release requires, the more likely an editor will be to accept it.

A news release should be *concise* and *straightforward;* it should contain no superfluous words. Nor should it contain confusing words: its meaning should be easily understood. Moreover, it should be written in an impersonal style. Your company, for example, should be referred to by name, not as "our company" or "we." Individuals, including oneself, should similarly be referred to by name—almost as if an outsider or reporter had written the story. References to dates and times, as well, should be specific. (Words like *today, tomorrow,* and *yesterday* are pointless when you can't be sure when your release will see print.)

The first, or lead, paragraph of a news release is the most important. Since an editor, if space is needed for a more newsworthy item, may chop away parts of your release from the bottom up, the lead paragraph should be capable of standing on its own. It should summarize the event and contain all the essential details. Following paragraphs should elaborate with additional information in order of importance. As in all business writing, ACCURACY and COMPLETENESS of details are essential; but in a news release even a spelling error could cause an editor to doubt your reliability and reject your story.

A news release may be prepared on either letterhead or standard typing paper. Ideally it should be limited to one page. If you must, however, use more than one sheet, the word *MORE* should be typed in the lower right corner of every page but the last, and all pages should be numbered successively in the upper right corner. The end of the release should be indicated with one of the following symbols:

-xxx-
000
# # #
-30-

The heading for a news release must include a release date:

FOR RELEASE
February 2, 19--

FOR RELEASE AFTER
4 P.M., February 1, 19--

FOR IMMEDIATE RELEASE

Also in the heading, if letterhead is not used, should be the company name and address as well as the telephone numbers of people whom an editor could contact for additional information. Following the heading you may either type a tentative title or leave an inch of white space for an editor to insert a title of her own.

The body of the news release should be double spaced; paragraphs should be indented five spaces. Margins of at least one inch should be left all around for copyeditors' comments. If photographs are enclosed with the release, they should be clearly labeled with a description of the event and the names of any people depicted.

Finally, the release should be addressed to The Editor, if sent to a newspaper, or to The News Director, if sent to a radio or television station. Of course, use the person's name if you know it. The envelope should bear the words: NEWS RELEASE ENCLOSED.

NEWS RELEASE

National Organization of Retired Persons
Fort Worth, Texas 76111
Zenaida Plonov, Publicity Director
(804) 771-1227

Marcia Hidalgo
The Editor
Fort Worth Gazette
(804) 771-2235

FOR RELEASE AFTER
3 P.M., April 7, 19--   4/4/--

ALVIN BANKS NAMED RETIRED PERSON OF THE YEAR

    Fort Worth, April 7, 19--. Alvin Banks, outgoing president of
the Fort Worth Chapter of the National Organization of Retired
Persons, was named "Retired Person of the Year" at a luncheon in
his honor on April 7.
    During his two years in office, Mr. Banks, the retired owner and
manager of Banks Building and Supply Company, helped the Fort Worth
Chapter grow from 53 members to its present high of 175 members. He
instituted a number of the organization's current programs, including
a part-time job placement service and a guest lecture series.
    Mr. Banks will be succeeded as president by Mrs. Beatrice Toller,
a retired buyer for Grayson's Department Store.
    The Fort Worth Chapter of the National Organization of Retired
Persons meets Wednesday evenings at 7 P.M. at the Presbyterian Church
on Humboldt Street. Meetings are open to the public and all retired
persons are welcome to join.

                              # # #

Figure 19-1

NEWS RELEASE

★ **PRACTICE**
For each of the following situations, prepare a publicity-minded news release.

A. As director of the accounting department of the Waterford Stores, send a news release to the company newsletter announcing the addition of a new member to your staff. Marlon Strong, a certified public accountant, earned his bachelor's degree at Brockton College, where he was president of the Young Accountants Club during his junior and senior years. Before coming to Waterford, he was a junior accountant with Moyer and Moyer, a private accounting firm. Quote yourself as praising Mr. Strong's background and expertise and welcoming him to the company.

B. On Saturday, July 31, at 11 A.M., the Paperback Power Bookstore at 777 Main Street, Little Falls, New Jersey, will host an autograph session for Lillian Lockhart, author of the current bestseller, *The Office Worker's Weekday Diet Book.* The book, published by Knoll Books at $13.95, was described in *The New York Times* as "a valuable, must-read book for anyone who works in an office." Ms. Lockhart, a registered nutritionist, is also author of *Eat and Run: A Diet for Joggers,* among other books. Emil Lazar, owner of Paperback Power, has said that Ms. Lockhart's appearance at the store will be the first of a series of autographing events. Prepare a news release for the *Little Falls Press* announcing the event.

C. The Reliable Drug Store, 120 Franklin Street, Roscoe, New York, has been serving the community for over twenty years. Monday, May 3, is the grand opening of a Health Food Annex to be located in what used to be Fred's Barber Shop, just to the right of Reliable's main store, at 118 Franklin Street. According to Marjorie Mansfield, present owner and daughter of the founder of Reliable Drug, Hiram Mansfield, the expansion was prompted by widespread interest in health foods as well as by increasing demand for top-quality vitamins and minerals. Ms. Mansfield said, "We intend to offer to small-town residents the variety of a big-city health food store and plan to carry everything from powdered yeast and protein to frozen yogurt and dried fruit." Write a news release to be sent to the local radio station making the expansion sound as newsworthy as possible.

20.
BUSINESS REPORTS AND PROPOSALS

Information plays a vital role in the business world, nowadays more than ever before. The latest advances in computers, information-processing systems, and telecommunications have in fact made information a commodity in itself and those who process information valued members of the business community.

The purpose of a *business report* is to convey essential information in an organized, useful format. And despite technological advances, the ability to accumulate data, organize facts, and compose a readable text remains a highly marketable skill.

A well-prepared business report will provide COMPLETE, ACCURATE information about an aspect of a company's operations. The subject of a report may vary from expenses to profits, production to sales, marketing trends to customer relations. The information provided by a report is often meant to influence decisions, to determine changes, improvements, or solutions to problems. Therefore, the report must also be CLEAR, CONCISE, and READABLE.

The *format* of a business report may vary, from a brief *informal report* intended for in-house use to a voluminous *formal report* intended for national public distribution. Some reports consist entirely of prose while others consist of statistics; and still other reports may employ a combination of prose, tables, charts, and graphs.

The *style* of a report depends upon the audience. An informal report to be read only by close associates may be worded personally; in such a report "I" or "we" is acceptable. A formal report, on the other hand, must be impersonal and expressed entirely in the third person. Note the difference:

Informal: I recommend that the spring campaign concentrate on newspaper and television advertising.

Formal: It is recommended that the spring campaign concentrate on newspaper and television advertising.

Informal: After discussing the matter with our department managers, we came up with the following information.

Formal: The following report is based upon information provided by the managers of the Accounting, Marketing, Personnel, and Advertising Departments.

Whether formal or informal, however, the wording of a report should be SIMPLE and DIRECT.

1. A Record Report merely states facts, describing the status of a company or of a division of a company at a particular point in time.
2. A Progress Report also states facts, tracing developments that have occurred over a period of time.
3. A Statistical Report presents numerical data, usually in the form of charts, tables, and graphs.
4. An Investigative Report is based on a study or investigation of a particular situation or issue. Such a report presents the newly accumulated data; it may also analyze the data.
5. A Recommendation Report is an investigative report taken one step further, providing specific recommendations based on the information provided.

Finally, there are three important *rules* to keep in mind when preparing any business report.

1. Cite your sources. *Always* let your reader know where your information comes from so that it may be verified.
2. Date your report. Business is volatile; facts and situations change daily, if not hourly. Your information could become outdated very quickly.
3. *Always* keep a copy of your report for your own reference.

INFORMAL REPORTS

The informal report is the most common form of business report. It is usually short, five pages or fewer, and is generally drafted in the form of a memo (Figure 20-1), or a variation of a memo. Sometimes, if sent to someone outside the company, the informal report may be written as a letter (Figure 20-2).

The tone and style of an informal report will vary according to the subject and audience. But whether friendly or impersonal, a report must always be worded with courtesy and tact.

An informal report must often be prepared quickly, requiring that information be gathered more casually and unscientifically than for a formal report. Nevertheless, no matter how minor the topic nor how short the time, any business report must be THOROUGH and FACTUAL.

The best approach to accumulating data is to begin by defining your *purpose.* If you can express precisely the reason for your report, you will know what information to look for.

Once your data are assembled, the second phase of report writing is *organization.* You must arrange your facts in a logical sequence that can be easily followed.

Finally, the nature of your data and your system of organization will determine your form of *presentation.* If your report calls for prose, organize your paragraphs:

First Pargaraph: Present the main idea clearly and concisely.

Middle Paragraphs: Develop the main point with supporting details and information.

Final Paragraph: State your *objective* conclusion. If called for, your own comments and recommendations may be included at the end.

TO: Mr. Marvin Dawson

FROM: Junzo Roshi

DATE: February 7, 19--

SUBJECT: Report on Secretarial Staff Overtime for January

As you requested, I have computed the number of overtime hours worked by the secretaries of the various departments and the cost of that overtime to the company.

Department	Employee	Hourly Wage	Number of Times	Total Hours	Total Cost @ Time & a Half
Executive	Ann Rogers	$15.00	6	15	$337.50
	Wilma Toynbee	15.00	5	14	315.00
Marketing	Maribel Cruz	10.00	8	17	255.00
Accounting	Nicole Foire	10.00	8	18	270.00
Personnel	Judy Hecht	10.00	10	21	315.00
	TOTALS		37	85	$1492.50

The cost of hiring a clerical assistant for 35 hours a week at $7.00 an hour would be $245.00, or $980.00 and 140 hours a month. This would save the company approximately $512.50 yet provide an additional 55 clerical hours.

JR

Figure 20-1

INFORMAL REPORT (MEMO)

Note: In a short, informal report, it is often a good idea to itemize your data. This may simply mean numbering your paragraphs, or it may mean arranging tables of statistics. However you do it, itemization makes a report seem more organized and easier to read.

International Industries, Inc.
3000 Avenue of the Americas
New York, NY 10019

Dear Shareholder:

Subject: Third Quarter Report

Third-quarter earnings continued at record levels due to a significant increase in International's petroleum operations. Earnings
for the first nine months exceeded last year's full-year results.

International Industries' third-quarter income from continuing
operations was $42,351,000 or $1.25 per common share, a 40%
increase over the income of $30,330,000 or 89 cents per common
share for the same period last year.

Operating income for International's petroleum operations increased
53% over the third quarter of last year, contributing over 79% of
International's income.

As a result of depressed conditions in the automotive and railroad
markets, International's earnings from fabricated metal products
continued to decline. International Chemicals' overall quarterly
earnings declined although full-year income from International
Chemicals should be substantially above last year's levels.

International Industries is a leading manufacturer of petroleum
equipment and services, metal products, and chemicals, with annual sales of $2 billion.

Laura M. Carson
Chairperson and Chief Executive Officer

Wayne G. Wagner
President and Chief Operating Officer

November 10, 19--

Figure 20-2

INFORMAL REPORT (LETTER)

INTERNATIONAL INDUSTRIES, INC.
Consolidated Statement of Income (Unaudited)
(In thousands, except per share)

	For the three months ended September 30	
	1992	1991
Revenues:		
Net Sales	$517,858	$454,866
Income from investments in other companies	8,729	4,046
Other income (loss), net	2,599	990
Total revenues	$529,186	$459,902
Costs and expenses:		
Cost of goods sold	$339,851	$303,893
Selling, general & administrative	111,384	91,597
Interest	9,456	13,001
Minority interest	1,600	705
Total costs and expenses	$462,291	$409,196
Income before items shown below	$66,895	$50,706
Taxes on income	24,544	20,376
Income from continuing operations	$42,351	$30,330
Income from discontinued operations, net of income taxes	--	2,346
Income before cumulative effect of accounting change	$42,351	$32,676
Cumulative effect of accounting change	--	--
Net income	$42,351	$32,676
Income per share of common stock (*):		
Income from continuing operations	$1.25	$.89
Net income per share	$1.25	$.96

NOTE: (*)   Income per share of common stock has been calculated
            after deduction for preferred stock dividend require-
            ments of $.03 per share of common stock for the three
            months ended September 30.

Figure 20-2 (Continued)

INFORMAL REPORT (LETTER)

FORMAL REPORTS

A formal report (Figure 20-3) is not only longer, but also more thorough than an informal report. It requires more extensive information gathering and is presented in a more stylized format. It is always presented objectively and relies on extensive details for documentation.

As for informal reports, begin preparing your formal report by pinpointing your topic. State the problem to be solved as precisely as you can. Then decide what information is needed to solve that problem and the techniques required to gather your information. Typical methods of information gathering include library research, surveys and interviews, and experimentation.

When your investigation is complete and your data are collected, you must organize and analyze the facts. Your interpretation may or may not be included in the final version of the report, but your own understanding and grasp of the material is essential before you begin to write.

When finished, your formal report will consist of the following parts:

1. *Title Page*

   This page will include the title of the report as well as the name of the person who prepared the report, the name of the person for whom it was prepared, and the date on which it was completed. The title page, therefore, will contain a great deal of white space.

2. *Table of Contents*

   This page will be outlined in advance, but it must be prepared last. It consists of a list of all the headings and subheadings in the report and the number of the page on which each section begins.

3. *Introduction*

   Unlike the introduction to a college term paper, this section is *not* an opening statement leading into your main topic. Rather, it is a statement of three specific facts:
   a. The purpose of your report (what the report demonstrates or proves);
   b. The scope of your report (what the report does and does *not* include);
   c. The method by which you gathered your information.

4. *Summary*

   This section is a concise statement of the main points covered in the report. Think of it as a courtesy for the busy executive who will not have enough time to read your entire report.

5. *Body*

   This is the essence of your report. It is the organized presentation of the data you have accumulated.

6. *Conclusion*

   This is an *objective* statement of what the report has shown.

7. *Recommendations*

   These should be made, when called for, on *the basis of the facts* included in the report. They should flow logically from the objective conclusion.

8. *Appendix*

This section consists of supplementary information, often in the form of graphs and charts, which does not fit into the body of the report but which is essential to substantiate the data.

9. *Bibliography*

A listing of references used in preparing the report is required whenever printed material has been consulted. Entries are listed alphabetically by author's last name. Proper format varies from field to field, so you should consult a manual or style sheet. The following examples, though, will serve as general models:

Book: Toffler, Alvin. *Powershift: Knowledge, Wealth, and Violence at the Edge of the 21st Century.* New York: Bantam, 1990.

Periodical: Rowland, Mary. "Sorting Through the Tax Changes," *The New York Times,* November 4, 1990, section 3, page 17.

```
                      RECENT DEVELOPMENTS IN
                        OFFICE MACHINES




                      Prepared by Rachel Orloff
                      Prepared for Mr. Winston Chin
                      February 22, 19--
```

Figure 20-3

FORMAL REPORT
Title Page

TABLE OF CONTENTS   2.

                                                     Page

Figure 20-3 (Continued)

FORMAL REPORT
Table of Contents

INTRODUCTION   3.

The purpose of this report is to examine the latest advances in office machines technology in order to determine what, if any, capital improvements should be made in the office equipment of the ANDMAR Corporation.

This report does not consider security systems or fire detection and control devices.

The information for this report was gathered from information supplied by the National Office Machines Dealers Association as well as from articles in several issues of Secretary's Press, Executive World, and Management Review.

SUMMARY

This report shows that, because of increasing emphasis on the use of very large-scale integrated circuits, major changes are anticipated in office machines during the next decade. These changes will primarily involve:

1.   electronic typewriters with memory functions;
2.   executive, as opposed to central, word-processing stations;
3.   high-speed and intelligent copiers;
4.   computers of increased speed, reliability, and memory capacity;
5.   electronic printing calculators;
6.   dual-voltage fax with memory.

Figure 20-3 (Continued)

FORMAL REPORT
Introduction and Summary

CONCLUSION AND RECOMMENDATIONS

4.

On the basis of the data in this report, it can be concluded that:

1. The installation of electronic typewriters and word-processing stations increases the productivity of secretaries and the efficiency of executives.
2. Medium-speed copiers and fax machines maximize cost-effectiveness when used on a departmental basis.
3. Programmable electronic calculators function at a fraction of the cost of electronic adding machines.

From these conclusions, it is therefore recommended that:

1. An in-depth investigation of currently available electronic typewriters, fax machines, and word-processing systems be conducted to determine the cost and feasibility of installing such equipment.
2. A cost analysis be made to compare the copiers presently in use at ANDMAR versus alternatives now on the market.
3. The services of an electronic calculator system sales specialist be engaged to determine the equipment best suited to ANDMAR's particular application.

Figure 20-3 (Continued)

FORMAL REPORT
Conclusion and Recommendations

When your report is complete and ready to be typed, keep in mind these guidelines for preparing the manuscript:

1. Use *standard manuscript form*—double space on one side of 8½ × 11″ paper.
2. *Number every page*—except the title page—in the upper right-hand corner.
3. Leave lots of *white space*—allow ample margins as well as space between subtopics.
4. Use lots of *headings and subheadings*—make your report logical by giving headings of equal weight parallel wording; surround headings with white space.
5. Pay attention to *paragraphing*—try to keep your paragraphs more or less equal in length. (A paragraph of 15 lines should not be followed by one of 6 lines; on the other hand, paragraphs of 15 and 11 lines, although unequal, would not be too unbalanced.) Also, give each paragraph, like the report as a whole, a logical structure; start with a topic sentence and follow with supporting details.

6. Be sure to *footnote* information that you take from other sources—quotations should be followed by a raised number[1] and at the bottom of the page a notation made:

> [1] Helen J. McLane, *Selecting, Developing and Retaining Women Executives* (New York: Van Nostrand Reinhold, 1980), pp. 71-73.

7. *Proofread* your report for errors in grammar, spelling, capitalization, and punctuation.
8. Bind the finished manuscript securely.

Proposals

A proposal is a sales pitch for an idea. Its purpose is to persuade someone to go along with your idea and put it into action.

Proposals are required in a variety of situations. For example, you may want to

- suggest an idea to your employer to change a company procedure, hire an additional employee, purchase new equipment, and so on;
- recommend an idea or project to a committee or board;
- apply for a grant to fund a project;
- solicit financial backing from investors for a new business or project.

The information you include and the format you choose for your proposal will vary with the situation. Some proposals, particularly grant applications, require the completion of extensive application forms and must follow a format prescribed by the organization offering the grant. In any case, all proposals must meet certain criteria:

1. *Define your idea.* Early in your proposal you must state CLEARLY your actual idea. You must define its purpose, as well as its scope and limitations. If you are presenting the idea to people unfamiliar with the background for the idea, you must fill them in, creating a context in which the idea fits logically.
2. *Be persuasive.* Offer specific reasons for your idea, including the benefits or advantages to be gained from it. Present these reasons logically, not just as a list, but as an organized progression that gradually builds an irrefutable case for your idea.
3. *Anticipate objections.* Provide answers to questions or doubts before they are raised. This may include credentials of people involved, justification of costs or expenditures, or refutation of alternative ideas.
4. *Explain how to proceed.* What must be done to implement your idea? What would you like your reader to do? Is there a deadline by which a decision must be made?

The size of your idea will determine the length of your proposal. If you are proposing the purchase of an extra computer terminal for your secretarial staff, you will need a briefer rationale than you would for a proposal for a bank loan to start up a new business. Still, all proposals must have:

- TITLE: This should be terse but clearly identify your idea.
- HEADINGS: Divide your persuasive argument into subtitled sections. You will make your proposal easier to read and your rationale easier to follow.

A *long* report may also include:

- SUMMARY: At the beginning, you will provide the busy executive with a synopsis of your idea and main supporting points.
- APPENDICES: Substantiating data can be attached at the end. Appendices may include resumes of the people involved in the project, tables and charts of financial figures or other relevant statistics, and any other information that would interrupt the flow of your persuasive argument but is nevertheless essential to the proposal.
- COVER: A long report should be bound in a plastic or cardboard cover.

Finally, you must consider the tone of your proposal. While you want the *logic* of your idea to predominate, supported by specific facts and information, you must also convey your own enthusiasm for the idea. You must communicate a sense of urgency if you want your reader to act. We began by saying a proposal is a sales pitch, and you will not successfully pitch an idea you don't believe in.

A Proposal to Speed Coverage
for Absent Employees

This is a proposal to provide the employees of Shoji International with a means of reporting anticipated absences during non-working hours. The purpose is to enable the Personnel Department to assign temporary coverage for absent employees by 9 A.M.

WHAT WE PROPOSE TO DO
We would install an answering machine in the Personnel Department, enabling employees throughout the company to call in sick any time between 5 P.M. the previous day and 8:30 A.M. the day of the absence. An assistant from Personnel will be rescheduled to work from 8:30 to 4:30 (instead of the present 9 to 5) to listen to the messages left on the machine, schedule the temporary assignments, and notify the substitute employees, who should be in place at their temporary workstations between 9 and 9:15 A.M.

WHAT WE WOULD LIKE TO SOLVE
Under the present system, an employee must report an absence to his/her supervisor. The majority of these calls, therefore, come in between 9 and 9:15 A.M., after the work day has begun. Next, the various department managers notify the Personnel Department, where temporary coverage is then arranged. The substitute employees may not arrive at their workstations before 10 A.M. An hour of down time, particularly in such departments as Sales and Customer Relations, can result in backlogs that last all day and may ultimately result in lost sales.

Figure 20-4
PROPOSAL

WHAT BENEFITS WE WILL ACHIEVE

The benefits will occur at four levels:

1. Employees will benefit by being able to report an expected absence at any time. They will be relieved of the need to rise from a sick bed at exactly 9 a.m. to call their office. They will experience enhanced self-esteem by not having to report their illness to their supervisor. We anticipate improved employee morale.

2. Supervisors and managers will benefit by no longer having to relay messages to Personnel about absent employees, a process that has taken time when a department was already short-handed. They will also benefit by having absentees' positions filled at the start of the work day, avoiding delays within their departments as well as added burdens on other employees. They will, further, be relieved of the need to discuss an employee's reasons for being absent until the employee returns to work (thereby losing no authority but reserving the authority to be used with those employees whose attendance records are questionable).

3. The Personnel Department will benefit by knowing early in the morning what rescheduling will be required that day. We will be relieved of the 9 a.m. rush of calls from managers that has until now slowed the process of assigning "temps." With adequate time, we will be able to make the most appropriate re-assignment to cover each absence, and we will be finished earlier, allowing more time to be devoted to our other responsibilities.

4. Finally, Shoji International will benefit. There will be reduced risk of lost sales or business due to the delays that, until now, have taken place in the morning. There will be the advantages of enhanced employee morale and more efficient morning operations throughout the company. (We anticipate that there might even be a reduction in absenteeism as a result of improved morale. This can be monitored as part of a follow-up study of the proposed change.)

WHAT THIS WILL COST?

The only cost of the proposed change is the price of a telephone answering machine. We have investigated a few models, all of which cost less than $60. With approval, we would like to buy the ANSO #229 at $49.95.

WHAT HAPPENS NEXT

With approval for the proposal, we will purchase and install the answering machine. On the day before it is installed, we will hold a brief managers' meeting to inform them of the change. On the next day, a memo will go out to all employees, explaining the new procedure for reporting absences. Finally, on the first day of full operation of the answering machine, Maribel Acevedo, Personnel Assistant, will begin working her new hours, 8:30–4:30.

We are ready to institute the proposal as soon as we receive an executive decision.

Figure 20-4 (Continued)

PROPOSAL

★ PRACTICE
The following activities require that you prepare either a formal report, an informal report, or a proposal. Be sure to employ an appropriate format.

A. Your employer has requested the latest closing prices on the following stocks (both preferred and common):

AT&T	General Motors
Eastman Kodak	IBM
Exxon	ITT

Consult a newspaper for the necessary information and present the data in an informal report.

B. A strike of the local transit workers union is anticipated in your community. In order to be prepared, your employer has asked you to investigate the cost of renting hotel rooms for the chief executives of the company. Contact a number of local hotels to find out their daily and weekly rates. Then present this information in an informal report. Include your recommendation for the most economical and convenient place to stay.

C. The budget for your department in the coming fiscal quarter includes funds for the purchase of a fax machine. Your supervisor plans to purchase a machine that is both state-of-the-art and appropriate for department needs. Prepare a formal report reviewing at least six different fax machines currently on the market. Consider such features as memory, resolution, half-tones, speed, as well as other available options.

D. The Counseling Department of the Fort Worth Business Institute has been establishing transfter-of-credit agreements with other educational institutions in the region. As the school's assistant director of counseling, prepare a formal report detailing the course requirements for the major programs of study in your school. Include a brief description of the course content and the number of credits awarded for each course.

E. Your local school board is seeking to raise funds to expand the high school library. It has turned to the business community for fund raising ideas. As a local business owner, you would like to suggest a town fair to be held in the school yard on a Saturday. Because local businesses as well as private citizens could rent space from the school board to run booths or games, the entire community could be involved in such a fund raising activity. Write a proposal to the school board suggesting your idea for a town fair. When you present your plan of action, be sure to include persuasive reasons for your idea. Also be sure to anticipate possible objections.

Part Three
WORDS AT WORK

The following lists include many of those words that might trip you up on your path toward successful writing in your career. Familiarity with these words, their spellings as well as meanings, will facilitate your composing effective business correspondence. The lists, however, are not a substitute for a dictionary, which you should always consult when in doubt about a word. Developing the dictionary habit, in fact, could be considered the final word on the subject of business English.

COMMONLY CONFUSED WORDS

accept	to receive willingly; to agree to
except	omitting
access	means of approach
excess	surplus
ad	advertisement
add	to contribute further; to find the sum
adopt	to take for one's own
adapt	to adjust
advice	recommended action
advise	to give advice; to counsel
affect	to influence
effect (*n.*)	result
effect (*v.*)	to bring about
all ready	completely prepared
already	ahead of or on time
all together	in complete unison
altogether	completely
allusion	reference
illusion	unreal appearance
alter	to change
altar	a sacred table
among	in the midst of several
between	in the interval connecting two
amount	quantity (as a unit or whole)
number	total (as a sum of parts)
appraise	to evaluate
apprise	to notify
balance	the difference between credits and debits
remainder	the amount left when part is taken away
beside	next to
besides	in addition to
bibliography	list of writings
biography	a life story

breath	respiration
breathe	to inhale and exhale
breadth	width
capital (*n.*)	money or property; a city that is the seat of government
capital (*adj.*)	chief in importance
capitol	the building in which a legislature meets
censor	one empowered to ban objectionable matter
censure	condemnation
cheap	of small value
inexpensive	of low price
choose	(present tense of *to choose*) to select
chose	(past tense of *to choose*) selected
cite	to quote; to summon
site	location
complement	to make complete
compliment	to praise
conscious	having awareness
conscience	moral sense
consul	government official in a foreign city
council	an administrative group of people
counsel (*n.*)	advice
counsel (*v.*)	to give advice
continually	repeatedly
continuously	uninterruptedly
costume	clothing
custom	habit
course	way; procedure
coarse	rough
credible	believable
creditable	worthy of credit or praise
decent	proper
descent	decline
desert (*v.*)	to abandon
desert (*n.*)	a barren wilderness
dessert	final course of a meal

device	a mechanism
devise	to create
disburse	to pay out
disperse	to scatter
elicit	to evoke
illicit	illegal
eligible	qualified
illegible	unreadable
eminent	renowned
imminent	impending
envelop	to surround
envelope	a paper mailer
farther	more distant
further	additional
fiscal	financial
physical	material; of the body
formerly	previously
formally	in accordance with the rules
immigrate	to settle in a new country
emigrate	to leave a country
imply	to suggest
infer	to assume or conclude
its	belonging to it
it's	*it is*
later	at a more advanced time
latter	last mentioned
leave	to depart; to allow to stay
let	to permit; to rent
led	(past tense of *to lead*) directed
lead (*n.*)	a heavy metal
lead (*v.*)	(present tense of *to lead*) to direct
legislator	a lawmaker, such as a senator
legislature	a lawmaking body, such as the Senate

lend	to let someone borrow
loan	the thing that is borrowed
less	a smaller amount
fewer	a smaller number
liable	responsible; likely
libel	slander
lose	to fail to win, keep, or find
loose	not tight
may be	to possibly be
maybe	perhaps
moral	having to do with right and wrong
morale	mental and emotional condition
overdo	to do too much
overdue	late
passed	(past tense of *to pass*) moved by
past	time gone by
persecute	to hunt down
prosecute	to carry on a legal suit
personal	individual, private
personnel	employees, staff
perspective	angle of vision
prospective	likely, possible
precede	to come before
proceed	to go on
proceeds	money acquired in a transaction
precedent	example or justification
president	highest officer
principle	a basic truth or rule
principal (*adj.*)	most important
principal (*n.*)	person with controlling authority
prophecy	prediction
prophesy	to predict
quiet	silent
quite	very

recent	new
resent	to be indignant at
respectfully	with esteem
respectively	individually
rout	to force out
route	road or course
root	anchoring part of a plant
stationary	not moving
stationery	writing material
suit	set of clothes
suite	an apartment
than	in comparison with
then	at that time
there	at that place
their	belonging to them
they're	*they are*
thorough	complete
through	via; over
though	despite; however
thought (*n.*)	an idea
thought (*v.*)	(past tense of *to think*) considered
to	toward; until
too	also; excessively
two	2; one plus one
undo	to annul
undue	inappropriate
whether	if
weather	atmospheric conditions
were	(past tense of *to be*) existed
where	what place
wear	to don clothes
ware	item for sale
who's	*who is*
whose	belonging to whom
your	belonging to you
you're	*you are*

SPELLING PROBLEMS

absence
absent
absurd
accede
acceptable
acceptance
accessible
accessory
accommodate
accompany
accrue
accumulate
accuracy
achieve
acknowledgment
acquaintance
acquire
adequate
adjacent
adjournment
advantageous
advertisement
affidavit
affiliated
afraid
against
aggravate
aggressive
airmail
all right
already
aluminum
amateur
analysis
analyze
anonymous
anxious
apologize
apparatus
apparent
appearance
applicable
appreciate
approval
approximate
architect
arrears
article

ascertain
attorney-at-law
author
auxiliary

bankruptcy
bargain
basically
beginner
belief
believe
beneficial
benefit
bookkeeper
boundary
brilliant
Britain
brochure
budget
bulletin
bureau
business

calendar
campaign
cancellation
capacity
captain
certain
changeable
character
chargeable
cigarette
clientele
colonel
column
commercial
commitment
committee
communism
comparative
competitor
complete
comptroller
concede
conceive
concentrate
concern

connote
conscience
conscientious
conscious
controlled
convenience
correlate
corrugated
counteroffer
criticism
criticize
cruel
curious
curriculum
curtain

dealt
deceive
defendant
definite
dependent
describe
description
desirable
despair
desperate
destruction
development
diagnosis
different
difficult
dilemma
diligence
disappoint
disastrous
disbursement
disciple
discuss
disease
disgust
disillusioned
dissatisfied
divide
divine
dominant

efficient
eight

eighth
eliminate
embarrass
emphasize
encyclopedia
endeavor
entire
environment
equipped
escape
evident
exaggerate
exercise
exhibit
existence
expenditure
expense
experience
experiment
explanation
extension
extraordinary
extreme

facilitate
facilities
facsimile
fallacy
familiar
fascinate
favorite
feasible
February
felicitate
fiction
fictitious
field
finally
finance
financial
financier
flexible
foreign
forfeit
forty
forward
franchise
freight
friend
fulfill

gaiety
gauge
generally
genius
genuine
government
grammar
gratuity
grief
grievance
guarantee
guidance

harass
height
hinder
hindrance
humor
humorous
hundred

ideal
illusion
immediately
immense
inaugurate
incident
incoming
inconvenience
independent
indispensable
individual
influence
influential
ingredient
initial
initiative
inquisitive
installation
intellect
interest
interfere
interpret
interrupt
irrelevant

jeopardy
jewelry
journey
judgment

justifiable

knowledge
knowledgeable

laboratory
leisure
length
liabilities
liaison
license
lien
lieutenant
lifetime
likable
likelihood
livelihood
loneliness
loose
lose
lost
loyalty
luxury

magnificent
maintain
maintenance
manufacturer
marriage
meant
mercantile
mileage
millionaire
minute
miscellaneous
mischief
mortgage

necessary
necessity
neutral
nickel
niece
ninety
ninth
notice
noticeable

occasion
occur

occurred
occurrence
omission
omitted
opportunity
oppose
opposite

pageant
paid
pamphlet
paralysis
paralyze
parliament
partially
particular
patience
peace
percent
perform
permanent
persistent
personnel
persuade
physician
piece
playwright
pleasant
possession
practice
precede
prefer
prejudice
prescription
presence
prestige
prevalent
prior
privilege
probable
procedure
proceed
professor
prominent
pronunciation
psychology
publicly
pursue

quality

quantity
questionnaire
quiet
quite

really
receipt
receive
recipe
recognize
recommend
referral
relative
relevant
relieve
remember
remembrance
representative
resource
restaurant
resume
rhyme
rhythm
ridiculous
roommate
routine

sacrifice
salable
satisfactorily
schedule
seize
sentence
separate
sergeant
shoulder
significant
similar
simultaneous
sincerely
sizable
specifically
specified
specimen
speech
strength
strict
subpoena
subtle
succeed

successful
sufficient
summarize
summary
superintendent
supersede
supervisor
surprise
surround
surveys
susceptible
symbol
synonym

tariff
technique
temperament
temperature
temporary
tendency
therefore
thorough
though
thought
through
tragedy
transferring
tremendous
tyranny

unanimous
undoubtedly
unique
unnecessary
until
usable

villain
voluntarily

warranty
weird
whole
wholesale
wholly
woman
women
write
writing
written

yield

A GLOSSARY OF BUSINESS TERMS

account *n.* (1) a bookkeeping record of business transactions; (2) a customer or client.

accrue *v.* to accumulate, as interest.

affidavit *n.* a written oath.

amortization *n.* the gradual paying off of a debt at regular intervals.

annuity *n.* an investment that provides fixed yearly payments.

appraise *v.* to evaluate.

appreciate *v.* to increase in value.

arbitration *n.* settlement of a dispute through a third party.

arrears *n.* overdue debts.

assessment *n.* evaluation for the purpose of taxation.

asset *n.* something that is owned and has value.

audit (1) *n.* the checking of a business's financial records. (2) *v.* to check a business's financial records.

balance (1) *n.* the difference between debits and credits. (2) *v.* to reconcile the difference between debits and credits.

bankruptcy *n.* the legally declared state of being unable to pay debts.

beneficiary *n.* a person stipulated to receive benefits from a will, insurance policy, etc.

bond *n.* a long-term debt security issued by a public or private borrower

brokerage *n.* a business licensed to sell stocks and securities.

capital *n.* money or property owned or used by a business.

cash flow *n.* a measure of a company's liquidity.

collateral *n.* property used as security for a loan.

compensation *n.* payment, reimbursement.

consignment *n.* shipment of goods to be paid for after they are sold.

corporation *n.* a business operating under a charter.

credit (1) *n.* the entry of a payment in an account. (2) *v.* to enter a payment in an account.

data processing *n.* the handling of information, especially statistical information, by computer.

debit (1) *n.* the entry of money owed in an account. (2) *v.* to enter money owed in an account.

debt *n.* money owed.

debug *v.* to remove errors from a computer program.

deficit *n.* a money shortage.

depreciate *v.* to decrease in value.

direct mail *n.* the sale of goods and services through the mail.

dividend *n.* a share of profits divided among the stockholders of a corporation.

endorse *v.* to sign the back of a check.

endowment *n.* money given, as a bequest.

equity *n.* the amount of money no longer owed on a purchase.

escrow *n.* written evidence of ownership held by a third party until specified conditions are met.

executor *n.* a person named to carry out someone else's will.

exemption *n.* money not subject to taxation.

expenditure *n.* an amount of money spent.

fiscal *adj.* financial.

flextime *n.* a system of flexible work hours.

forfeiture *n.* loss of property as a penalty for default or neglect.

franchise *n.* a special right to operate a business granted by the government or a corporation.

goodwill *n.* the value of a business's public image and reputation.

gross (1) *adj.* total, before deductions. (2) *v.* to earn a certain amount before deductions. (3) *n.* the total before deductions. (4) *n.* twelve dozen.

hardware *n.* the physical machinery of a computer.

information processing *n.* the "marriage" of data processing and word processing.

input *n.* data fed into a computer.

insurance *n.* the guarantee of compensation for a specified loss.

interest *n.* the fee charged for borrowing money.

inventory *n.* an itemized list of property or merchandise.

investment *n.* money put into a business or transaction to reap a profit.

invoice *n.* a list of goods shipped.

journal *n.* a written record of financial transactions.

lease (1) *n.* a contract for renting property. (2) *v.* to rent or let.

ledger *n.* a record book of debits and credits.

legacy *n.* money or property left in a will.

liability *n.* a debt or obligation.

lien *n.* a claim on property as security against a debt.

liquidity *n.* ability to turn assets into cash.

list price *n.* retail price as listed in a catalog.

margin *n.* difference between cost and selling price.

markup *n.* the percentage by which selling price is more than cost.

merger *n.* the combining of two or more companies into one.

middleman *n.* a businessperson who buys from a producer and resells at wholesale or retail in smaller quantities.

monetary *adj.* relating to money.

monopoly *n.* exclusive control of a commodity or service.

mortgage (1) *n.* the pledging of property as security for a loan. (2) *v.* to pledge property as security for a loan.

negotiable *adj.* transferable.

net (1) *n.* an amount left after deductions. (2) *v.* to clear as profit.

networking *n.* the establishing of business and professional contacts.

option *n.* the right to act on an offer at an established price within a limited time.

output *n.* data provided by a computer.

overhead *n.* the costs of running a business.

par value *n.* the face value of a share of stock or a bond.

payable *adj.* owed.

personnel *n.* employees, staff.

petty cash *n.* money kept on hand for incidental purchases.

portfolio *n.* the various securities held by an investor.

power of attorney *n.* the written right to legally represent another person.

premium *n.* a payment, usually for an insurance policy.

productivity *n.* rate of yield or output.

proprietor *n.* owner.

prospectus *n.* a statement describing a business.

proxy *n.* authorization to vote for a stockholder at a meeting.

quorum *n.* the minimum number of persons required to be present for the transaction of business at a meeting.

receivable *adj.* due.

remittance *n.* the sending of money in payment.

requisition *n.* a written request for supplies.

resume *n.* an outline of a job applicant's qualifications and experience.

rider *n.* an amendment to a document.

royalty *n.* a share of the profits from a book or invention paid to the author or patent holder.

security *n.* (1) funds or property held as a pledge of repayment; (2) a stock or bond.

shareholder *n.* one who owns shares of a corporation's stock.

software *n.* set of programs for a computer.

solvent *adj.* able to pay debts.

spreadsheet *n.* a table of numbers arranged in rows and columns for computer calculations.

stockholder *n.* one who owns stock in a company.

subsidy *n.* a monetary grant.

tariff *n.* a tax on imports or exports.

telecommunications *n.* high-speed communications via wire or microwave.

turnaround time *n.* time taken to complete a task.

trust *n.* a monopoly formed by a combination of corporations.

vita *n.* an outline of a job applicant's qualifications and experience, a resume.

word processing *n.* the handling of narrative information by computer.

ANSWERS TO EXERCISES IN "GRAMMAR AND SENTENCE STRUCTURE"

1. Identifying Verbs and Subjects (page 4)

Exercise 1

1. opens
2. greeted
3. adjourned
4. looks
5. has

6. ordered
7. called
8. reduced
9. deserved
10. retyped

Exercise 2

(Answers may vary; the following are suggestions.)

1. is
2. is
3. works
4. sees
5. takes

6. is
7. works
8. refers
9. seeks
10. work

Exercise 3

ordered
was
cost
received
arrived

listed
is
enclose
credit
appreciate

Exercise 4

1. has worked
2. has been auditioning
3. must be
4. has been rising
5. will have finished

6. has worked
7. took
8. am looking
9. have been hired
10. has moved

Exercise 5

am writing
would like
have been
have been working
have included

have studied
have completed
am enclosing
is included
will be provided

Exercise 6

1. studied, looked
2. has driven, delivered, sold
3. asked, told
4. went, bought
5. typed, proofread
6. called, took
7. was offered, accepted
8. saved, quit, opened
9. placed, received
10. retired, moved

Exercise 7

1. John is
2. He likes
3. He had planned
4. computer science is
5. His plans had to be changed
6. Marie is
7. She enjoys
8. Mathematics had been
9. she went, developed
10. atmosphere salary are satisfying

Exercise 8

1. Mr. and Mrs. Price are buying
2. agent banker are helping
3. agent lawyer disagree
4. Prices banker are
5. agent banker lawyer Prices will be
6. Regina boss were discussing
7. Accuracy thoroughness conscientiousness were
8. sales expenses were
9. Regina employer met
10. raise will begin

Exercise 9

We would like
Dark Lady is named
bouquet is steeped
drop mingles
Rosemary violets pansies evoke
loves lyrics blend
perfume cologne are
we are offering
purse-atomizer pouch are
this purchases can be charged ordered

Exercise 10

1. had known
2. is tired
3. saw
4. apologized
5. was repaired

6. is
7. is filled
8. is
9. will be torn
10. missed

Exercise 11

1. Bicycling keeps
2. Writing makes
3. Balancing makes
4. To answer is
5. To admit indicates

6. To lose is
7. Waiting infuriates
8. Smoking is
9. To find demands
10. To operate requires

Exercise 12

(Answers may vary; the following are suggestions.)

1. a. Walter is selling insurance.
   b. Selling insurance has been his job for the last ten years.
   c. The selling point of his insurance is its low premium.
2. a. I will be speaking to the Chamber of Commerce next Friday.
   b. Speaking to groups is not my strongest skill.
   c. Speaking engagements make me nervous.
3. a. The customer is paying cash for her purchase.
   b. Paying bills is always unpleasant.
   c. Paying customers deserve courteous service.
4. a. Mary is writing a novel.
   b. Writing can be a highly marketable skill.
   c. My writing skills need improvement.
5. a. I was looking at myself in a mirror.
   b. Looking at one's reflection is enlightening.
   c. My looking glass is broken now.

Exercise 13

(Answers may vary; the following are suggestions.)

1. a. My dog was lost.
   b. The lost dog found his way home.
2. a. Having danced all night, Wendy was tired.
   b. The tired dancer went home to sleep.
3. a. The wedding invitations were printed on parchment.
   b. The printed word is a powerful tool.
4. a. The old jar was opened after much prying.
   b. The opened jar required refrigeration.
5. a. The job was advertised in the newspaper.
   b. The advertised vacancy was filled quickly.

REVIEW EXERCISES

A.
1. Mr. Munson <u>was studying</u>
2. He <u>was considering</u>
3. money <u>had been</u>
4. money <u>is</u>
5. it <u>earns</u>
6. Mr. Munson <u>would like to be earning</u>
7. account <u>would have paid</u>
8. he <u>wants to invest</u>
9. he <u>knows</u>
10. he <u>will be</u>

B.
1. offices <u>are</u>
2. households <u>will contain</u>
3. people <u>perform</u>
4. They <u>run</u>
5. people <u>do</u>
6. they <u>may manage</u>
7. workers <u>are</u>
8. people <u>do</u>
9. technology <u>has made</u>
10. Employees <u>can communicate</u>
11. computers <u>are used</u>
12. workers <u>rely</u>
13. technology <u>enables</u>
14. businesses <u>are</u>
15. they <u>may find</u>

C. Americans <u>are reconsidering</u>
I <u>am submitting</u>
readers <u>may find</u>
article <u>is</u>
It <u>suggests</u>
It <u>recommends</u>
places things <u>are listed</u>
details prices <u>have been researched</u>
consideration <u>is appreciated</u>
you <u>are</u>

D. I <u>have investigated</u>
places <u>are equipped</u>
two <u>are</u>

Villa di Rome <u>serves</u>
band <u>is provided</u>
cost <u>is</u>
Blossom's <u>offers</u>
floor <u>is</u>
cost <u>is</u>
I <u>will be</u>

E. Lorna Tellman <u>wins</u>
Lorna Tellman <u>was awarded</u>
She <u>was selected</u>
Ms. Tellman <u>was</u>
event <u>brought</u>
income <u>doubled</u>
winner <u>will be honored</u>
This <u>will take</u>
Tickets <u>are</u>
Ms. Tellman <u>remarked</u>
I <u>was</u>

2. Sentence Completers (page 17)

Exercise 1

1. <u>roving</u> reporter
2. <u>growing</u> controversy
3. <u>demanding</u> editor
4. politician <u>accused</u>
5. <u>provoking</u> questions
6. <u>alleged</u> criminal
7. <u>tempting</u> bribe
8. <u>Refusing</u> he
9. <u>suspected</u> politician
10. <u>honest</u> man

Exercise 2

1. <u>difficult</u> job
2. <u>good</u> boss
3. <u>quiet</u> boss
4. <u>low</u> profile
5. <u>dynamic</u> boss
6. <u>long</u> hours
7. <u>high</u> salaries
8. <u>fair</u> situation
9. <u>smart</u> individuals
10. <u>rare</u> positions

Exercise 3

(Answers may vary; the following are suggestions.)

1. careful
2. expressive
3. lovely
4. lucky
5. biblical
6. boastful
7. admissible
8. spinal
9. photographic
10. infinite
11. senseless
12. magical
13. comparable
14. terrible
15. verbal
16. glorious
17. biological
18. insistent
19. moody
20. planetary

Exercise 4

1. The woman ~~in charge~~ (is) Ms. Skelton.
2. She (is) the president ~~of the company.~~
3. The suite ~~on the sixth floor~~ (is) her office.
4. The telephones ~~inside her office~~ never (stop) ringing.
5. The people ~~around her~~ (work) hard.
6. The man ~~by her side~~ (is) her partner.
7. He (is) chairman ~~of the board.~~
8. They (work) very closely ~~at the office.~~
9. The success ~~of her career~~ (took) much effort.
10. She (is) a woman ~~of determination.~~

Exercise 5

1. desperately wanted
2. cautiously asked
3. answered regretfully
4. seriously needed
5. patiently explained
6. had been wandering aimlessly
7. had been getting done sloppily
8. looked hesitantly
9. calmly told
10. politely thanked

Exercise 6

(Answers may vary; the following are suggestions.)

1. silently: The lovers looked at each other silently.
2. excitedly: I opened the package excitedly.
3. merrily: The children sang merrily.
4. horribly: He died horribly in a plane crash.
5. wearily: We worked on wearily till dawn.
6. patiently: I explained the answer patiently.
7. studiously: She prepared studiously for the exam.
8. correctly: She answered every question correctly.
9. joyfully: We celebrated the holidays joyfully.
10. boastingly: He told us boastingly of his accomplishments.

Exercise 7

for damages	*adjective*
to my car	*adjective*
on February 13	*adverb*
on Elm Street	*adverb*
during the night	*adjective*
on the ice	*adverb*
of my car	*adjective*
at $950	*adverb*
for the repair costs	*adjective*
at Al's Auto Body Shop	*adverb*

Exercise 8

1. never <u>asks</u>
2. often <u>makes</u>
3. <u>will</u> sometimes <u>correct</u>
4. always <u>appreciates</u>
5. <u>does</u> not <u>show</u>
6. always <u>conceals</u>
7. <u>should</u> not <u>hide</u>
8. <u>can</u> always <u>perceive</u>
9. also <u>recognizes</u>
10. <u>should</u> not <u>neglect</u>

Exercise 9

1. important	*adjective*
2. should market	*verb*
3. carefully	*adverb*
4. must outline	*verb*
5. should include	*verb*
6. salable	*adjective*
7. well	*adverb*
8. should be typed	*verb*
9. worded	*adjective*
10. readily	*adverb*

Exercise 10

1. memo
2. it
3. topic
4. information
5. copy
6. memo
7. questions
8. copy
9. details
10. memo

Exercise 11

1. PN
2. PA
3. PA
4. PN
5. PA
6. PN
7. PN
8. PA
9. PN
10. PA

REVIEW EXERCISES

A. <u>High</u> interest rates
<u>overdue</u> accounts
<u>personal</u> check
<u>current</u> bill <u>overdue</u>
<u>great</u> lapse
<u>prompt</u> customer
<u>delayed</u> payments
<u>troublesome</u> way
<u>sound</u> credit rating

B. have looked <u>carefully</u>
are receiving <u>belatedly</u>
is addressed <u>improperly</u>
is sent <u>initially</u>
must be forwarded <u>later</u>
handle <u>promptly</u>
get <u>slowly</u>
cannot cover <u>efficiently</u>
must be dealt <u>immediately</u>
are mounting <u>daily</u>

C. OF ESCO, INC.
OF THE MEETING
OF DECEMBER 13, 19--
to order
at 1:45 P.M.
by Mr. Griffen
of the meeting
Among the proposals
of time-sharing
in a slow turnaround time
within two years
of a computer
for itself
in savings
to the company
of a computer
at 3:00 P.M.

D.

1. PN	6. PA	11. DO
2. PA	7. DO	12. PN
3. DO	8. PN	13. PN
4. PA	9. DO	14. PA
5. DO	10. PN	15. PA

3. The Sentence vs. Fragments vs. Run-ons (page 31)

Exercise 1

(Answers may vary; the following are suggestions.)

1. accountant, *or* he
2. job, *and* he
3. carefully, *so* he
4. discouraged, *but* he
5. job, *so* she
6. relieved, *but* she
7. unemployed, *and* she
8. job, *for* she
9. back, *or* she
10. secretary, *yet* she
11. advance, *and* she
12. boss, *for* he
13. plans, *and* she
14. her, *so* she
15. careers, *or* nothing
16. jobs, *and* they
17. patient, *but* they
18. large, *so* you
19. workers, *but* first
20. best, *and* you

Exercise 2

1. S
2. F
3. S
4. F
5. F
6. S
7. F
8. S
9. S
10. F

Exercise 3

1. F
2. S
3. S
4. F
5. F
6. F
7. F
8. S
9. S
10. S

Exercise 4

(Answers may vary; the following are suggestions.)

1. substantially *although* the economy
2. prospering *because* they benefit
3. busy *since* more
4. well *whether* the stock
5. possessions *before* they spend
6. sales *while* department
7. now *because* they
8. discover *how* recession
9. services *that* people
10. situation *while* others

Exercise 5

(Answers may vary; the following are suggestions.)

1. wardrobe *before* you
2. thought *because* first
3. best *since* you
4. comfortable *because* you

5. choice *although* a
6. idea *unless* they
7. tie *whether* the
8. chances *before* you
9. mirror *before* you
10. best *so that* you

Exercise 6

(Answers may vary; the following are suggestions.)

1. *Although* James . . . immediately, he
2. *Because* he . . . forgotten, he
3. *So that* he . . . practice, he
4. *When* he . . . job, he
5. *Because* Judy . . . school, she
6. *While* that . . . weeks, she
7. *As* she . . . interviews, she
8. *When* the . . . along, she
9. *Because* she . . . practice, nervousness
10. *Because* James . . . ahead, their

Exercise 7

(Answers may vary; the following are suggestions.)

1. *While* some . . . time, others
2. *If* you . . . done, effective
3. *Unless* you . . . planning, you
4. *After* you . . . planning, you
5. *If* you . . . deadlines, you
6. *When* you . . . activity, you
7. *Unless* you . . . relaxation, you
8. *Because* overcommitment . . . ineffectiveness, **you**
9. *If* you . . . morning, schedule
10. *If* you . . . time, you

Exercise 8

1. S	6. RO
2. S	7. RO
3. S	8. S
4. RO	9. RO
5. RO	10. S

Exercise 9

1. RO	6. RO
2. S	7. S
3. S	8. RO
4. RO	9. S
5. RO	10. S

REVIEW EXERCISES

A.

1. S	6. RO	11. S	16. F
2. RO	7. F	12. F	17. S
3. F	8. S	13. RO	18. F
4. S	9. RO	14. F	19. RO
5. F	10. S	15. RO	20. S

B. Along with the many other employees of Rome Industries, I would like to offer you my sincere good wishes on the occasion of your retirement. We will truly miss you.

Because of your outstanding performance as assistant public relations director, we would like to express our appreciation with a small gift. You will find a check for $1000 enclosed.

In addition, you will be cordially invited to the annual executive banquet, at which you will be presented with a gold watch symbolizing your many years of loyal service.

I hope that your retirement will be healthy and rewarding and that you will visit us whenever you have a chance. It will not be easy to replace a colleague as amiable and efficient as you have been these nineteen years.

C. Thank you for inviting Dr. Marcus to speak at your health club. Physical fitness through psychotherapy is a topic in which he is very interested.

Unfortunately, Dr. Marcus will be out of town through the month of August. Therefore, he will be unable to speak to your members until the fall. Moreover, he will be traveling through southern Italy. Consequently, I will not be able to inform him of your invitation for several weeks.

Nevertheless, I am sure Dr. Marcus would appreciate your invitation. I will convey it to him as soon as he returns. Our offfice will get in touch with you at that time. I hope we will be able to arrange a date for the lecture then.

D. In reply to your inquiry of July 31, 19--, regarding Ms. Ruby R. Hood, I am pleased to supply the information you requested.

Ms. Hood was in our employ for three years. She was a visiting nurse in our midtown district. Her principal responsibility was to tend to a number of elderly patients whose needs included domestic assistance as well as medical attention and bedside care.

Ms. Hood was an outstanding nurse. Many of her patients looked upon her with grandmotherly affection. She related well to even the most crotchety of them and was capable of performing under the most difficult, even dangerous, of conditions.

It is entirely without hesitation that I recommend Ms. Hood for the position of Head Nurse at your institution.

E. 1. Public relations letters, a highly specialized mode of business communications, are written to influence public opinion. A public relations writer prepares news releases as well as advertisements, speeches, and other written forms that promote an organization's positive image. To become a public relations writer, one must be clever with words, but a knowledge of sales technique and a sense of timing are further requirements. A persistent competitive spirit will also help, for public relations is a difficult field to break into.

2. Experiencing rapid growth in the past decade, the paralegal profession offers many opportunities. To become a paralegal can take as little as three months in one of the hundreds of paralegal training programs across the country. Paralegals are legal assistants who work with lawyers and other legal professionals. The paralegal's duties include legal research as well as drafting and indexing legal documents and assisting in trial preparation. Employed by local, state, and federal governments, by private law firms, and by corporations, there are over 80,000 paralegals in the United States. Nearly 80 percent of them are women.

4. Subject-Verb Agreement (page 43)

Exercise 1

dismiss	bliss	discuss
happiness	cross	boss
moss	class	toss
dress	address	sadness
fuss	readiness	helpless

Exercise 2

Singular	Plural	Singular	Plural
cost	costs	factory	factories
journey	journeys	safe	safes
buzz	buzzes	life	lives
inquiry	inquiries	fox	foxes
money	monies	banana	bananas
anniversary	anniversaries	loss	losses
request	requests	cargo	cargoes
finance	finances	trustee	trustees
success	successes	phony	phonies
ax	axes	banjo	banjos

Exercise 3

1. This company's policy
2. All employees' salaries
3. An employee's performance
4. An immediate superior's opinion
5. The administration's objectivity
6. An employee's loyal service
7. A raise's merit
8. someone's outstanding performance
9. This company's employees
10. their workers' satisfaction

Exercise 4

1. Airports employ
2. The pilots fly jets
3. The navigators keep
4. The flight attendant takes
5. The ground crews check
6. The baggage handler tosses
7. The ticket agent arranges
8. The customs officials open
9. Tower control directs
10. The security agent watches

Exercise 5

1. offers
2. hire
3. need
4. clean
5. employs
6. have
7. comes
8. pay
9. employ
10. is

Exercise 6

1. is
2. are
3. are
4. are
5. are
6. are
7. were
8. are
9. were
10. are

Exercise 7

1. is
2. travel
3. take
4. drive
5. has
6. walk
7. rains
8. take
9. is
10. have

Exercise 8

1. satisfy
2. are
3. covers
4. are
5. have
6. augment
7. help
8. meets
9. break
10. are

Exercise 9

1. is
2. are
3. does
4. makes
5. provides
6. is
7. prepares
8. say
9. help
10. are

Exercise 10

1. wants
2. pays
3. is
4. remains
5. has
6. seems
7. volunteers
8. is
9. moves
10. is

Exercise 11

1. have
2. are
3. qualify
4. seem
5. have
6. is
7. are
8. contribute
9. are
10. are

Exercise 12

1. has
2. were
6. are
7. was

3. are
4. is
5. has

8. need
9. is
10. are

Exercise 13

1. seems
2. are
3. is
4. appears
5. are

6. is
7. has
8. seems
9. are
10. is

Exercise 14

1. have
2. were
3. were
4. was
5. appears

6. has
7. are
8. is
9. are
10. has

Exercise 15

1. offers
2. feel
3. disagrees
4. has
5. feel

6. are
7. provides
8. obstructs
9. wants
10. is

Exercise 16

1. have
2. is
3. has
4. induce
5. are

6. needs
7. put
8. leads
9. encourage
10. depends

Exercise 17

1. is
2. were
3. has
4. is
5. provide

6. increases
7. grow
8. require
9. are
10. makes

Exercise 18

1. offer
2. include
3. was
4. supplies
5. show

6. provides
7. are
8. is
9. meet
10. is

REVIEW EXERCISES

A.

1. consist	6. are	11. is
2. is	7. make	12. is
3. frighten	8. worries	13. have
4. discourage	9. wait	14. realizes
5. prefer	10. depends	15. is

B.

1. is	6. ceases	11. plans
2. are	7. provides	12. alleviate
3. are	8. is	13. enriches
4. put	9. reduces	14. does
5. are	10. compounds	15. becomes

C. As you know, job hunting in this day and age is a difficult proposition. . . .

Now, Integrity Careers, Inc., has the help you need. Our career guidance kit, "Know Thyself," provides the answers to your biggest questions: What job do I really want? What are my most marketable skills? What factors have kept me from reaching my goals up to now? What do I do to finally land the job of my dreams?

This kit, including job lists and model resumes, is not available in any store. . . . Only those who receive this letter even know the kit exists.

So why not send us $50 postage paid to receive your Integrity Career Guidance Kit? . . .

D. Corro Communications is pleased to announce the promotion of Augusta Samuels to assistant vice president of marketing. The former advertising director of our south and midwest divisions brings to her new job a wealth of dedication and experience.

Ms. Samuels' new office will be located in the New York headquarters building at 1 Sixth Avenue.

To mark the occasion, Corro requests the pleasure of your company at a reception honoring Ms. Samuels. . . .

E. . . . We appreciate your interest in a position with our company.

Although we received over 200 responses to our advertisement for an administrative assistant, we have given each applicant's resume careful consideration. Because your background and experience meet our company's criteria, we would like to invite you to come in for an interview. . . .

5. Verb Forms
(page 63)

Exercise 1

type	is talking	have worked	has been going
are	is going	have fallen	has been driving
sing	is trying	have sung	has been saying
try	is typing	have wanted	has been asking
answered	was saying	had spoken	had been doing
wrote	was falling	had remembered	had been crying
danced	was holding	had smelled	had been going
worked	was walking	had worked	had been laughing
will walk	will be typing	will have gone	will have been walking
will type	will be filing	will have sung	will have been studying
will study	will be studying	will have talked	will have been typing
will file	will be walking	will have eaten	will have been filing

Exercise 2

1. spoken
   written
   been
   done
   said
   forgotten
   gone
   taken

2. types
   works
   says
   laughs
   knows
   argues
   speaks

3. answering
   laughing
   typing
   filing
   speaking
   working
   trying

4. typed
   filed
   forgot
   worked
   decided
   transcribed
   corrected

5. fought
   argued
   bickered
   cooperated
   disagreed
   conferred

Exercise 3

Present Tense	Past Tense	Past Participle
arise	arose	arisen
bear	bore	born
begin	began	begun
bend	bent	bent
bet	bet	bet

Present Tense	Past Tense	Past Participle
bid	bid	bid
bind	bound	bound
bleed	bled	bled
blow	blew	blown
break	broke	broken
bring	brought	brought
burst	burst	burst
buy	bought	bought
cast	cast	cast
catch	caught	caught
choose	chose	chosen
come	came	come
cost	cost	cost
creep	crept	crept
cut	cut	cut
dig	dug	dug
do	did	done
draw	drew	drawn
drink	drank	drunk
drive	drove	driven
eat	ate	eaten
feed	fed	fed
feel	felt	felt
fight	fought	fought
find	found	found
flee	fled	fled
fly	flew	flown
forget	forgot	forgotten
get	got	gotten
give	gave	given
go	went	gone
grow	grew	grown
hang	hung	hung
have	had	had
hear	heard	heard
hit	hit	hit

Present Tense	Past Tense	Past Participle
hold	held	held
hurt	hurt	hurt
keep	kept	kept
know	knew	known
lay	laid	laid
lead	led	led
lend	lent	lent
lie	lay	lain
lie	lied	lied
light	lit	lit
lose	lost	lost
make	made	made
mean	meant	meant
meet	met	met
pay	paid	paid
put	put	put
quit	quit	quit
read	read	read
rid	rid	rid
ride	rode	ridden
ring	rang	rung
rise	rose	risen
run	ran	run
say	said	said
see	saw	seen
seek	sought	sought
sell	sold	sold
send	sent	sent
set	set	set
shake	shook	shaken
shed	shed	shed
shine	shone	shone
shoot	shot	shot
sing	sang	sung
sit	sat	sat
sleep	slept	slept

Present Tense	Past Tense	Past Participle
slide	slid	slid
speak	spoke	spoken
speed	sped	sped
spend	spent	spent
split	split	split
spread	spread	spread
stand	stood	stood
steal	stole	stolen
stick	stuck	stuck
swear	swore	sworn
sweep	swept	swept
swim	swam	swum
swing	swung	swung
take	took	taken
teach	taught	taught
tear	tore	torn
tell	told	told
throw	threw	thrown
win	won	won
wind	wound	wound
write	wrote	written

Exercise 4

1. wanted
2. loved
3. read
4. asked
5. majored
6. changed
7. been
8. continued
9. attends
10. studying

Exercise 5

1. work   meet   prepare
   rest   study   apologize
   try

2. sleeping   typing   writing
   planning   cooking   studying
                         working

3. gone   finished   graduated
   tried   learned   rested
   recovered

4. talking	walking	writing
typing	working	studying
sleeping		trying

Exercise 6

(Answers may vary; the following are suggestions.)

1. can
2. would
3. must
4. should
5. had better

6. should
7. will
8. may
9. should
10. could

Exercise 7

1. Sylvia
2. Mrs. Ortiz
3. May
4. Max
5. Amy

6. Ann
7. Henry
8. Judy
9. Mr. Toshiro
10. Steve

Exercise 8

1. face: Foreign investors in China faced . . .
2. snarl: Bureaucratic delays frequently snarled . . .
3. threatens: The eventual death of Den Xiaoping threatened . . .
4. jeopardize: American trade sanctions also jeopardized . . .
5. fear: American companies feared . . .
6. do: They did . . .
7. consider: Still, many foreign companies considered . . .
8. has: China has . . .
9. offers: China's domestic market offered . . .
10. is: Underlying this investment boom was . . .

Exercise 9

1. P
2. P
3. A
4. P
5. A

6. A
7. P
8. P
9. P
10. A

Exercise 10

1. A new copier was ordered by Allbright Enterprises on Tuesday.
2. It was delivered by the Allied Trucking Company on Thursday.
3. The bill was sent by the manufacturer immediately.
4. The bill was received by Allbright on Friday.
5. It was paid by them promptly.
6. However, a malfunction in the machine was discovered by a secretary on Monday.

7. The mechanism was being jammed by paper.
8. Stopping payment on their check was considered by Allbright.
9. But its merchandise is guaranteed by the manufacturer.
10. The copier was repaired by them Tuesday afternoon.

Exercise 11

1. Harold Dawson constructed that porch.
2. Emma Hobbs contracted him to build it.
3. Mr. Dawson's father had taught him carpentry.
4. So he crafted the porch expertly.
5. He laid the floorboards evenly.
6. He hand-notched the railings.
7. He even hand-carved the molding.
8. His final product pleased Mrs. Hobbs.
9. She paid him handsomely.
10. A machine cannot match the work of a fine craftsperson.

Exercise 12

is   (active)
has not been paid   (passive)
is   (active)
have been sent   (passive)
have been ignored   (passive)
know   (active)
have been   (active)
have been paid   (passive)
is   (active)
do force   (active)
send   (active)

. . . We have sent you two statements and three letters regarding your balance. Yet you have ignored them.

We know that you have been a reliable customer for many years although you have paid your bills slowly on occasion. . . .

Please do not force us to close your account or to turn this matter over to our attorneys. . . .

REVIEW EXERCISES

A. 1. expected
2. pursued
3. paid
4. become
5. trained
6. work
7. performed
8. obstructed
9. required
10. provide

B.

1.	wanted	6.	trained	11.	began
2.	been	7.	advised	12.	arrived
3.	learned	8.	seemed	13.	were
4.	served	9.	combined	14.	offered
5.	taken	10.	preparing	15.	begun

C. 1. Justin <u>wanted</u> to become an airline reservations agent. He <u>enjoyed</u> working with the public, and he <u>had</u> the necessary qualifications. He <u>was</u> a high school graduate, <u>spoke</u> two foreign languages, <u>typed</u> 55 words per minute, and <u>had worked</u> with computers. He <u>had been</u> a salesperson for the <u>previous</u> two years, which <u>was</u> also helpful. Most importantly, he <u>related</u> well to people.

2. Alicia <u>is</u> a flight attendant, a job which <u>involves</u> serving others. Her position <u>requires</u> patience and tact since she <u>deals</u> with potentially irritable passengers. She <u>has</u> to keep passengers calm as well as serve them food and beverages. She not only <u>caters</u> to their needs, but also <u>maintains</u> their safety. Because she <u>performs</u> her duties well and <u>has</u> often <u>been</u> complimented by passengers, she <u>is being</u> promoted to Supervisor of Flight Training.

3. Donna <u>entered</u> corporate management immediately after finishing college. She <u>started</u> as a product manager and moved up to assistant vice president for finance. <u>Now</u> she <u>wants</u> to open her own business. She <u>has considered</u> cosmetics, a traditionally "women's field," but she <u>prefers</u> to invest in a "mainstream" industry. So she <u>has investigated</u> computer software. She <u>has found</u> the field attractive and so <u>is planning</u> to quit her job in the near future.

D. It is my great honor to inform you that you have been name<u>d</u> . . .

Words cannot express our deep appreciation . . . and good judgment save<u>d</u> . . . that would have been los<u>t</u> had the robbers escape<u>d</u>.

. . . it must have create<u>d</u> . . . you to spen<u>d</u> . . . we will be please<u>d</u> . . . to be hel<u>d</u> on Friday . . .

E. . . . has announce<u>d</u> plans . . . is schedule<u>d</u> to . . .

including retire<u>d</u> persons . . . Delaney explaine<u>d</u>: "Job . . . and convince local . . . ."

are bei<u>ng</u> schedule<u>d</u> for . . . is urge<u>d</u> to . . . be experience<u>d</u> but . . .

employers interest<u>ed</u> in . . . .

6. Pronouns (page 90)

Exercise 1

1.	us	6.	They
2.	they	7.	them
3.	I	8.	them
4.	me	9.	me
5.	me	10.	she

Exercise 2

1. me	6. he
2. her	7. me
3. me	8. me
4. me	9. she
5. I	10. me

Exercise 3

1. I am	6. she does
2. she can	7. she is
3. she has	8. he corrects me
4. they gave her	9. recommend me
5. for her	10. I am

Exercise 4

1. Whoever	6. Whoever
2. whom	7. who
3. who	8. whomever
4. who	9. who
5. whom	10. Who

Exercise 5

staff and I would like
happier than we that your
a colleague who has been
wishes for your continued success

Exercise 6

1. his	6. Their
his	Theirs
2. her	7. Their
hers	Theirs
3. her (or his)	8. His (or Her)
hers (or his)	His (or Hers)
4. Their	9. our
Theirs	ours
5. His (or Her)	10. your
His (or Hers)	yours

Exercise 7

hope that our association will
account makes your shopping more
preceding month. Its clear, itemized
sales receipts. There's never a
Enclosed is your Trumbel's credit
you on your next visit

Exercise 8

1. me
2. himself
3. I
4. him
5. ourselves

6. us
7. ourselves
8. us
9. him
10. he

Exercise 9

1. economy its
2. company itself
3. accounts their
4. department its
5. sales their
6. manager his
7. company its
8. Suppliers their
9. accountant her
10. members their

Exercise 10

(Answers may vary; the following are suggestions.)

1. As I walked into the office, I broke my foot by hitting it against the glass door.
2. Wendy enjoyed working in the publicity department because her co-workers were so patient.
3. The merchants accused of cheating a group of tourists say they are not guilty.
4. After searching through the files all morning, Laura realized she would never find the file she was looking for.
5. The president and his assistant, concerned with cutting costs and increasing productivity, studied the reports carefully.
6. A desk-top copier would be more economical for this office than for a larger office.
7. Trying very hard to relax didn't help me once the interview began.
8. Before Mr. Douglas retired, he had worked for Mr. Lancaster for ten years.
9. If you are well trained, you will find it easier to get a well-paying job.
10. Amelia worked part-time for a pediatrician and enjoyed her job very much.

Exercise 11

(Answers may vary; the following is a suggestion.)

... Mr. Brand began with our firm as assistant to the vice president in charge of marketing, Mr. Goodman. When Mr. Goodman was promoted nine months later, Mr. Brand served under the new vice president, Mr. Brown, who retired three years later. At that point, Mr. Brand himself was made vice president. . . .

I can therefore wholeheartedly recommend him as a consultant for your company, for marketing is a field in which he outshines all competition.

Exercise 12

1. his	6. us
2. their	7. your
3. one	8. you
4. it	9. her
5. he	10. her

Exercise 13

(Answers may vary; the following is a suggestion.)

have been <u>my</u> family's physician
and that <u>her</u> working conditions
me about <u>them</u> or suggest
me with <u>them</u>? Or can
me and <u>my</u> brothers in

REVIEW EXERCISES

A.

1. me	6. he's
2. I	7. his
3. who	8. me
4. he	9. It's
5. He	10. who

B. *(Answers may vary; the following are suggestions.)*

1. Since Ralph finished technical school, he hasn't seen his friend Calvin.
2. C
3. Ralph's job took his family and him to Cincinnati.
4. Calvin was saddened by his leaving.
5. But then Calvin himself got a job in Boston.
6. Both men are computer programmers, and each enjoys his work.
7. Now Ralph is being transferred, and he and his family will be moving to Boston.
8. So Ralph and Calvin are looking forward to their reunion.
9. C
10. But they hope to resume their friendship where it left off.

C. *(Answers may vary; the following is a suggestion.)*

I have reviewed the recent employee complaints and find that <u>employees</u> are primarily unhappy with office conditions. . . .

1 The air conditioning and heating systems are inadequate, and <u>they</u> are usually out of order. . . .

3 Larger offices are not assigned by merit or seniority; rather <u>they're</u> assigned by favoritism.

4 Secretaries are not permitted to reorder supplies until <u>supplies</u> are exhausted.

The first two complaints involve capital repairs <u>which</u> will require authorization. The second two complaints concern policy, <u>and</u> I am currently investigating both matters. . . .

D. *(Answers may vary; the following is a suggestion.)*

When a person has made an expensive purchase, <u>he</u> is right to be angry when <u>his</u> order is mishandled. . . .

I have checked your purchase order and confirmed <u>your</u> complaint. . . . If you call this department for an appointment, our delivery team will pick up <u>the Kirman</u> and lay the correct rug for you at no extra charge.

To show you how sorry <u>we</u> at Van Dyke's Carpets are, we would like to offer you a gift of a 2′ × 3′ Bukhara. When placed in an entryway or foyer, this area rug, a $250 value, will make a lovely complement to your new rug. . . .

E. *(Answers may vary; the following is a suggestion.)*

Only an idiot would leave <u>his</u> car unlocked in New York City. . . .

That is why we'd like to take this opportunity to advise you of another simple means of protecting <u>your</u> car—the Crookproof Cutoff Switch. . . .

By installing a Crookproof Cutoff Switch on your car, <u>you</u> will make theft virtually impossible. . . . Even a thief with a key will be stopped dead in <u>his</u> tracks. . . .

For only $19.95, you'll protect <u>your car</u> for a long, long time.

7. Advanced Sentence Structure (page 107)

Exercise 1

(Answers may vary; the following are suggestions.)

1. Finding a job in today's economy requires ingenuity, perseverance, and flexibility.
2. Traditional ways to get a job included mailing resumes, using a school placement counselor, or registering with employment agencies.
3. These methods don't always work in the face of a weak economy, high unemployment, and vast competition.
4. With experience in sales, public relations, and supervision, Lewis sought a position as a store sales manager.
5. Instead of using resumes, agencies, or even help-wanted ads, he personally visited every major store in his community.
6. One store owner was impressed by Lewis's assertiveness, determination, and personality.
7. Due to her present volume of business, staff size, and overhead costs, she didn't need a sales manager.
8. Instead, she offered Lewis a job as a salesperson, with a reasonable starting salary, commission structure, and benefits.
9. Lewis was concerned about income, security, and advancement.
10. He accepted the job, confident he could impress his employer, increase her sales, and achieve his own career goals in time.

Exercise 2

(Answers may vary; the following are suggestions.)

1. Having started a family and been able to finish school at the same time, Beth was prepared for the pressures of her new job.
2. Still, holding a job and trying to raise her family were difficult.
3. Her ambitions were to nurture her children, her career, and her husband.
4. Beth succeeded because of her children's understanding, her husband's support, and her family's respect.
5. Sometimes Beth's husband was the housekeeper, dishwasher, babysitter, and also cook.
6. Beth reciprocated by doing the shopping and the laundry and making time to be alone with her husband.
7. The children learned to clean their own room, make their own lunch, and be independent.
8. On weekends, they all made a point of spending time together and discussing their feelings.
9. Beth had explained her hopes for the family, her goals for her career, and her reasons for wanting to work in the first place.
10. As a result of Beth's working, the family has benefited socially, financially, and emotionally.

Exercise 3

(Answers may vary; the following are suggestions.)

1. Many small investors would rather save their money than risk it in the stock market.
2. They are more interested in financial security than large profits.
3. They think they must either jeopardize all they own in the stock market or settle for 3½% interest.
4. Actually, small investors can afford neither low interest rates nor the risk of the stock market.
5. So, both recession and low-interest savings accounts have led many people to other areas of investment.
6. These people are looking not only for security but for a high return.
7. Many, therefore, have put their money into mutual funds rather than savings accounts.
8. Mutual funds not only provide high yield but offer reasonable security.
9. They provide the investor with not only professional management but also diversification.
10. Thus, the investor is neither taking an enormous risk nor giving up to recession.

Exercise 4

(Answers may vary; the following are suggestions.)

1. Employees all through the company were curious about the executive board meeting.
2. Secretaries around the water cooler could not figure out why the president had been so nervous.

3. On Monday, he had explained to his assistant why the company was in trouble.

4. He began the meeting by saying, "Customers who buy our products are frequently discovering defects."

5. The meeting, which stretched on for hours, was attended by all executive personnel.

6. An assistant delivered cold dinners in cardboard boxes to hungry board members.

7. After much discussion behind locked doors, they pinpointed the source of the problem.

8. They agreed to institute new procedures on the following day.

9. The board decided that each product, after going through the assembly line, would be inspected by an expert.

10. They are trying to devise a set of foolproof standards for employees.

Exercise 5

(Answers may vary; the following are suggestions.)

1, 2. C

3. They fixed the typewriter, only six months old but already unreliable, in our reception area.

4. C

5. The precision of this man, who seemed to know exactly what he was doing, greatly impressed our office manager.

6. We watched as he returned the machine to perfect working order in less than ten minutes.

7. So little company time was lost due to a broken typewriter.

8, 9. C

10. Their bill, which was very reasonable, was on our office manager's desk Tuesday.

Exercise 6

(Answers may vary; the following are suggestions.)

1. As I was settling down at my desk, the day started.

2. The morning passed quietly while I prepared reports and filed them away.

3. When I was nearly finished with the last report, the telephone rang.

4. I answered it promptly as a salesman walked in.

5. To run an office smoothly often requires tact.

6. Asking the salesman to have a seat, I took the caller's message.

7. As the salesman was about to give his sales pitch, two customers arrived.

8. As I was listening to one customer's complaint, the salesman continued pushing his products.

9. I tried to keep an eye on the second customer, who was wandering around the showroom.

10. I finally handled each in turn, and the day resumed its leisurely pace.

Exercise 7

(Answers may vary; the following are suggestions.)

1. C
2. Al single-handedly served dozens of customers who were walking in and out all day long.
3. C
4. However, when first starting up the business, he required help.
5. C
6. Also, pricing and displaying the merchandise himself, he set up the boutique for opening day.
7. But, to incorporate the operation, he needed legal assistance.
8. To set up his system of record keeping, he relied on an accountant's advice, too.
9. C
10. To get a business going, one should not avoid the expense of a team of professionals.

Exercise 8

1. Pat told the personnel officer that she was applying for a position as an administrative assistant.
2. The personnel officer replied that they had no such opening at that time.
3. Pat said that she would like to make out an application for their waiting list anyway.
4. While she was writing, the man said that they were looking for an executive secretary.
5. He continued that the position was with the assistant vice president of marketing.
6. Pat said that she was willing to begin as a secretary if there were opportunities for advancement.
7. The personnel officer assured her that they filled most higher positions from within the company.
8. Then he added that, if her skills were appropriate, he would arrange an interview for her.
9. Pat informed him that she could type 80 words a minute and take dictation at 120.
10. Now, she tells people that within an hour she had the job.

Exercise 9

1. The program director began by asking me if I had had any previous experience in an old age home.
2. Then she asked if I could tell them about my relevant education.
3. The director's assistant wanted to know how I found working with people much older than myself.
4. A third person queried about what special approaches were necessary when working with an elderly population.
5. Next, the director again asked what I would do if I thought someone were having a heart attack.

6. Another member of the panel inquired into what musical instruments I play.
7. Then the assistant asked if I felt I could work on my own.
8. She further questioned if I was willing to work long hours.
9. The director then asked what salary range I would consider acceptable.
10. Finally, she inquired when I could start.

REVIEW EXERCISES
(Answers may vary; the following are suggestions.)

A. I would like to order a desk advertised in your fall catalog. The model is number 15C-2J, comes in solid oak, and is priced at $495.

Please charge the desk to my account, number 7651-38-801, and send it immediately to the following address:

96 Lakeview Drive
Riverdale, New York 11232

B. It is with great pleasure that we have contracted with your executive council to provide refrigeration and stove repair services. . . .

We have agreed to assume reponsibility for all malfunctions of refrigerators, freezers, and gas ranges for an annual fee of $150 per apartment. There will be no additional charge to you for repairs, even if the cost of these services should exceed $150. . . .

Therefore, please let us know if you are interested in securing our Kitchen Insurance for your home. . . .

C. . . . In checking our records, we find you have indeed owned the set for only six weeks.

We can clearly understand your anger at having a television break down so soon after purchase. . . .

On your behalf, we have contacted the factory repair service, who informed us that they will get in touch with you immediately to arrange for free repair of your set. . . .

D. . . . A standard review of credit applications includes checking accounts, savings accounts, and outstanding debts. Having investigated your ability to assume such credit, we find that your current obligations are substantial. . . .

E. On Tuesday, October 12, you instructed me to find out which telephone-answering equipment will best suit our office needs. You asked me to find the three top models. . . .

1 Dictaphone, model #108B—equipped with 30-second announcement cartridge, 90-minute message cassette, and remote control message receiver; available at Berkeley's Office Equipment, Inc., for $165.

2 Ansaphone, model #26-60—equipped with 30-second announcement cartridge, 60-minute message cassette, fast-forward device, and remote control message receiver; available at Audrey's Audio for $100.

3 Quadraphone, model #XJ9—equipped with 20-second announcement cartridge, 90-minute message cassette, message length switch, and remote control message receiver; available at all Taylor Discount Stores for $125. . . .

8. Mechanics (page 129)

Exercise 1

1. ?	6. .
2. !	7. ?
3. .	8. !
4. .	9. .
5. ?	10. .

Exercise 2

product.
magazine, we
you. Should
rates. Our
delay! Call

Exercise 3

1. 6:45	6. remark:
2. breakfast;	7. mail;
3. ways:	8. response;
4. routine:	9. billing;
5. o'clock;	10. arrives:

Exercise 4

1. engineer, she
2. people, she . . . bridges, dams, and
3. job, Lydia
4. construction, and
5. However, Lydia's
6. improvement, water quality, and
7. system, so
8. exciting, and

9. fact, she . . . management, accounting, and
10. future, Lydia

Exercise 5

1. Transport, Ltd., is . . . Street, Rockville, Maine
2. company, founded in 1949, is
3. Forman, a . . . School, was
4. August, 1962, she [or August 1962 she]
5. woman, one would imagine, had
6. Today, Ms. . . . 1,200 women, many
7. Forman, it . . . drivers, not her own achievement, that
8. road, she believes, has
9. Transport, of course, employs . . . men, too.
10. women, not the men, who

Exercise 6

1. ✓
2. Mr. Chu, who . . . success, must
3. ✓
4. Mr. Alvarez, which . . . lunch, Mr. Chu
5. client, Ms. Murphy, was
6. Mr. Chu, confident . . . manner, enjoys
7. ✓
8. breakfast, which . . . overlooked, can
9. ✓
10. contract, which . . . signing, will

Exercise 7

1. anybody's guess
2. Rosemary's responsibility
3. the policemen's weapons
4. the actresses' roles
5. Gus's dog
6. Iris's cat
7. the cars' transmission
8. the bus's tires
9. Alex and Sid's partnership
10. the passer-by's reaction

Exercise 8

1. company's
2. c.o.d.'s
3. haven't
4. M.D.'s
5. Adler's
6. We've
7. Moses'
8. ✓
9. ✓
10. it's

Exercise 9

1. "The Affordable . . . the People"
2. "Computers enable . . . to do."

3. "Computers provide . . . store it."
4. "Lap-top computers," she explains further, "enable . . . go."
5. "The Affordable PC,"
6. "Because my . . . days."
7. "By storing . . . my knees."
8. "Many . . . clubs."
9. "Without . . . with words."
10. "With spelling . . . and precision."

Exercise 10

1. an X-rated movie
2. a four-star restaurant
3. a hand-sewn garment
4. a mind-boggling question
5. home-grown vegetables
6. all-night negotiations
7. a tea-stained tablecloth
8. a seventeen-year-old graduate
9. a career-oriented student
10. a polka-dotted dress

Exercise 11

1. bank-rupt-cy
2. cor-por-a-tion
3. X
4. de-pre-ci-a-tion
5. li-a-bil-i-ty
6. fis-cal
7. sell-ing
8. fran-chise
9. mort-gage
10. mo-nop-o-ly

Exercise 12

1. (1870–1965)
2. financier—he . . . thirty—he
3. (national defense adviser)
   (special . . . Byrne).
4. Trust"—a
5. (U.S. . . . Commission).
6. (formerly . . . College)
7. (see *Baruch* [2 volumes, 1957–60]).

Exercise 13

"Flexible Work Hours" (or Flextime for short) is one of the biggest innovations in employment policy in the past few decades. Under Flextime, employees choose the times at which they arrive at and depart from work within limits set by management. Usually core hours are established: during this midday period all employees must be present. They may choose, however, to come in early or to stay late. Under Flextime, absenteeism has dropped significantly, and productivity has risen. As a result, the Public and World Affairs Committee predicts, "Flextime is going to be with us in the coming years."

Exercise 14

1. Secretarial and Office Procedures for College
2. Principles of Data Processing
3. How to Marry a Millionaire
4. "So You Want to Be a Legal Secretary?"
5. "How to Ask for a Raise"
6. "One Hundred Ways to Supplement Your Income"
7. How to Find the Job You've Always Wanted
8. "Avoiding Three O'Clock Fatigue"
9. "How to Work Around a Candy Machine Without Gaining Weight"
10. Take the Money and Run

Exercise 15

1. On June 28, 1778, the Battle of Monmouth was fought. The last major battle in the North during the Revolutionary War, it took place north of Monmouth Court House in New Jersey. There, George Washington led an army of 13,500 troops to victory against the British troops, who were led by Henry Clinton.
2. Born on February 11, 1847, in Milan, Ohio, Thomas Alva Edison became one of America's greatest inventors. . . . Edison also built the first central electric power station, erected on Pearl Street in New York City. Known as the "Wizard of Menlo Park," he considered his genius to be "one percent inspiration and ninety-nine percent perspiration."

Exercise 16

Dear Mr. Jackson:

I would like to offer my hearty congratulations on your promotion to president of the Empire Stove Company. All of us at Seymour's Service Centers, Inc., are pleased that your years of hard work have been rewarded.

Seymour's appreciates the fine quality and serviceability of American-made stoves and appliances. That is why we have always confidently offered Empire Stoves to our customers.

In closing, President Jackson, let me say that we look forward to a long and mutually rewarding business relationship with E.S.C.

Sincerely yours,

Exercise 17

1. The meeting to explore ways of increasing tourism in Greenwood, North Dakota, was called to order at 7:15 P.M.
2. Mr. Ashley introduced the guest speaker, the Honorable J. R. Buckley, mayor of Greenwood.
3. CORRECT
4. Buckley began his speech with an anecdote about ancient Rome in the year 129 B.C.
5. CORRECT
6. The mayor surprised the audience by announcing plans to spend $2,550,000 on restoring the town's landmarks and historical sites.

7. He also announced the intentions of ITT to erect a Sheraton Hotel on Broad Street in the center of town.
8. After Buckley's address, Lana Stephens, C.S.W., asked a question.
9, 10. CORRECT

Exercise 18

On Tuesday, March 17, which happened to be St. Patrick's Day, I purchased four pounds of Muenster cheese from your supermarket on Grand Street in Grahamsville, New Jersey. . . .

The manager of the Grand Street store refused to refund my money. . . . I would like you to know that if my claim is not satisfied, I intend to take the matter to the Department of Consumer Affairs.

Exercise 19

1. $8.12
2. CORRECT
3. 49 West 11 Street
4. August 10, 1980
5. CORRECT
6. ten men, eight women, and sixteen children *or* 10 men, 8 women, and 16 children
7. 2 sixty-cent fares
8. 9:30 A.M.
9. CORRECT
10. P.O. Box 21

REVIEW EXERCISES

A. There will be a meeting of the Sales Department on Friday, November 8, in room 110. Mr. Arthur Parker will address the meeting on the topic, "Improving Your Sales Through Self-Hypnosis."

Mr. Parker, a certified psychoanalyst who has studied at the Alfred Adler Institute, is the author of several books, including the best-seller *It's a Snap* (New York, 1991). . . .

B. Dear Tenant:

Please be advised that, pursuant to the 1992–93 Rent Guidelines Board, the percentages covering lease renewals effective July 1, 1992, have been changed. . . .

5% for one-year renewal
9% for two-year renewal
13% for three-year renewal

. . . Please sign and return both copies, along with the additional security of $20.41. . . .

C. On the basis of information provided by your physician and at your request, you have been placed on medical leave of absence as of May 30, 1993.

To maintain your leave, company policy requires additional written statements from your physician at thirty-day intervals. These statements should be sent directly to the Personnel Insurance Coordinator, at the downtown office.

Failure to return to work on the date indicated by your physician will be considered a resignation.

Feel free to contact me for further information regarding this policy.

D. Policy No. 43 681 345
Date: September 5, 1991

Dear Mr. and Mrs. Chou:

. . . Because you made five claims in the past four years, we cannot provide $500 deductible comprehensive coverage on the 1990 Ford Probe that replaced your old car. Nevertheless, bodily injury and property damage on the old car have been transferred to your new car. . . .

You will be covered by the protection only until 12:01 A.M. on September 26, 1991. You will therefore have a three-week period in which to apply for the protection elsewhere.

Please understand, Mr. and Mrs. Chou, that our decision was made after thorough consideration of your case and based upon the underwriting rules and regulations of our company.

All of your other coverage remains in full force as it was before your request.

E. Dear Dr. Christopher:

Not long ago, I spoke with you on the telephone about a possible teaching position with you next semester. You suggested I mention this in my letter.

The man who referred me to your school was Professor Helmsley of the Accounting Department.

My most recent job was in the Secretarial Skills Department at Bronxville Community College. I was a part-time instructor there for four consecutive semesters. . . .

Thank you.

Sincerely yours,

INDEX